T5-BCB-909

# African-American Perspectives On:

## Crime Causation, Criminal Justice Administration And Crime Prevention

Edited by Anne T. Sulton, Ph.D., J.D.

**AFRICAN-AMERICAN PERSPECTIVES ON CRIME CAUSATION, CRIMINAL JUSTICE ADMINISTRATION, AND CRIME PREVENTION**

Edited by
Anne Thomas Sulton

Published by
Anne Thomas Sulton
Sulton Books
Post Office Box 3748
Englewood, Colorado 80155
(303) 773-1164



Publication Design: Network Graphics, Denver, Colorado

Printed in the United States of America

Library of Congress Catalog Card Number: 93-87085

ISBN 0-9639633-0-9

1st Hardback Printing
October 1994

*This book is dedicated to the memories of:*

*Raymond Ellis*
*(Coppin State College)*

*Gwynn Pierson*
*(Howard University)*

*Lloyd Sealy*
*(John Jay College of Criminal Justice)*

# CONTENTS

# PREFACE

Since beginning work on this project in early 1993, over 20 million crimes were committed in this country, including over 40,000 murders. Clearly, this book is too late and too little to prevent or ease the pain suffered by these victims and their families. Hopefully, this collection of articles, authored by leading African-American criminologists and practitioners, will help prevent future crimes. Should some of the dozens of innovative recommendations included in these articles be implemented, surely this nation will experience a reduction in crime.

These articles suggest fresh and exciting new ways of thinking about a wide range of contemporary crime problems. But they offer more than a glimmer of hope for achieving domestic peace and tranquility. Read together, as a whole, they provide a partially completed blueprint for a safer and more just society.

While working on this book, my thoughts frequently turned to those days when my mother, Esther Phillips, and her friends walked along the darkened streets of my hometown, Racine, Wisconsin. They had no fear of crime. Their only concern, as they hurried down the streets, was arriving at work on time. Now they, like millions of other senior citizens across America, huddle behind locked doors fearing for their safety.

All of the authors contributing articles to this book really understand this fear and the crime occurring in our neighborhoods. These authors, as well as other African-Americans, are desperately trying to have their voices heard so that rational and effective public policies can be fashioned. Rational public policies, with a real promise of effectively preventing crime, must be fashioned to protect our elderly. They deserve to be and feel safe, as do our small children.

As editor and publisher of this book, I sincerely appreciate the work of the contributing authors. And I am deeply indebted to my husband, Dr. James E. Sulton, Jr., for his support and encouragement.

Anne T. Sulton, Ph.D., J.D.
Englewood, Colorado

# EXCLUDED: THE CURRENT STATUS OF AFRICAN-AMERICAN SCHOLARS IN THE FIELD OF CRIMINOLOGY AND CRIMINAL JUSTICE

*Vernetta Young is a tenured professor. She teaches criminology and criminal justice courses at Howard University. Young received her doctorate degree in criminal justice from the State University of New York in Albany.*

*Anne Sulton is an attorney and a criminologist. She received her doctorate degree in criminology and criminal justice from the University of Maryland and her law degree from the University of Wisconsin.*

Crime and delinquency are raging out of control in every major urban area in this nation. Dead bodies on street corners, young gangsters flashing "signs," and drug sales are nearly as commonplace as children boarding school buses, postal employees delivering mail, and sanitation workers collecting garbage.

Since the turn of the century, African-American criminologists have studied these issues. Hundreds have written books, articles, or monographs describing or explaining these phenomena. They also have delivered theoretical- or research-oriented papers at scores of conferences and professional meetings. Yet their contributions have been virtually ignored.

When reading supposedly comprehensive reviews of major theoretical paradigms, the unsuspecting observer would conclude that African-American criminologists have no ideas about crime and delinquency. When examining lists naming scholars awarded substantial sums of money to conduct large-scale research projects, one might assume that African-American criminologists have no interest in conducting empirical investigations. Lists naming scholars to serve as members of groups recommending public policies rarely include the names of African-American criminologists. And seldom are African-American criminologists included on the editorial boards of criminology journals, on the policymaking boards of criminology organizations, or on the criminology faculties of colleges and universities. Even the news media disregard the perspectives advanced by African-American criminologists.

On the other hand, ideas advanced by white criminologists have assumed prominent positions in the field of criminology. Millions of dollars each year are spent developing, testing, and refining their theories. And literally billions of dollars are spent implementing programs based on their ideas. Yet the ideas advanced by white criminologists have consistently produced utterly impractical, obscenely costly, shockingly inefficient, and wholly ineffective results. By all accounts, crime and delinquency are unraveling the nation's basic social fabric, straining its capacity to finance criminal justice administration, taxing its ability to respond quickly to challenging social problems, and testing its resolve to respond humanely to offenders.

The pace of this nation's progress in understanding and controlling crime and delinquency is dreadfully slow. This unfortunate situation exists, in part, because the field of criminology has developed with little recognition of the perspectives advanced by African-Americans.

This article, therefore, represents an initial step toward quickening our pace toward progress. Its primary objective is to encourage scholars and policymakers to include the perspectives advanced by African-American criminologists.

## AFRICAN-AMERICAN PERSPECTIVES

Whether there is a distinct theoretical paradigm that can be classified as the "African-American perspective" is subject to debate. Varying views are expressed on a wide range of topics. However, since the turn of the century, several dominant themes have emerged from the writings of African-American criminologists. Among the most prominent is that crime and delinquency in African-American neighborhoods can be attributed to whites' segregative and discriminatory attitudes and practices against African-Americans (Greene 1979).

African-American criminologists, as a group, consistently argue that racism, discrimination, and segregation are inextricably interwoven with crime and delinquency. For example, Vontress (1962) argues that crime can be attributed to "a melange of causes stemming from the patterns of segregation and discrimination uniquely imposed on the minority group by the dominant group" (p. 108), while J. Davis (1976) viewed crime as "a complex reaction to oppression." Many writers have pointed to specific economic, social, or political problems such as poverty, illiteracy, unemployment, over-crowded housing, inadequate nutrition, and differential law enforcement (Vontress 1962; L. Davis 1976; Banks 1977; Barnett 1977; Bell and Joyner 1977; Brown 1977; Edwards 1978; Primm 1987; Sulton

1989). Of particular note are the 1987 issue on race and crime in Volume 16 of *The Review of Black Political Economy,* Myers and Simms' (1989) *The Economics of Race and Crime,* and discussion in a special issue of *Social Justice* guest edited by Headley (1989) and containing works by Coramae R. Mann and Daniel Georges-Abeyie.

In general, African-American criminologists adhere to the notion that social structural inequities produce variations in opportunity structures which cause differential pressures for criminal conduct. Thus, the incidence of illegal behavior in African-American neighborhoods is significantly related to and affected by those social structures that substantially influence the life experiences and are outside the immediate control of the individuals involved in such behavior.

Particular characteristics of individual offenders or groups of offenders are infrequently the target of African-Americans' analyses. Offenders usually are viewed as victims of society's indifference to the plight of the poor, oppressed, and downtrodden (Miller 1909; Vontress 1962; Headley 1989; Perry 1989). However, African-American criminologists seldom suggest that individual offenders are not responsible for their conduct, citing the fact that most African-Americans are law-abiding citizens (Bell and Joyner 1977; Sulton 1989). Rather, they usually argue that because crime is a social phenomenon, it requires that offenders' behavior be evaluated within the context in which it occurs. In other words, "to understand the phenomenon of crime we must cast it against a socioeconomic backdrop" (Conyers 1977, p. 21; Myers and Simms 1989).

In essence, many if not most African-American criminologists take a holistic approach. Crime is not viewed as an isolated social problem, completely separate and distinct from other social ills plaguing the African-American community. Rather, crime is viewed as a symptom of other social problems and occurring within a multidimensional and dynamic setting (Sulton 1989).

African-American criminologists also have challenged the theoretical adequacy of existing explanations of crime and victimization in the African-American community. Some have argued that these explanations are based on misconceptions and myths about the African-American community derived from untenable assumptions about the historical impact of slavery on the African-American family (Young 1980). Moreover, although the myths have not received empirical support, the popularly accepted negative characteristics of African-American women and complementary characterizations of African-American men have been employed to deny them equitable treatment (Young 1986). Others have argued that theories of crime causation purporting to explain the involvement of African-Americans have negated the impact of cultural and racial identity by assuming that variables which tend to explain the behavior of non-African-American individuals are necessarily adept at explaining the behavior of African-Americans (Covington 1984, 1986; Austin 1989).

In addition to studying the etiology of criminal and delinquent behavior, African-American criminologists have focused their attention on describing the statistical dimensions of the crime problem. They, like their white counterparts, examine available data such as the Federal Bureau of Investigation's annual *Uniform Crime Reports*. However, unlike many of their white counterparts, most African-American criminologists question the usefulness of available data. They proceed cautiously, noting that the data provide little insight into the relationships between variables or the meaning of such relationships. And most of these scholars steadfastly argue that the data should not be used to assert that African-Americans are more criminal than whites (Vontress 1962; Brown 1974; Davis 1976; Scott 1976; Napper 1977; Bell and Joyner 1977; Sulton 1989).

Many African-American criminologists reject arguments that African-Americans are disproportionately involved in crime. By examining a broader array of data, such as the U.S. Census reports, these scholars conclude that African-Americans are *proportionately* represented in crime statistics as offenders. For example, the National Minority Advisory Council on Criminal Justice (1980) concluded that the relative involvement of African-Americans in crime is more in line with their ranking on the "misery index" than in their contributions to the total population. And Bell and Jenkins (1990) asserted that although poverty is related to homicide, when holding income constant, "racial/ethnic differences in homicide are greatly reduced or disappear" (p. 146).

African-American criminologists generally are frustrated by their white counterparts' insistence on using available crime data to show that African-Americans are disproportionately involved in crime, arguing that it is unprofessional to make such an allegation because the concept of "disproportionality," as employed by many white criminologists, is based on the groundless assumption that the contribution of African-Americans to the total population should somehow influence their contribution in other areas. Completely ignored by these white criminologists is the qualifier: "all things being equal." Totally disregarded is the fact that all things are not equal. And masterfully understated is the fact that the vast majority of African-Americans are not involved in any type of crime.

In our view, white criminologists intentionally present the relationship between race and crime in a superficial and nonscientific manner because it is consistent with their stereotypical view of the African-American community. It supports their belief that whites are superior to non-whites and that race is the primary determinant of human traits and capacities.

African-American criminologists frequently base their assumptions on a broader view of America and more carefully consider the relationships between or among crime, poverty, unemployment, illiteracy, and a host of other social ills. They often argue that when comparisons are based on a wider variety of variables, which describe the conditions under which African-Americans live, then the involvement of African-Americans in crime is not, in fact, "disproportionate."

In other words, African-American criminologists generally maintain that if one is going to make comparisons, it is necessary to first make certain that the groups compared are, in fact, comparable. This is not an unknown concept. The technique of carefully "matching" subjects for the purpose of comparison is used extensively by white criminologists, except when the issue of race is raised. Somehow, this concept mysteriously vanishes.

In addition to identifying causes of crime and examining methods by which it can be measured, African-American criminologists have explored ways in which it can be prevented. Many recommendations have been offered (Sulton 1989; Bell and Jenkins 1990). The following are among those most frequently noted:

1. Equal and just administration of criminal laws
2. Equal access to educational opportunities
3. Economic revitalization of African-American neighborhoods
4. Community control of institutions and agencies providing services to African-American neighborhoods
5. Improvement in African-Americans' quality of life
6. Teaching African-Americans conflict resolution skills
7. Providing productive activities for African-American youngsters
8. Enacting legislation aimed at curbing handgun sales
9. Improving African-Americans' racial identity.

Brown (1988) concisely summarized and accurately reflected the position held by most African-American criminologists when he stated:

> Thus, any sincere effort to deal with the crime problem must address the problems of unemployment, underemployment, substandard housing, inadequate health care, physical deterioration, teenage pregnancy, economic development, self-esteem, drugs, family deterioration, racism and discrimination, plus other social and economic ills. (p. 104)

## EXTENT OF EXCLUSION

### *Exclusion by White Criminologists*

Despite the fact that African-American criminologists have been interested and active, their perspectives generally are not included in the vast majority of criminology or criminal justice textbooks authored or edited by white criminologists. For example, Greene (1979) compiled and published *A Comprehensive Bibliography of Criminology and Criminal Justice Literature by Black Authors from 1895 to 1978,* which contains over 300 entries. But few of these works are incorporated in reviews of major theoretical paradigms or in major treatises on the policies and procedures of criminal justice agencies.

Even where African-American criminologists have made immensely important contributions to the field, contributions that would rival any of those made by the most outstanding and often noted white criminologists or criminal justice practitioners, their works are largely ignored in textbooks authored or edited by white criminologists. For example, Dr. Lee Brown, an African-American criminologist and the nation's current drug czar, is among the most prolific writers in the field, having authored several books and numerous articles. He has long been recognized as one of the most outstanding experts in the area of policing. Dr. Brown has served as police chief for Atlanta, Houston and New York City. He has served on several national commissions and is frequently interviewed by members of the press. However, seldom are his views among those discussed in white criminologists' supposedly comprehensive reviews of issues pertaining to policing. Similarly, the late Lloyd Sealy's contributions have been ignored by white scholars. Before serving as a department chair at John Jay College of Criminal Justice, Professor Sealy was a high-ranking officer in the New York City Police Department. He coauthored one of the best written and most important books in the area of police-community relations and authored numerous articles. Yet references to his works rarely are found in white criminologists' books.

Articles published in criminology and criminal justice journals reflect a similar pattern of exclusion. African-Americans seldom find their articles among those published in the 30 refereed journals most frequently read by criminologists and criminal justice practitioners.

The lack of African-American criminologists on the editorial boards of these journals may account for this discrepancy. Editorial boards determine which topics are worthy of consideration and which voices are heard. For example, when examining the membership lists of ten of the leading refereed journals' editorial boards, we found that only two of the 157 members listed are African-Americans.

Publications in refereed journals and citations to these publications are substantial measures of professional acceptance and success. Membership on committees of professional organizations is another important indicator of a scholar's accomplishments. In recent years, the Academy of Criminal Justice Sciences and the American Society of Criminology have increased the number of African-American scholars serving on committees. Although some progress has been made, more must be done to ensure that African-American criminologists are assigned to committees which set policy and determine the organizations' agenda.

At nearly every juncture, white criminologists have excluded African-American perspectives on crime and delinquency. As a result, the participation of these scholars in the field has been severely limited. According to the National Minority Advisory Council on Criminal Justice (1980),

> This kind of self-indulgence on the part of white social scientists continues only because many of them have carefully avoided genuinely challenging new intellectual thrusts from minority scholars which would force them into a real confrontation with their own contradictions and myopia. (p. 7)

Whether the exclusion is conscious and deliberate or unconscious and unintentional is subject to debate. The fact remains the same: African-American perspectives on crime and delinquency are absent.

*Exclusion by Criminal Justice Practitioners*

The idea that criminal justice agencies discriminate on the basis of race is one of the field's most controversial issues. Policing in African-American neighborhoods has been under tremendous scrutiny, as have prosecutors' charging decisions, judges' sentences, and prison guards' treatment of inmates. Yet seldom are African-American scholars invited by these agencies to provide technical assistance, to develop training programs, or to conduct studies. The millions of dollars spent each year by these agencies are used to retain the consulting or research services of white criminologists.

A refreshing change from this pattern of exclusion can be found when agencies contract with the National Organization of Black Law Enforcement Executives or the Police Foundation. African-American criminologists frequently participate in these two organizations' technical assistance and research activities. As a result, in policing, we have seen a number of substantial changes. For example, there have been significant increases in the numbers of African-American line officers and chief executives. We also have observed the development and implementation of policies promoting better police-community relations as well as policies aimed at controlling police misconduct. Although many problems remain, the evidence clearly suggests that the participation of African-American criminologists has played an important role in these advances.

Although local police departments can point to many instances when they have worked with African-American criminologists, the progress of courts and corrections agencies in this regard is unremarkable. These agencies rarely include African-American criminologists among those consulted or commissioned to conduct studies.

*Exclusion by Policymakers*

Elected and appointed government officials often solicit the opinions of criminologists. Criminologists frequently are appointed to commissions or receive contracts to conduct research on specific crime problems, such as drug abuse or youth gang violence. When reviewing lists naming those consulted or commissioned by policymakers, we found that policymakers typically seek advice from white criminologists. African-American criminologists are seldom consulted or commissioned.

There are several instances where "minority commissions" have been established. For example, the National Minority Advisory Council on Criminal Justice (NMACCJ) was established in 1976 by the Law Enforcement Assistance Administration (LEAA). NMACCJ's membership was comprised of African-Americans, Hispanics, American Indians, and Asians. However, NMACCJ's report, as well as other reports authored by African-American scholars, have not been widely circulated. Some allege that these reports were intentionally "buried" because the conclusions reached by commission members were politically unpopular.

*Exclusion by Funding Sources*

Public and private sector funding sources have awarded research grants to African-American criminologists. However, there are only a few cases in which the amounts received by these scholars exceeded $100,000. It is the rare occasion when African-American criminologists are cited as principal investigators on large-scale projects; seldom are they included as project consultants or data collectors by white criminologists receiving the large grants.

For example, NMACCJ (1980) found that during 1975 and 1980, the federal government's Office of Juvenile Justice and Delinquency Prevention awarded nearly $55 million to researchers. Not one grant was awarded to a non-white researcher. NMACCJ (1980) stated that

> historically, especially since 1965, the groundswell of research funds on all governmental levels earmarked for investigative inquiry on or about minorities have, in the main, gone to white institutions of higher education, governmental or private agencies. The myopic research perspective of this group of social scientists has precluded any significant minority participation in the subsequent projects which these funds supported. (p. 8)

Without adequate financial resources to conduct research, African-American criminologists are unable to empirically test their theories or to explore the policy implications of their ideas. When white criminologists do not provide African-American criminologists opportunities to work on major research projects, the latter's views are excluded and they are unable to gain the experience needed to manage similarly-sized research projects. More important, the quality of the research conducted is seriously compromised.

Much of the research conducted by white criminologists on inner-city crime problems is suspect. Frequently, the theoretical bases, research methods, and data manipulation techniques that they employ are seriously flawed. In other words, there is a lack of professionalism because "contemporary social science techniques have been little more than modern sophistry designed and developed to further legitimize institutional instruments of racist and classist ideology of the status quo" (NMACCJ 1980, p. 8).

First, white criminologists "bring with them professional habits, and ideological baggage that are incompatible with what concerned minority investigators feel is satisfactory social science research" (NMACCJ 1980, p. 8). As a result, their research questions are inappropriate, their hypotheses frequently incorrect and their research methods "insensitive" to African-Americans' culture and values (NMACCJ 1980).

Even if white criminologists clearly understood these issues, formulated relevant research questions, and developed appropriate research methods, their research reports on inner-city crime problems must be carefully scrutinized. It is difficult at best for white criminologists to collect accurate information from African-Americans. One of the effects of racism and discrimination is that African-Americans, particularly those living in inner-city neighborhoods, deeply distrust whites. These individuals either refuse to participate in research projects or provide less than candid responses to questions posed by white researchers.

Given the fact that very few white criminologists understand the African-American community, most misinterpret the data they do collect.

Few white criminologists have direct experience with African-Americans beyond a mere cordial greeting or brief conversation. White criminologists generally lack familiarity with the history, languages, gestures, values, and cultures of the African-American community. They simply do not have an in-depth knowledge of the African-American experience.

On the other hand, African-American criminologists were raised in predominantly African-American neighborhoods and continue to reside in or regularly visit relatives or friends living in these neighborhoods. As a result, these scholars not only have better access than their white counterparts to those African-American populations that are frequently "objects of scholarly inquiry" but possess a broad and deep understanding of African-Americans. For these reasons, African-American criminologists are better equipped than their white counterparts to conduct research on inner-city crime problems.

Some observers might argue that African-American criminologists have an equal opportunity to obtain sizable research grants because grants are awarded through a competitive process. Only the naive believe that the playing field is level. Many research grants are awarded from discretionary funds — there is no competition for these grants.

When there is competition, the manner in which the requests for proposals are written effectively exclude African-American criminologists' participation. Funding agencies usually shape the requests for proposals based on the theories advanced by white criminologists. African-Americans frequently disagree with these theories, and their rejection of the basic assumptions included in the requests for proposals places African-Americans at a distinct disadvantage. In other words, African-American criminologists essentially begin "the race" several yards behind their white counterparts because they must start by challenging the theoretical framework in which the grant applications will be evaluated.

Consequently, African-American criminologists often are discouraged from submitting grant applications to many public and private funding agencies because of their fundamental disagreement with the perspectives advanced in these agencies' requests for proposals. Discouragement also results from realization that funding agencies are inclined to fund those criminologists having published extensively in refereed journals or having completed other major research projects.

### *Exclusion by Members of the Press*

The editorial boards and assignment editors of news organizations are interested in crime and its control. When stories are prepared, news reporters often seek information from criminal justice practitioners. But they also frequently look to those sitting on the faculties of colleges and universities to provide detailed explanations about the causes of crime or to offer opinions about long-range strategies to control it.

Criminology and criminal justice faculties are predominantly white; most have no African-American scholars. Consequently, the public receives the perspectives of white criminologists. Much of the information given to the press by these scholars is based on their personal perceptions of the crime problem in African-American neighborhoods rather than on the results of rigorous empirical research. The public is provided little information by white criminologists with which to challenge the completely unfounded notion that crime and race are inextricably intertwined. Consequently, the public is led to believe that African-Americans are responsible for most of the crime.

This is a particularly disturbing situation. Atlanta's former mayor, Maynard Jackson (1977) contended that

> we have cultivated an environment through the press and other forms of mass media which promotes aspects of crime that tend to give support to the myth that blackness and criminality are synonymous terms. (p. 30)

He maintained that race should not "raise a presumption of criminality" (p. 29).

## EFFECTS OF EXCLUSION

There are several obvious effects of excluding African-American perspectives and limiting their participation in the field of criminology. First, the field has developed with little recognition of the ideas advanced by African-Americans. As a result, the issues have been defined without the benefit of the knowledge possessed by those most likely to understand important components of the phenomena under investigation. Consequently, few theories on crime causation have any practical value (Brown 1977).

Second, there is a disturbing overreliance on data published in the *Uniform Crime Reports*. Criminologists are preoccupied with "crunching numbers" generated for wholly other purposes. Too frequently, available data are first examined and then theories are developed. This is simply unprofessional. Theory formulation should precede data collection. Otherwise, as we too often observe, criminologists fail to even consider whether they are seeking answers to questions relevant to the issues at hand. And as Napper (1977) succinctly reminds us, this approach "blatantly generates false perceptions of crime and ... provides the basis for believing that criminality is synonymous with blackness" (p. 15).

Third, there is an emphasis on funding large-scale data collection efforts, nearly all of which are conducted by white criminologists. As a result, money frequently is not available to fund the advancement of alternative theoretical or policy-oriented perspectives. Smaller, innovative, issue-specific proposals offered by African-American criminologists are not funded, supposedly because no money is available. Consequently, the quest to establish the field as a legitimate academic discipline is stymied.

Fourth, there is a tendency for criminologists to respond to irrelevant questions posed by criminal justice practitioners, policymakers, funding sources, and members of the press. These parties encourage criminologists to ask "how many fit into this category?" before asking why the categories were developed and if the categories are appropriate for the issues under consideration. And these same parties too readily adopt policy recommendations without understanding the targets of those policies. The obvious absence of African-American perspectives, as well as their possible contribution to the development of appropriate questions and the recommendation of policies suitable to the targets of those policies, are unquestioned.

Perhaps the most telling effect of excluding African-American perspectives is the fact that criminologists and criminal justice practitioners have made very little progress in understanding crime or its causes. Scholars and practitioners are even unable to accurately describe the nature and extent of the crime problem. We still do not know how much crime occurs, and there is little consensus about what causes it. Indeed, the most practical recommendations for controlling crime frequently come from individuals outside the field.

## HOW TO INCLUDE THE AFRICAN-AMERICAN PERSPECTIVE

Obviously, the perspectives of African-American scholars must be included if this nation is to make progress in understanding and controlling crime and delinquency. We propose that the following steps be taken:

1. White scholars should include the perspectives advanced by African-American scholars when they write books or other major treatises, edit books, and compile bibliographies.
2. White scholars and funding agencies should make certain that African-American scholars are included as consultants or researchers when large-scale research projects are conducted, particularly those focusing on inner-city crime problems.

3. Professional organizations and refereed journals must include African-American scholars on their policymaking committees and editorial boards.
4. Criminal justice practitioners and policymakers must include African-American scholars when seeking advice or technical assistance and when establishing commissions.

We anticipate that arguments will be made concerning the difficulty of locating adequate numbers of African-American scholars to participate in the aforementioned activities. While acknowledging that the number of these scholars is small, we reject arguments that they cannot be found.

## SUMMARY AND CONCLUSIONS

We realize that some readers might attempt to dismiss our argument that African-American criminologists are excluded by pointing out that we lack empirical evidence to substantiate our claims. Others might contend that our argument is no more than impressionistic musings of two disgruntled African-American criminologists. We challenge these critics to provide evidence to the contrary.

Certainly, there are some African-American criminologists noted in a few white criminologists' books. There are some with publications in refereed journals. There are some sitting on the editorial boards of refereed journals or occupying important positions in criminology organizations. There are some having received sizable research grants, as well as some serving on commissions and being contacted by the news media. But for the most part, African-American criminologists' perspectives are being totally ignored. The number of those *included* is so small that they can be counted on one hand and called by name.

While we believe that collecting data to help analyze the reasons for African-Americans' exclusion would be a worthy endeavor, it is not our intention to encourage this type of research. Frankly, because crime and delinquency are such pressing problems in our neighborhoods, we believe that both time and money would be better spent exploring ways to reduce these problems.

Our purpose in taking time to write this article is to remind criminologists and policymakers that African-American perspectives are virtually absent. We encourage them to listen to more voices so that this nation can make progress in reducing crime and delinquency.

African-American perspectives are virtually excluded from major treatises on criminology and criminal justice. We are seldom consulted, appointed to commissions, or invited to conduct research. We believe that we have been excluded primarily because we challenge many of the basic assumptions proposed by white scholars and because including us requires distribution of financial resources for consulting, technical assistance, and research among a broader group of scholars.

Whether or not one concludes that racism is the basis for African-American scholars' exclusion is immaterial to a resolution of the issues raised in this article. A finding that our white colleagues are racists is simply not relevant to the question of how this nation can benefit from the expertise of African-American criminologists.

Unquestionably, this nation will make little progress in controlling crime and delinquency if it follows its current course. Clearly, the field of criminology and criminal justice will not receive standing as a respectable academic discipline until it demonstrates that it is making worthwhile contributions to this nation's efforts to control crime and delinquency. History suggests that neither goal will be accomplished without the full participation of African-American criminologists and inclusion of African-American perspectives.

One would err by concluding that the foregoing discussion suggests that white criminologists are unable to make useful contributions. We are not suggesting that these scholars are incapable of studying crime or are unfit for service as consultants or researchers. Rather, we argue that this nation's ability to control crime and delinquency is stymied because of a reluctance to include the ideas advanced by African-American criminologists.

This article demonstrates that African-American scholars have been excluded. We argue that we must be included and that we can be to the extent that white criminologists, criminal justice practitioners, funding agencies, policymakers, and members of the press are willing to broaden the scope of inquiry and include new voices.

African-American scholars have made and continue to make valuable contributions to the field of criminology. Our contributions must be acknowledged. Our voices must be heard.

## REFERENCES

Austin, R. 1989. "Family Environment, Educational Aspiration and Performance in St. Vincent." *Review of Black Political Economy* 17:191-22.

Banks, T. 1977. "Discretionary Justice and the Black Offender." In *Blacks and Criminal Justice*, edited by C. Owen and J. Bell. Lexington, MA: Lexington Books.

Barnett, S. 1977. "Researching Black Justice: Descriptions and Implications." In *Blacks and Criminal Justice*, edited by C. Owen and J. Bell. Lexington, MA: Lexington Books.

Bell, C. and E. Jenkins, 1990. "Preventing Black Homicide." In *State of Black America 1990*, edited by the National Urban League. New York: National Urban League, Inc.

Bell, J. and I. Joyner. 1977. "Crime in the Black Community." In *Blacks and Criminal Justice*, edited by C. Owen and J. Bell. Lexington, MA: Lexington Books.

Brown, L. 1974. "Crime, Criminal Justice and the Black Community." *Journal of Afro-American Issues* 11:87-100.

_______. 1977. "Causes of Crime." In *Black Crime: A Police View*, edited by H. Bryce. Washington, DC: Joint Center for Political Studies.

_______. 1988. "Crime in the Black Community." In *State of Black America 1988*, edited by the National Urban League. New York: National Urban League, Inc.

Conyers, J. 1977. "Crime as a Concern of Congress." In *Black Crime: A Police View*, edited by H. Bryce. Washington, DC: Joint Center for Political Studies.

Covington, J. 1984. "Insulation from Labelling: Deviant Defenses in Treatment." *Criminology* 22:619-43.

_______. 1986. "Self-Esteem and Deviance: The Effects of Race and Gender." *Criminology* 24:105-36.

Davis, J. 1976. "Blacks, Crime and American Culture." *Annals of the American Academy of Political and Social Science* 423:89-98.

Davis, L. 1976. "Historical Overview of Crime and Blacks Since 1876." In *Crime and Its Impact on the Black Community*, edited by L. Gary and L. Brown. Washington, DC: Howard University Institute for Urban Affairs and Research.

Edwards, W. 1978. "The Minorities' Relation to Crime: A Concept of Social Deprivation." *Western Journal of Black Studies* 2:275-81.

Headley, B. 1989. "Racism, Powerlessness and Justice." *Social Justice* 16:1-19.

Jackson, M. 1977. "Crime as a Concern of City Hall." In *Black Crime: A Police View*, edited by H. Bryce. Washington, DC: Joint Center for Political Studies.

Miller, K. 1909. "Crime Among Negroes." Paper presented at the Hampton Negro Conference.

Myers, S. and M. Simms. 1989. *The Economics of Race and Crime.* New Brunswick, NJ: Transaction Press.

Napper, G. 1977. "Perceptions of Crime: Problems and Implications." In *Black Perspectives on Crime and the Criminal Justice System*, edited by R. Woodson. Boston: Hall.

National Minority Advisory Council on Criminal Justice. 1980. *The Inequality of Justice: A Report on Crime and the Administration of Justice in the Minority Community.* Washington, DC: National Minority Advisory Council on Criminal Justice.

Perry, R. 1989. "Re-examining the Black on Black Crime Issue: A Theoretical Essay." *Western Journal of Black Studies* 13:66-71.

Primm, B. 1987. "Drug Use: Special Implications for Black America." In *State of Black America 1987*, edited by the National Urban League. New York: National Urban League, Inc.

Scott, E. 1976. "Black Attitudes Toward Crime and Crime Prevention." In *Crime and Its Impact on the Black Community*, edited by L. Gary and L. Brown. Washington, DC: Howard University Institute for Urban Affairs and Research.

Sulton, A. 1989. *Inner-City Crime Control.* Washington, DC: Police Foundation.

Taylor Greene, H. 1979. *A Comprehensive Bibliography of Criminology and Criminal Justice Literature by Black Authors from 1895 to 1978.* Hyattsville, MD: Ummah Publications.

Vontress, C. 1962. "Patterns of Segregation and Discrimination: Contributing Factors to Crime Among Negroes." *Journal of Negro Education* 31:108-16.

Young, V. 1980. "Women, Race and Crime." *Criminology* 18:26-34.

_______. 1986. "Gender Expectations and Their Impact on Black Female Offenders and Victims." *Justice Quarterly* 3:305-27.

# A DICHOTOMIZATION: CRIME AND CRIMINALITY AMONG TRADITIONAL AND CHRISTIANIZED IGBO

*Sampson Ike Oli is an associate professor. He coordinates the criminal justice program and teaches criminal justice courses at Bethune-Cookman College. Oli received his doctorate degree in criminal justice from the City University of New York. He also holds law degrees from the Nigerian Law School in Lagos and the University of Nigeria in Enugu.*

## INTRODUCTION

In recent years, several studies, reports and commissions have examined the apparently rising rate of crime in some of the independent African countries (Carter and Merenin 1981; Brillon 1983). Concern has also been expressed over the seeming propensity of African Americans to commit crime in the United States. Several crime causation theories have been advanced by criminologists in the effort to provide explanations.

This paper examines the social history of the Igbo in Nigeria. Its purpose is to determine the nature and degree of criminality exhibited by the people of this society. Such information will shed light on questions concerning these Africans' involvement in crime as well as their involvement in criminal behavior in other countries in which they now reside.

## THE IGBO

The Igbo are found mainly in Anambra, Enugu, Imo, Abia and the eastern fringes of Delta states of Nigeria. This corresponds roughly with north of Nsukka highlands to parts of the Atlantic coast.

The words "Ibo" and "Igbo" are now used interchangeably. In the past, Igbo referred to the people while Ibo was used to describe the language. Because of diversity and lack of centralization, some Igbo still refuse to use the word Igbo as descriptive of themselves. This is because the word

"Igbo" was until recently used derisively to apply to less civilized persons who live in the hinterland (Ogbalu 1979).

The meaning and origin of the word "Igbo" is as unknown as the origin of the people. Bohannan and Curtin (1979) suggest that the word "Ibo" was a classification applied from outside and that the Igbo themselves might not even have been conscious of their common identity. After more than fifteen years work among the Igbo, Basden (1921) lamented, "All my attempts to trace the origin of the name Ibo have been unsuccessful."

Writing on the origin of the Igbo, Stride and Ifeka (1971) note that oral evidence and settlement patterns suggest that in about A.D. 1300 to 1400, the Igbo began to move south and east from the region of Awka and Orlu. Henderson (1972) refers to another set of legends which trace the origin of the Igbo to Nri and Agulu. Ogbalu (1981) and Nzimiro (1972), while agreeing with the above, suggest that allowance be made for recent migrations of some Igbo from Benin. Anyasodo (1975) on his part maintains that the Igbo people migrated from Abysinian highland areas which encompassed present-day Ethiopia around the fourth century B.C. Oral traditions, myths, folklore and songs indicate, however, that Igbo people did not migrate from any other distant parts of the world. There is consensus among the Igbo themselves that God Chineke, Chukwu, Obasi or Olisa created and planted them in places where they now occupy, and that they have no ancestral links with any other people (Ejidike 1991).

## IGBO SOCIAL AND POLITICAL SYSTEM

Among the Igbo, religion and law are so closely interwoven that their social and political life is highly influenced by a pantheon of supernatural powers which operate within the human sphere in various ways and to varying degrees. These supernatural forces are grouped into two broad categories: 1) those that occupy and control the heavens under the general supervision of God Chineke, Chukwu, Olisa, or Obasi di nelu; and 2) those that occupy and control the earth, led by the earth goddess Ani, Ala, or Obasi di nala. There are also several minor deities representing water and agriculture, fortune, destiny, wealth, strength, evil spirits and other natural phenomena. And there are spirits that represent departed ancestors, controlling the fortunes of their living descendants.

Although the Igbo would rate the God of the heavens Obasi di nelu or Chineke as more powerful, in actual fact, they hold the earth goddess Obasi di nala as more sacred. She controls the earth on which they live, from which they draw resources vital to life, and into which they are buried when they die (Ani 1991).

## MAP OF NIGERIA SHOWING IGBOLAND

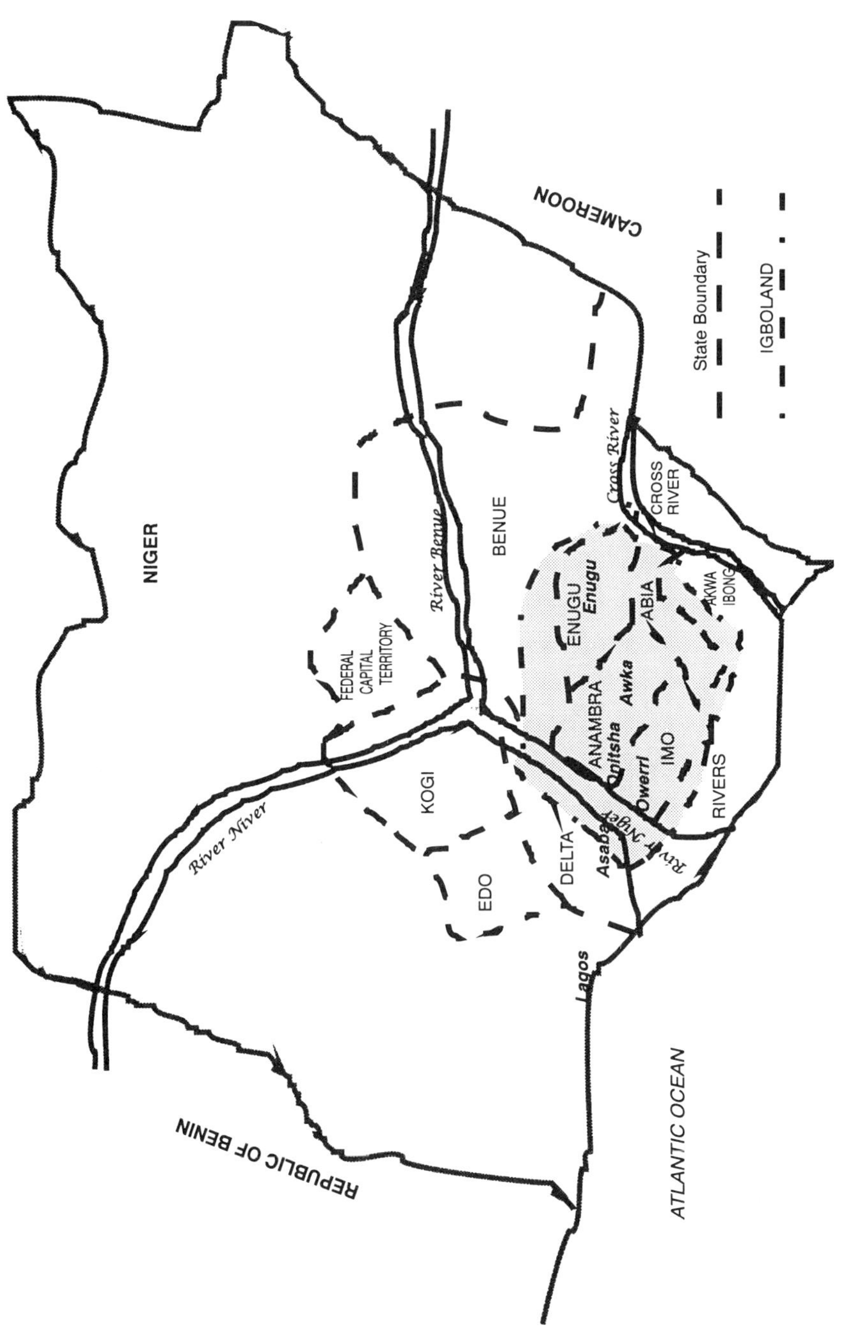

The Igbo are more concerned with achieved leadership position than with advantages of birth or ascribed leadership. Individual initiative and achievement determine the position each person assumes within the Igbo sociopolitical system. Flowing from and giving added meaning to this equality is a spirit of competition in every sphere of life. Individuals are respected for their ambition in seeking power, status or prestige (Ezenwa 1991).

Igbo culture perceives a dynamic world in which all things are subject to change, even their relation with the spiritual world (Achebe 1959). As a result, the underlying world view of the Igbo emphasizes the very essence of change within society.

The family ezi na ulo is a very important institution among the Igbo. It is closer to what has been considered the extended rather than the nuclear family. Thus, it differs from the English concept of family in that it is not limited to a husband, his wife and their children. It includes other relations such as in-laws, uncles, cousins, nephews (distant and near) and even maids and servants. The Igbo believe that they owe a great deal of responsibility to all with whom they are related.

Law among the Igbo begins in the family where the process of regulating the behavior of the individual member is first put into effect. The Igbo child, unlike his counterpart in some of the western societies, is exposed to regulations which incorporate all the ramifications of Igbo law, custom and religion from an early age. The training of children among the Igbo is everybody's responsibility and every adult is expected to correct and protect a child, whether related to the child or not, for, according to Ogbalu (1984), a child is the child of all, *Nwa bu nwa ora.*

## IGBO LEGAL SYSTEM

The source of each Igbo law often determines how it is published, and the legal process needed to ensure compliance. There are three major sources of Igbo law. First, those ordained by the gods. Second, those handed down by the ancestors. And, third, those decreed by the living.

Laws ordained by the gods are announced: (1) by the chief priest, in person or through the town crier; (2) by the gods themselves, usually at night by masquerades; or (3) as in the case of the long juju, from the depth of a cave (Stride and Ifeka 1971). These laws must be obeyed because they cannot be questioned. Among these are laws about planting and harvesting of crops, laws about the seasons and protocol for worship of particular gods, and sanctity of human life. The Igbo believe that their gods are capable of enforcing their own laws directly without intervention by mortals (Achebe 1959, p.32).

Laws handed down by the ancestors are kept in circulation through fables, songs and stories, and through regular declarations by elders and family heads. These are primarily what departed ancestors considered as good or bad during their time on earth. Among these are laws relating to interpersonal relations, care of the elderly, welfare of children, crime and warfare. Such laws, together with laws decreed by the living, are enforced by chief priests, age grades and masquerades (Achebe 1959, p.32).

Laws decreed by the living are made up of rules and regulations which the present generation consider sufficiently important to govern their interaction with one another. Among these are laws relating to marriage, welfare of children, property, disputes over land, fishing in prohibited streams, and similar laws.

The Igbo believe that abominations stick to the body *alu na atado na aru*. This means that when an abomination is committed by one member, the entire community bears the sin. Therefore, in order to avoid the stigma, there is intense pressure on the offending member and his family to perform all the necessary ceremonial covering of abomination. Otherwise, the entire community suffers the consequences of the misdeeds of its member (Achebe 1959, p.32).

Generally, offenses are handled by the elders as follows: A complaint is brought before the elders by the offended party in a ritual context. The elders arrange for a public hearing if the offense is of a serious nature. Otherwise, they listen to both parties and then pronounce judgment *ka ikpe*. On the other hand, if the dispute is without substance, they may simply advise both parties to be of good behavior *dua ha odu*, after blaming each to the extent of his contribution to the dispute. Quarrels between members of the same family are settled by the family heads. Quarrels between individuals from different families are settled before the entire community *ama ala*, with the elders acting as arbiters. More serious disputes, especially between different families, require the attention of spirits in the form of masquerades (Achebe, 1959 pp. 87-89; Ogbalu, 1979 pp. 102-104).

## ENFORCEMENT OF IGBO LAW

Law and authority are so closely interwoven with the social and political fabric of the Igbo people that it is often difficult to separate one from the other. Law, politics, family relationships and conduct are equally and simultaneously emphasized within the immediate family as they are outside it (Okafor 1978).

For example, the most serious crime among the Igbo is homicide ochu. If the slaying was intentional, the offender would be put to death. Murder was very rare among the Traditional Igbo (Aniekwe 1990).

Involuntary or inadvertent killing ochu oghom were treated differently. The punishment for inadvertent killings is one which gives the offender an opportunity to flee the village with his entire family for a period of not less than seven years (Achebe 1959, p.117). Other less serious offenses such as stealing, adultery, battery, and fishing in prohibited streams, are punished by ostracism, ridicule or fine.

The Igbo concept of punishment does not include incarceration. The only practice that resembles incarceration in the Igbo legal system is when a prisoner is handed to a leading member of the community for safe keeping pending determination of his fate (Achebe 1959, p.29).

Igbo society includes the dead no less than the living. The ancestors therefore continue to be a guiding force in the maintenance of law and order. The ofo was the symbol of authority and continues to represent evidence of the presence of the ancestors and a means of ensuring that equity and justice are available to all. The whole system of magic and taboo serve as a solid buttress of law and a means of ensuring security and protecting property. According to Okafor (1978), "Belief in divine moral code, and the ability of the gods to punish any deviations from or violations of the divine law, was the most powerful mechanism of social control in African society."

In modern times, the Nigerian criminal justice system responds to crime by arresting, prosecuting and punishing offenders. But Igbo traditional law still operates to ensure that the family of the offender assuage the sin of their family member by paying compensation to the victim or his family (Oli 1991, p.7).

The Igbo attach great importance to the principles of equity. They also recognize the need to take extenuating circumstances into account in individual cases. They are more concerned with maintaining the cohesion of their communities than with the unequivocal affirmation and enforcement of the rights of an individual which may upset the harmony of the group. As Meek (1970) notes:

> Trials, therefore, were often nothing more than an organized expression of public opinion, and served the purpose of allowing grievances to be aired, a litigant's object being, frequently, to vindicate his character publicly, rather than mulct his opponent in damages.

Infringement of laws are dealt with by elders or by the entire community depending on the seriousness of the offense. For example, if a member is accused of committing a crime, he is summoned to appear before the elders of the community. Trials are usually held before family heads, elders and spirits, or at the shrine of particular gods. During a trial, a defendant is given every opportunity to confront his accusers, to produce evidence and witnesses in his defense, and to ask questions of the accuser. He may also offer to take an oath at the shrine of a god selected by the community (Ogbalu 1981, p.103). The defendant is given every opportunity to adduce evidence to show that he acted within his rights, or that there are mitigating circumstances. Traditional Igbo trials are made easy by the fact that everyone believes that the gods saw what happened and would punish any person who tells lies at trials (Ogbalu 1981, pp.99-104).

Where the offense was committed flagrantly and the offender found guilty, he is expected to comply with the imposed punishment without waiting for further intervention by the community. Failure to comply within a specified time will result in a visit by an age grade representative assigned the duty of collecting the fine or of executing the judgment. If the age grade fails to accomplish all or part of its tasks, spirits are then invoked to enforce the decision. It is believed that intervention by spirits will result in extensive damage to the property and person of the offender. No offenders will wait for such a visit from spirits to take place (Achebe 1959, p.117).

## AGE GRADES

Age grades are traditional organizations to which all Igbo males (and females in some Igbo communities) belong by virtue of birth. Actual membership is sometimes preceded by formal application and an elaborate induction ceremony. Members are arranged according to age, to which specific duties and privileges are assigned. Each age grade functions as an arena within which Igbo traditions and customs are expounded and the importance of respect for authority and service to the community are emphasized.

Age grades are organized in every Igbo community. The age span for each grouping varies between communities, depending on the population of the community and the customs inherited from their ancestors. For example, in Agulu, Awka, Nise and Nri communities, the age span is from three to seven years. In Onitsha, Obosi, Oba and Ogidi communities, the age span is from three to six years. In Enugu, Awgu and Udi communities, the age span is from three to five years. As a general rule, age grades remain unorganized until potential members reach the age of puberty (Ogbalu 1979, p.29).

The most important function of age grades in Igbo society is the guarding of public morality. They emphasize compliance by members to codes of community conduct, and they serve as tools for enforcement of such codes. Each age grade acts as a venue for controlling the behavior of its members, and through them, the entire community. An age grade is the arena in which the virtue of striving and prosocial behavior itself is inculcated and emphasized (Oli 1992, p.13).

Age grades take concerted action against any member found guilty of committing an offense. For example, if a member steals, he would be compelled by his age grade to return the stolen property and to pay a fine to the age grade for dragging its name in the mud (Ani 1991).

## CRIME AMONG THE IGBO

In recent years, increasing concern has arisen over the fact that Igbos seem to represent a higher percentage of incarcerated criminals than their total population in Nigeria. According to the Annual Abstract of Statistics (1990), there are more Igbos in prisons in Igbo states and non Igbo states in Nigeria. For example, while the number of Igbos from Anambra state in Oyo state prisons is 178, the number of Yorubas from Oyo state in Anambra state prisons is only two. Also, while Anambra state Igbos in Lagos state prisons is 1,006, the number of Lagos state Yorubas in Anambra state prisons is seven (See Table 1).

Questions are being asked by many Igbo scholars about the impact of the continuing disregard of traditional values. Specifically, if traditional social control systems had served the Igbo so well in the past, why have such control systems failed to serve them now? In particular, such questions are being directed at the growing loss of interest by Christianized Igbos in their traditional religions, laws and customs (Ogbalu 1979).

## CHALLENGES TO RESEARCH

Attempts to explain the rise in the incidence of crime among the Igbo present myriad difficulties. An explanation of the factors that contribute to crime does not by itself explain why the Traditional Igbo are underrepresented in the crime population. Of the 4,295 persons in prison in three Igbo cities of Awka, Onitsha and Enugu, 3,221 were Christian and 1,074 were traditionally oriented (Nigerian Prison Services 1990). Nor do they explain why the Traditional Igbo appear to be involved in a different category of crime than their westernized counterparts (Ogbalu 1981). Nor is it possible to identify a single causal factor. Such explanations can only become valid when presented in connection with a carefully considered study of the cultural and traditional peculiarities of the people involved.

**PRISON ADMISSION IN STATES CLASSIFIED BY STATE OF ORIGIN**

| State / State of Origin | Anambra | Bauchi | Bendel | Benue | Borno | Cross River | Gongola | Imo | Kaduna | Kano | Kwara | Lagos | Niger | Ogun | Ondo | Oyo | Plateau | Rivers | Sokoto | TOTAL |
|---|---|---|---|---|---|---|---|---|---|---|---|---|---|---|---|---|---|---|---|---|
| Anambra | 5,381 | 219 | 419 | 593 | 247 | 122 | 266 | 449 | 747 | 802 | 172 | 1,006 | 345 | 77 | 351 | 178 | 766 | 329 | 136 | 12,605 |
| Bauchi | 16 | 3,741 | 104 | 75 | 407 | n.a. | 96 | 1 | 417 | 168 | 34 | 526 | 78 | 4 | 2 | 31 | 369 | 3 | 31 | 6,103 |
| Bendel | 47 | 33 | 4,574 | 127 | 54 | 45 | 35 | 24 | 493 | 355 | 217 | 991 | 279 | 132 | 364 | 434 | 204 | 185 | 37 | 8,630 |
| Benue | 50 | 74 | 5 | 7,195 | 165 | 60 | 360 | 8 | 555 | 170 | 157 | 638 | 337 | 42 | 84 | 87 | 1.286 | 8 | 22 | 11,303 |
| Borno | 47 | 229 | 38 | 78 | 8,044 | 2 | 499 | 1 | 413 | 296 | 31 | 612 | 108 | 15 | 2 | 54 | 196 | 9 | 17 | 10,691 |
| Cross River | 138 | 85 | 131 | 268 | 3 | 7,250 | 16 | 118 | 243 | 138 | 42 | 671 | 64 | 51 | 150 | 152 | 184 | 722 | 24 | 10,450 |
| Gongola | 31 | 177 | 99 | 241 | 959 | 6 | 7,212 | 12 | 482 | 558 | 15 | 577 | 32 | 7 | 96 | 58 | 241 | 17 | 29 | 10,849 |
| Omo | 1,013 | 86 | 207 | 388 | 128 | 140 | 184 | 6,336 | 589 | 272 | 94 | 1,089 | 311 | 69 | 186 | 208 | 271 | 1,080 | 38 | 12,698 |
| Kaduna | 52 | 97 | 125 | 123 | 32 | 3 | 152 | 10 | 6,558 | 1.151 | 155 | 757 | 319 | 76 | 138 | 72 | 346 | 31 | 104 | 10,301 |
| Kano | 57 | 252 | 111 | 116 | 1,149 | 3 | 406 | 2 | 1,366 | 5,654 | 125 | 854 | 275 | 56 | 63 | 102 | 296 | 34 | 61 | 10,982 |
| Kwara | 11 | 48 | 70 | 50 | 7 | 4 | 6 | 3 | 403 | 112 | 1,733 | 659 | 252 | 92 | 204 | 187 | 155 | 9 | 83 | 4,088 |
| Lagos | 7 | 4 | 51 | 59 | 63 | 12 | 6 | n.a. | 202 | 37 | 59 | 872 | 47 | 173 | 83 | 102 | 182 | 6 | 7 | 1,972 |
| Niger | 1 | 10 | 128 | 60 | 3 | 4 | 15 | n.a. | 340 | 100 | 107 | 694 | 2,415 | 10 | 53 | 23 | 221 | 1 | 121 | 4,306 |
| Ogun | 9 | 3 | 98 | 37 | 3 | 3 | 13 | 1 | 525 | 457 | 70 | 816 | 39 | 2,248 | 452 | 505 | 103 | 12 | 43 | 5,437 |
| Ondo | 13 | 16 | 116 | 60 | 2 | 34 | 5 | 2 | 477 | 132 | 78 | 705 | 26 | 111 | 1,657 | 412 | 88 | 11 | 68 | 4,013 |
| Oyo | 2 | 43 | 96 | 83 | 75 | 11 | 58 | 4 | 446 | 120 | 182 | 914 | 119 | 293 | 430 | 3,596 | 122 | 31 | 71 | 6,696 |
| Plateau | 5 | 142 | 70 | 225 | 195 | 10 | 163 | 15 | 723 | 362 | 41 | 486 | 163 | 8 | 5 | 50 | 5,762 | 21 | 46 | 8,492 |
| Rivers | 18 | 23 | 95 | 71 | 1 | 40 | 39 | 19 | 152 | 127 | 51 | 454 | 29 | 23 | 64 | 54 | 52 | 3,600 | 418 | 5,330 |
| Sokoto | 23 | 59 | 90 | 65 | 431 | 4 | 115 | 4 | 1,102 | 99 | 219 | 651 | 417 | 95 | 26 | 221 | 217 | 20 | 6,633 | 10,891 |
| Foreigners | 16 | 133 | 243 | 105 | 1,393 | 26 | 961 | 1 | 591 | 82 | 89 | 1,202 | 50 | 182 | 5 | 123 | 224 | 57 | 339 | 5,822 |
| Total | 6,937 | 5,474 | 6,870 | 10,019 | 13,361 | 7,788 | 10,607 | 7,010 | 16,824 | 11,592 | 3,671 | 15,174 | 5,705 | 3,764 | 4,415 | 6.649 | 11,285 | 6,186 | 8,328 | 161,659 |

Source: Nigerian Prison Service, Federal Ministry of Internal Affairs.

Note: n.a. = Not Available

Many of the social problems among the Igbo today seem to be linked to the growth of Christianity and a concomitant growth of urbanization and the urge to acquire money, property and prestige. As more and more Igbo sons and daughters join the ranks of Christian converts, old ideas and customs lapse into disuse and eventually disappear (Achebe 1959; Ogbalu 1979).

For example, the fear of spirits is gradually replaced by belief in expiation of sins, and an increased resort to devious means for achieving greatness. Control by tradition is replaced by police control. The English legal system notion that one is presumed innocent until detected and proven guilty, replaces fear of the omnipresence of spirits, admission of guilt and certainty of punishment (Okafor 1978).

A study of the Igbo people presents its own peculiar problems. Few scholars have attempted to study social control systems among the Traditional Igbo. Such reluctance has to a large extent been due to the Igbo culture. The absence of a centralized authority and lack of a uniform Igbo dialect make it difficult for Igbo and non-Igbo researchers to know where to begin. And many scholars of Igbo language have difficulty understanding important Igbo proverbs.

Because it is customary for the Igbo to precede their expressions with proverbs, it is virtually impossible to understand Igbo thought without first understanding Igbo proverbs. And to understand Igbo proverbs, one must first understand the Igbo and their language. According to Echeruo (1971), "...there is absolutely no other way."

Research also has been restricted by factors such as geographical area and survey respondents' suspicion about the researcher's real intentions. The Igbo often attach a special value to time spent with a researcher, and would deliberately fail to appear at prearranged locations. It then became necessary for the researcher to visit their houses to plead with them, or to solicit the intervention of an influential member of the community. This gave the respondent added prestige in his neighborhood as one whose views are of considerable importance (Henderson 1972).

Research efforts are further complicated by the introduction of different Igbo orthographies by the two major Christian denominations in Nigeria. The Roman Catholic Mission (R.C.M.) and the Church Missionary Society (C.M.S.) have each come up with orthographies so different that persons trained in one often experience difficulty reading books written in the other.

Another major problem encountered during research was how to distinguish Christianized from Traditional Igbos. This problem was resolved by reliance on the Igbo custom of naming their children. It is customary for an Igbo child to receive a name that corresponds with the week day on which he or she was born. There are four days in an Igbo week namely, Oye, Afor, Nkwo and Eke. Thus, it is possible to distinguish a Traditional from a Christianized Igbo. Males born to Traditional Igbo families are given names like Nwoye, Nwafor, Nwankwo or Nweke, while females receive names like Mgbooye, Mgboafor, Mgbankwo, or Mgboeke (Ogbalu 1981, p. 26).

The Christianized Igbo usually abandons this traditional naming custom and adopts a Christian name at baptism along with some other Igbo middle name. For example, a person whose traditional name at birth was Nweke Emenike (a son born on Eke day to the Emenike family) may adopt the name Stephen Chukwuma Emenike (Stephen being a biblical name, and Chukwuma a modernized Igbo name which means God knows best). This practice of adopting names after conversion to Christianity offered the best means for the researcher to avoid problems in identifying Traditional and Christianized Igbo (Ogbalu 1981, pp. 26-29).

There have been no comprehensive studies that evaluate the amount of criminal activity resulting from attachment to or participation in or involvement with Traditional Igbo social organization. However, in his book *Things Fall Apart*, Achebe (1959) sheds some light on this question. He dramatized Traditional Igbo life in its encounter with colonialism and Christian life among the Igbo and shows how the coming of white men led to the breaking up of old ways in Traditional Igbo communities. In *Arrow of God*, Achebe (1969) also provides the reader with a classic account of the spirituality of ceremony of Igbo traditional life, laws and customs, and the tragic result of their contact with European culture and collision with British colonial authority.

In *Igbo Institutions and Customs*, Ogbalu (1979) carefully describes various Igbo traditional institutions and customs. He maintains that "There is an urgent need to arouse interest and to pave the way for more accurate and elaborate information that benefits the Igbo and their descendants."

Other studies of the Igbo have been either collections of Igbo proverbs, translations of Igbo fables or accounts of some epochs in Igbo history (Davids 1980).

This paper is an effort to supplement the limited materials developed by earlier scholars. It also expands the range of study to include crime, social control, and the effects of the introduction of foreign religions and social control systems on the behavior of Igbos and their descendants.

## METHODOLOGY

Much of the data referred to in this paper comes from members of the Igbo in Nigeria. The Igbo were selected because Traditional Igbo societies seem to emphasize control of their individual members through various traditional organizations. Also, results of a study of this nature could have external validity when used with reference to descendants of Traditional Igbos who have become Christianized and now live outside Traditional Igbo communities.

Prior research has shown that people's judgment on such matters as moral issues, aesthetic preferences, and religious questions are often influenced by what they are told or what they believe to be the majority view (Henshel and Silverman 1975). Given these factors, it is difficult to predict behavior without taking into account the views of the people in the communities within which the behavior is most likely to occur. Since precise measurements of such views are virtually impossible, the nearest suitable method that can produce reliable information on the subjects is a perception study.

A survey group comprised of 360 persons of Igbo origin in Nigeria and abroad were interviewed. Direct observation, face-to-face interviews, and a mailed survey questionnaire were used to collect data. Since the formal underlying structural principles of the Igbo social system could not easily be obtained through the use of these data collection activities, data from official records served in several ways to enhance and clarify information obtained. Data from the Nigerian Police, Nigerian Prison Services and Courts in the cities of Enugu, Onitsha and Awka, and other official sources in Nigeria, including the Federal Office of Statistics, were obtained. The combination of methods made possible a closer examination of the empirical fit between actual Igbo behavior and the formal rules of their social life. In other words, the methods employed helped clarify differences between what Igbo people say or feel they do and what they actually do.

Because age grades exist and play important roles in every Traditional Igbo community (Ogbalu 1979), this study also examined the operational strategies of that social institution in order to determine the degree of its effectiveness in advancing law-abiding behavior among Traditional Igbos.

To accomplish this, two major areas of concern were considered. One related to the respondents' general perception of traditional law enforcement agencies. The other related to perception of the role, functional problems, and degree of influence of age grades on subsequent behavior among members.

The first concern was of a general nature. The research questions were made sufficiently open-ended to enable respondents to provide as much information as possible. Open-ended questions also made it possible for subjects to include other information on age grades that would otherwise not be obtained in a rigidly structured closed-ended format.

The second concern involved core issues. The questions were designed to elicit as many direct responses as possible without arousing any suspicions or hostility based on fear that the questioning was intended for purposes other than the declared ones.

The population of incarcerated convicts in Awka, Onitsha and Enugu was also examined. Primary interest was in two areas: (a) the religious orientation of the inmates in each incarceration facility of the cities studied; and (b) the opinion of subjects with regard to effectiveness of age grades as agents of social control.

A total of 1,805 inmates in the three cities were Christian and 1,047 were traditionally-oriented in their religious beliefs. When compared with populations of the cities, just over 50 percent of the total population of the three cities are Christian, while the prison population is 74.6 percent Christian.

Even though the city of Awka has a greater concentration of Traditional Igbos than Christianized Igbos (43,200 to 33,600), significantly more Christianized Igbos are in prison than Traditional Igbos in that city (387 to 162) (Anambra State Ministry of Information 1985; Oli 1991). This information tends to support the original hypothesis that Traditional Igbo social control systems are more compelling on behavior.

The 360 members of the sample group were asked to respond to the question: "Do age grades control crime?" Of the 160 Christians who responded, 133 or 83 percent agreed that age grades do control crime. Of the 171 Traditional Igbos responding, 157 or 92 percent stated they felt age grades control crime. Apparently, a very high percentage of Igbos surveyed, regardless of their religious orientation, believe that age grades control crime.

To the question: "To what extent do age grades influence positive behavior?," of the 309 responses, 161 were from Christianized and 148 were from Traditional Igbos. Eighty two percent of the Christian and 93 percent of the Traditional Igbos indicated that age grades do influence behavior toward conformity with law. A chi-square analysis showed that the differences between the two groups were not significant. Hence, religious orientation is not a critical factor in determining if an Igbo believes that avoiding crime is a result of the age grade activities.

Overall, the questions and responses dealt with diverse areas of the Igbo social system and the influence of age grades on behavior. A majority of respondents, irrespective of religious orientation or residence, indicate that the more involved a person is with traditional organizations, religion and customs, the more likely he is to avoid anti-social behavior.

## CONCLUSION

To assume that everything traditional has been changed or forgotten so that traces of it are no longer visible among Nigerian Igbo would be incorrect. If anything, such changes, wherever they occurred, have been generally superficial, affecting the material side of life, and only beginning to reach the deeper levels of thinking patterns and responses of the people. In fact, traditional concepts still form the essential cultural background of many Igbo, and they are often quick to revert to such concepts when faced with serious personal problems. These concepts represent a major link with their past and offer an essential source of information about their history and tradition.

Three major questions were examined: Why was crime so insignificant during the early days in Igbo communities when traditional social institutions were intact? Why are the Igbo presently over represented in the criminal population in Nigeria? And, why are Christianized Igbos overrepresented in the population of incarcerated criminals in Nigeria? Answers to these questions may provide an insight into factors responsible for rising crime in independent African countries.

What this paper has shown is that traditional social control systems have helped and are helping the Traditional Igbo to deal with problems of crime and other types of anti-social behaviors. Obviously, some amount of crime existed and continues to exist among the Traditional Igbo, but the number pales in comparison with what exists among Christianized Igbos today.

Because traditional systems of social control have been neglected, crime and anti-social behavior are increasing among the Igbo. And since there is a higher incidence of crime and criminality among Christianized Igbo than Traditional Igbo, modernization and neglect of traditional customs and values may be responsible for crime.

Evidence presented in this study indicates that delinquency and crime rates have not been major problems for Igbos who maintain traditional lifestyles. Thus, in the absence of such a comprehensive social control system, crime is more likely to increase. This might explain why some Africans and African-Americans are involved in crime. More specifically, where they internalize the norms and social systems of foreign societies and cultures, with fewer traditional social control mechanisms, increased participation in crime occurs.

This seems to suggest that there is an urgent need for change in Nigeria. Nigeria's leaders should consider reemphasizing traditional values and invite the world to take a closer look at its rich traditional heritage. Otherwise it may risk decay.

## REFERENCES

*Abstract of Statistics 1988*. Lagos, Nigeria: Federal Office of Statistics.

Achebe, C. 1959. *Things Fall Apart*. New York: Fawcett Crest Books.

Ani, F. 1991. Interview with Chief Ani the Omeokachie of Nneogidi on July 15th.

Aniekwe, P. 1990. Interview with Chief Aniekwe of Adazi Nnukwu on July 20th and 21st.

Anyasodo, U. 1975. *Ebolachi-Have You Survived The Night?* Michigan: Habo Press.

Basden G. 1921. *Among the Ibo of Nigeria*. London: Seely Service.

Bohannan, P. and P. Curtin, 1971. *Africa and Africans*. New York: Natural History Press.

Brillon, Y. 1983. "Juridical Acculturation In Black Africa and Its Effects on the Administration of Criminal Justice." *International Summaries NCJ-78583*.

Carter M. and O. Merenin. 1981. "Law Enforcement and Political Change In Post-Civil War Nigeria." *Journal of Criminal Justice* 9:125-149.

Davids, P. 1980. *Ilulu Igbo*. Onitsha: University Publishing Co.

Echeruo, M. 1971. "Igbo Thought Through Igbo Proverbs: A Comment." *The CONCH III* 2:63-75.

Ejidike, E. 1990. Interview with Chief Ejidike the Igwe Eze Onyeolulu of Agulu on July 30th.

Ezenwa, P. 1991. Interview with Chief Ezenwa the Eze Okpoko I of Oba in June.

Henderson, R. N. 1972. *The King In Every Man*. New Haven: Yale University Press.

Henshel, R. and R. Silverman. 1975. *Perception in Criminology*. New York: Columbia University Press.

Nzimiro, I. 1972. *Studies In Igbo Political System*. Los Angeles: University of California Press.

_______ 1981. *Omenala Igbo*. Onitsha, Nigeria: University Publishing Co.

Ogbalu, F. 1979. *Igbo Institutions and Customs*. Onitsha, Nigeria: University Publishing Co.

_______ 1981. *Ndu Ndi Igbo*. Onitsha, Nigeria: University Publishing Co.

Okafor, F. 1978. *Africa At The Crossroads*. New York: Vintage Press.

Oli, S. 1991. *Crime And Social Control Among The Igbo*. Unpublished Manuscript.

_______ 1992. *Age Grades Agents of Social Control In Igboland*. Unpublished Manuscript.

Stride, G. and C. Ifeka. 1971. *Peoples and Empires of West Africa*. Lagos, Nigeria: Thomas Nelson (Nigeria) Ltd.

U.S. Department of Justice. 1991. *Sourcebook of Criminal Justice Statistics*. Washington D.C.: U.S. Government Printing Office.

# THE COLONIAL MODEL AS A THEORETICAL EXPLANATION OF CRIME AND DELINQUENCY

*Becky Tatum is an assistant professor at North Carolina Central University. She teaches criminology and criminal justice courses. Tatum currently is completing her doctorate degree at the State University of New York in Albany.*

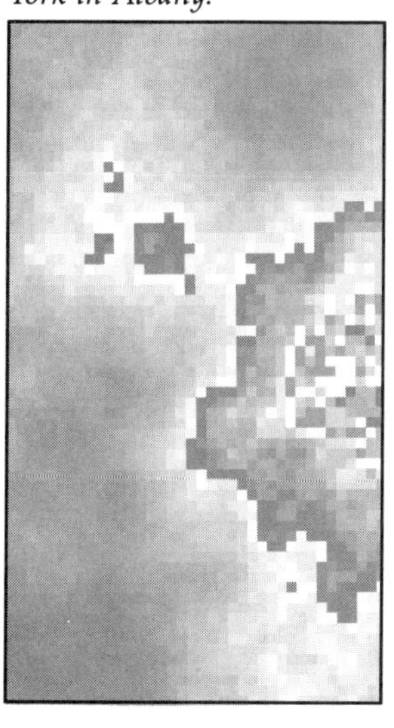

## INTRODUCTION

Empirical research on the relationship between race and crime spans many decades. Historically, the findings of this research reveal a disproportionate involvement in criminal activity by people of color in comparison to their representation in the population. Most of the crime statistics point to young African-American males as being the major perpetrators of crime.

National arrest statistics in 1991 suggest that African-Americans under 18 years of age account for 29 percent of the Part One Index crimes which include murder, forcible rape, robbery, aggravated assault, larceny-theft, arson, burglary and motor vehicle theft (FBI 1992). However, in 1991, these youths comprised only four percent of the total U.S. population (U.S. Bureau of the Census 1992).

The overrepresentation of African-Americans in crime and delinquency is reaffirmed by victimization and self-report data. Victimization data in 1991 show that African-Americans account for 28 percent of single-offender victimizations and 38 percent of multiple-offender victimizations, which include rape, robbery and assault (U.S. Department of Justice 1992). Self-report data (National Youth Survey) stress the importance of distinguishing between prevalence and incidence rates of delinquency. While prevalence comparisons in delinquent behavior show few differences between African-American and White youth from lower, working and middle class backgrounds, the incidence of delinquent behavior appears to be greater among low-income and African-American youths (Elliott and Ageton 1980).

Numerous theoretical models have attempted to explain the association between race, crime and delinquency. Traditional theoretical models range from anomie, social disorganization and relative deprivation to differential involvement in crime, biological determinism and a subculture of violence. One theoretical model that has not been fully examined and is absent from mainstream criminology is the theory of internal colonialism.

The colonial model is a socio-psychological perspective. It assesses the impact of the social context which an individual experiences on the psychological factor of alienation. In particular, the theory examines the relationship between structural oppression, alienation and three adaptive forms of behavior — assimilation, crime or deviance, and protest.

According to this model, individuals who are the victims of social, economic and political oppression are likely to perceive that oppression, and as a result develop feelings of alienation in which the commission of crime is an adaptive response. In the colonial model, race or color is the ascriptive criterion for differences in subjection to situations of oppression.

The purpose of this paper is to review the original version of the colonial model and the application of the model (internal colonialism) to the United States. Second, this paper will address the adequacy of internal colonialism in explaining the association between race and crime.

## THE COLONIAL MODEL

Colonialism is a social system traditionally characterized by a state's establishment of political control over a foreign territory and the settlement of those foreigners in the territory for purposes of exploitation and political hegemony (Staples 1989). Colonialism has existed for centuries and has involved territories originally inhabited by White and non-White people.

The colony theory, as developed by Frantz Fanon (1963 and 1967a), is concerned with the colonization of non-Western or non-White people by European nations. A psychiatrist and activist from Martinque, Fanon writes about the racial relations that exist between Blacks and Whites in the third world countries of Asia and Africa.

Colonization is a process which has four distinct phases. The clearest delineation of the four phases of colonization is discussed by Blauner (1969). The first phase involves a forced, involuntary entry of a foreign racial group into the geographical territory of the society being colonized. Specifically, a small minority of outsiders enters a country and establishes control over its majority population. The primary objective of the outsiders is to obtain valuable economic resources. First contact between the two groups usually involves a system of trade where the outsiders trade relatively worthless items for more expensive and valuable items. Observing that the native inhabitants are unaware of the value of their goods, the outsiders move to subjugate and exploit them for their own economic gain (Davidson 1976).

The second phase of colonialization involves the establishment of a colonial society. This society can be characterized by three interrelated processes of cultural imposition, cultural disintegration and cultural re-creation. In a colonial society, actors from two different social worlds come together in a situation where one set of actors are citizens of a powerful technologically superior European state. These Europeans possess social and economic privileges that are not shared by the native people. The unequal distribution of power and special privileges of Europeans result in the creation of two distinct social actors — the colonizers (immigrants) and the colonized (native).

Cultural disintegration occurs when the colonists alter the cultural and social organizations of the colonized people. This alteration is more than a result of the natural processes of contact and acculturation. The colonizing power institutes a policy which constrains, transforms or destroys indigenous values, orientations, and ways of life (Fanon 1963). Due to economic and political power, the colonizers are able to carry out a process of cultural imposition in which their culture and values have ascendancy over native culture and values. In the colonial society, it is necessary to re-create or re-define the culture of the native. The colonizer paints the native as the quintessence of evil (Fanon 1963). Native society is described as lacking values and as being insensible to ethics. The customs of the native people, their traditions, and their myths are defined as signs of the poverty of spirit and constitutional depravity. Zoological terms are used to describe the native. The colonizer speaks of the native's reptilian motions, the stink of the native quarters, those children that seem to belong to no one, and that laziness stretched out in the sun (Fanon 1963).

The colonizing power also remakes history by referring to the history of the mother country. Schools teach colonized children to negatively view their culture. These children are taught the colonizer's history, language, values and life styles. They are told that this life style is superior to that of the children's parents or elders. In essence, native children are taught to reject their own culture and to accept those images of themselves and their social world which the colonizer has created and maintained.

The third phase of colonization involves a relationship by which members of the colonized group tend to be governed by representatives of the colonizer's power. A colonial society is divided into two separate groups — the colonized and the colonizer — who are pitted against each other. In the colonies, the police and the soldiers are the official maintainers of the colonizers and their rule of oppression. The police and the soldiers maintain frequent and direct contact with the native. Their role in the colonial social system is to put oppression and domination into practice, with the clear conscience that they are the "upholder of the peace" (Fanon 1963). Yet, they are the messengers of violence which disrupt the home and the mind of the native (Fanon 1963).

The development of a caste system based on racism is the fourth phase of colonization. Racism is a principle of social domination by which a group seen as inferior or different in terms of alleged biological characteristics is exploited, controlled and oppressed socially and psychologically by a superordinate group (Blauner 1969). Racism occurs within the political, social and economic institutions. The government and its laws protect the interests of the colonizers. The prosecution of injustices against the native receive little governmental support and the native learns that he should expect nothing from the colonizer's justice system.

For the colonizer, the colony is a place where jobs are guaranteed, wages are high, advancement is rapid and businesses are profitable (Memmi 1968). In this society, the cause is the consequence. As Davidson (1976) explains:

> If the living conditions of the colonizer are high, it is because those of the colonized are low; if he can benefit from plentiful and undemanding labor servants, it is because the colonized man who can be exploited will not be protected by the laws of the colony; if he can easily obtain administrative positions, it is because they are reserved for him and the colonized are excluded from them; the more freely he breathes, the more the colonized are choked.

Despite the fact that colonial privileges are unequally distributed among the colonizers, those at the bottom of that ladder retain their allegiance to the colonial administration for their positon in the colony is superior to their previous position in the mother country. Although they also may be victimized, those colonizers who occupy the bottom rung enjoy privileges superior to the colonized people. In order to reserve their limited advantages, they must identify with the very same economically powerful interests whose victims they are themselves (Zahar 1974).

In his theory, Fanon does not directly address the issue of perceived oppression. However, from examining his works, it is evident that the colonized are likely to perceive themselves as being oppressed and are also likely to be cognitive of this oppression. According to Fanon (1967a), the oppressive conditions that the colonized experience constantly remind them that they are "different" and emphatically show them their "place."

Although race is the major emphasis of the colonial model, Fanon does recognize a social class hierarchy among the colonized. All colonized individuals do not suffer from the oppressive conditions of the social order to the same extent. In fact, the bourgeois fraction of the colonized people represent the part of the colonized nation that is necessary and irreplaceable if the colonial machine is to run smoothly (Fanon 1963). Although their position in society is lower than the colonizers of any status, in regards to the natives, they enjoy more privileges. As a result, there is an antagonism which exists between the native who is excluded from the advantages of colonialism and his counterpart who manages to turn colonial exploitation to his account (Fanon 1963). The colonialists make use of this antagonism by pitting one against the other.

To summarize, the colonial process is initiated when members of one racial group forcefully enter the territory of another for the purpose of economic exploitation. The political and economic dominance of the immigrants enable them to create a society in which their culture and values are more salient than those of the native people. The native culture is systematically destroyed and is re-defined in negative terms. The relationship between the two groups - the colonizers (immigrants) and the colonized (natives) - is maintained by representatives of the colonizers. The colonizers establish a caste system based upon racism in which political power and social and economic privileges are reserved for members of the dominant power structure. As a result of their structural exclusion, the colonized are likely to perceive that they are oppressed and be cognitive of their oppression. A social class hierarchy exists among the colonized in regards to colonial privileges.

## PSYCHOLOGICAL CONSEQUENCES OF COLONIALISM

The colonization process produces a state of alienation within the colonized people. Although Fanon's work *Black Skin, White Masks* is a study of alienation, Fanon never defines the concept. It is clear from Fanon's work, however, that when he speaks of alienation, he is describing the separation of a person from his individuality, his existential condition, his culture or community or his essential self.

Robert Staples provides a definition of alienation using the colonial model. According to Staples (1989), alienation is a feeling of psychological deprivation arising from the belief that one is not a part of society and that the values of a nation are not congruent with the individual's own orientation. Alienation, as utilized by Staples and Fanon, differs from the Marxists' concept of alienation in that the alienated state of mind is the result of social and political exploitation as well as economic exploitation. Colonized individuals are deprived of an investment or stake in economic, social and political institutions. Moreover, Fanon and Staples argue that this exploitation is a result of race not class.

Fanon describes five types of alienating experiences that colonized people undergo: self-alienation, alienation against significant others (or one's racial group), alienation against general others, cultural alienation, and alienation against the creative social praxis. Self-alienation involves alienation from one's corporeality and personal identity. It is also a condition of separation or attempted separation of the individual from himself. The example of "separation" that Fanon (1967a) provides is a Senegalese who learns Creole in order to pass as an Antilles native. Being "Senegalese" is part of the existential self of a native of Senegal, and to run away from this is to manifest alienation.

Alienation against significant others involves estrangement from one's family and social or racial group. Here, the individual hates in others those characteristics he hates most in himself. His expressed contempt for and attacks against his family, social or racial group are the means by which he refrains from recognizing and expressing his self-contempt (Wilson 1990).

Estrangement between different racial groups characterizes alienation against general others. This aspect of alienation involves the notion of superordination and subordination in which all relations between the colonized and the colonizer are determined. Violence, paranoia and distrust are characteristic of this type of alienation. Violence and distrust can be displayed by both the colonizer and the colonized, however, the victims of the violence of the colonized are usually not members of the dominant group. The victims of the violence of the colonized are usually other colonized individuals.

Cultural alienation involves estrangement from one's language and history. Fanon argues that language and education are two of the most potent instruments that are utilized in the systematic alienation of the colonized. Language is more than a medium of communication. Language is viewed as a system of symbols and as a conserver of intergenerational experience which has great potential for influencing thought and action. Diversity of languages in the world has led to a diversity of cultures-namely the totality of such institutions as religion, kinship, social stratification and ideology (Jinadu 1986). To adopt the language of the dominant group is to assume the dominant group's cultural forms and thought patterns.

According to Fanon (1967a), the fact that the culture is different from the group into which one is born is evidence of separation from oneself. This separation is enhanced through the system of formal education. The colonized are taught the history of the dominant group. The symbols of "good guys" are the dominant group; the symbols of "bad guys" are the colonized. As a result, the colonized views his culture negatively and embraces the language, culture and history of the dominant group. Fanon (1967a) recognizes, however, that the adoption of the dominant culture by the colonized is often the key that can open doors (politically, socially or economically) which previously have been closed to him.

Last, alienation against the creative social praxis is concerned with the denial or abdication of self-determining socialized and organized activity which is the very foundation of the realization of human potential (Bulhan 1985). The colonized believes that he does not have a measure of choice, influence or control in what happens to him or in what he can make happen. The colonized is full of self-doubt and has a readiness to compromise.

Fanon (1967a) notes the colonizer is also alienated. The alienation of the colonizer is the result of the kinds of social relations that are present in the colonial society. Characterizing and treating the colonized as inhuman results in the colonizer assuming inhuman features (Zahar 1974). Other than denoting the dual alienation of the colonizer and the colonized, Fanon unfortunately does not fully address the alienation of the colonizer in his theory.

Colonized people react to their alienation in one of three ways. First, colonized individuals may choose to imitate the oppressor and assimilate into his culture. What Fanon discusses is behavioral assimilation or acculturation in that the values, attitudes and behavior of the dominant group are adopted. This process is called "identification with the aggressor." According to Fanon (1963):

> The "inferior race" denies itself as a different race. It shares with the "superior race" the convictions, doctrines, and other attitudes concerning it. Having judged, condemned and abandoned his cultural form, his language, his food habits, his sexual behavior, his way of sitting down, or resting, of laughing, of enjoying himself, the oppressed flings himself upon the imposed culture with the desperation of a drowning man.

The ideal of identifying with the colonizer can also be manifested in the relationship of the colonized to each other, especially if one enjoys a higher status. The colonized individual with higher status dislikes colonized individuals of lower status and he may express some of the most racist stereotypes about the colonized.

Second, the colonized individual may defend assaults on his personality by turning his anger and frustration against himself or his people. This is displaced aggression which results in a higher incidence of alcoholism, psychiatric disorders, hypertension and crime — particularly homicide — among the oppressed. As Fanon (1963) explains:

> The colonized man will manifest this aggressiveness which has been deposited in his bones against his own people. This is the period when the niggers beat each other up, and the police do not know which way to turn when faced with astonishing waves of crime.

Since the colonized cannot defend his personality in the larger social arena, the last resort is to defend his personality via other colonized individuals. In the eyes of the colonizer, this type of auto-destruction is evidence of the inherent inferiority of the colonized individual.

Third, the colonized may defend assaults on his personality by openly resisting the colonial order. These "radical" individuals seek to restore traditions, self and group confidence among the oppressed. Horizontal violence turns into vertical counterviolence. Destructive behaviors give way to proactive revolutionary praxis and anger and tensions find appropriate targets and constructive avenues of discharge (Bulhan 1989).

It may be argued that individuals who engage in protest are no longer alienated. They have regained their identity and they have reclaimed their history and culture. They work to restore self and group confidence and they promote group cohesion among the oppressed. These individuals, however, still feel that they are not a part of society and that the values of the nation are not congruent with their own orientation. Thus, they are still alienated. Rather than internalizing the alienation, the alienation is externalized and redirected in the service of personal and collective liberation (Bulhan 1985).

Fanon (1963a) advocates violence as being indispensable in the decolonization process. He maintains that colonialism is inherently violent and will only yield when it is confronted with greater violence. He further argues that colonialism creates in the native a perpetual tendency toward violence. The advocation of violence as a tool for liberation is where Fanon's sociological argument loses much of its support among critics who view Fanon's recommendation as an advocation for barbarism and terrorism. Others argue that Fanon is seeking "whatever means necessary" to end the exploitation of man by man (Smith 1973).

## INTERNAL COLONIALISM

Internal colonialism occurs when foreign control of a state or territory is eliminated and the control and exploitation of subordinate groups passes to the dominant group within the newly created society. Although there is no forceful entry by a foreign group, internal colonialism has the other identifying characteristics of classical colonialism (e.g. caste system based upon racism, cultural imposition, cultural disintegration and re-creation, and members of the colonized being governed by representatives of the dominant power). Moreover, internal colonialism is a social system which is deeply grounded in the sharp differentiation of White and non-White labor (Feagin 1978). Groups are brought into a society of internal colonialism by force which includes enslavement, incarceration and annexation (Feagin 1978).

Internal colonialism in North America predates the Revolutionary War of 1773-1777. The process of systematic subordination of non-Europeans in North America begins with the genocidal attempts of colonizing settlers to uproot native populations and force them off desirable lands (Feagin 1978). Unlike other racial minorities, the analogy between classical and domestic colonialism for Native Americans involves the forced entry of a foreign force.

Other examples of internal colonialism include Pacific and Asian people who were imported as indentured servants or annexed in the expansionist period of United States development; slave labor from Africa which was utilized as a dominant source of labor in the agricultural South; the utilization of cheap Mexican labor in the Southwest; and groups such as the Filipinos and Hawaiians who were brought in as contract labor due to the fact that their homelands are United States possessions. Although each group entered the society of internal colonialism differently, the common underlying factor is that the start of their subordination is linked to economic exploitation and incorporation, which is a major factor in classical colonialism.

The model of internal colonialism has often been used to explain the African-American experience in the United States (See Frazier 1957; Blauner 1969, 1972; Carmicheal and Hamilton 1967; Staples 1975, 1989). Internal colonialism analysts examine how the subordination or colonized status of African-Americans is linked to economic, political and social incorporation. Specifically, they are concerned with the establishment and persistence of a racial stratification system and the social processes which maintain subordination (Feagin 1978). A summary of the historical, economic, political and social exploitation and subordination of African-Americans is presented below.

## ECONOMIC SUBORDINATION

Unlike other racial and ethnic groups entering the United States, the economic (as well as social and political) subordination of African-Americans began with the institution of slavery. Some of the first Africans who were brought to the American colonies in 1619 were treated as indentured servants. However, by the mid 1600's, the slave status of Africans had been fully institutionalized into the laws of several colonies and was even reflected in the U.S. Constitution. For the next two and one-half centuries, virtually all African immigrants were brought by force to serve in involuntary servitude. In the agricultural South, slaves formed an important source of forced labor. Slaves were classified as being "property" and could be sold or passed as a tract of land, horse or ox. With the average maintenance cost of $19 per year, the slave represented the lowest and the worst of the modern laborers (Dubois 1962).

The economic exploitation of African-Americans continued after the institution of slavery was abolished. Emancipation did not change the economic structure. The lack of land reform and the absence of economic changes resulted in most freed slaves being forced to sell their labor to the same agricultural system that had prospered when it enslaved them. What emerged was actually a form of semi-slavery. Tied to one farm and economically exploited by the system of sharecropping tenant farming, it was virtually impossible for African-American laborers to gain any type of independence.

To ensure a cheap and controlled labor supply for plantations, vagrancy laws (Black Codes) allowed police officers to pick up itinerant African-American laborers to provide forced labor on local farms under threat of imprisonment on chain gangs (Feagin 1978; Wilson 1973). Black Codes further relegated "persons of color" to the occupation of farmer or servants unless they secured a special license and paid an annual tax (Frazier 1957).

Outside the agricultural system, African-Americans were segregated into "unskilled Negro jobs," and were prohibited from participating in the expanding industrial sectors in the South. African-Americans in northern cities, both prior to and after the Civil War of 1861-1865, faced similar situations, with African-American laborers often being displaced by European immigrant workers or forced into lower-level unskilled occupations. In short, the African-American worker was denied access to money, jobs and technology that would assure economic advancement within the dominant social structure.

European immigrants suffered from similar forms of economic exploitation. European immigrants also were relegated to unskilled, lower-paying occupations and were paid less than their Anglo-Saxon White counterparts. For the Irish, there was evidence of wage slavery in which Irish coalminers worked for groceries and rent (commonly called "bobtail checks"), equaling their wages (Feagin 1978). However, a major difference between the economic exploitation of European immigrants and the "Negro freedman" can be seen in regards to economic displacement based upon race and the intensity of the economic exclusion.

African-Americans provided a serious form of labor competition for poor and working class Whites. African-Americans worked cheaply, partly from custom and partly as their own defense against competition (Dubois 1962). To eliminate this competition, both the North and South enacted legislation to create a color-caste labor system. This type of legislation was not created for European immigrants, although there were laws passed in the American colonies to discourage Irish immigration. In essence, the racial stratification system that was developed in this country placed European laborers above African-American laborers and afforded them greater opportunities in which to move up the economic ladder.

The decline of the significance of cotton and the industrial growth in northern cities led to the migration of African-Americans northward after World War I in 1914-1918. The drastic curtailment of European immigrants during World War I resulted in an acute labor shortage in the northern factories. In need of unskilled and semi-skilled labor, northern industrialists began a campaign to attract African-American labor from the South. African-American laborers were offered free transportation and high wages if they agreed to migrate North (Wilson 1973).

African-American migrants represented the younger and better-educated segment of the southern African-American population (Feagin 1978; Jaynes and Williams 1989). These individuals saw northern cities as an economic "promised land." Instead of economic promise, what many African-Americans found was an urban economy which exhibited oppressive economic conditions similar to those experienced in the South. The better-paying or foreman jobs were frequently reserved for White workers. Thus, there was a slow shift from tenant farming and sharecropping to unskilled and semi-skilled jobs in the industrial sectors.

A relatively small number of professional African-Americans were present, having primarily been educated at one of the 117 predominantly African-American colleges. Reconstruction had increased the educational opportunities for African-Americans. Although their schools were grossly inferior to those of Whites, African-Americans became teachers, lawyers, physicians, inventors and ministers. The services of these professionals, however, were confined to the African-American community because of racism or the reluctance of Whites to use their services. *De facto* and *de jure* segregation also restricted these individuals to residences in predominantly African-American neighborhoods.

This pattern of occupational subordination of African-Americans into the secondary and lower-skilled job market continues with the effects of these long-standing discriminatory practices still seen today. Data show that African-Americans are disproportionately employed in low-wage jobs that are unprotected by tenure and seniority, and in manufacturing and goods-producing industries that are particularly sensitive to upward and downward business cycles which affect layoffs and unemployment (Blackwell 1985; Jaynes and Williams 1989).

Although some of the disparity may be explained by differences in levels of education, part of the disparity can be explained by continuing patterns of discrimination in hiring practices and salaries (Blackwell 1985; Hacker 1992). African-Americans are perceived to lack basic skills or work experience, or to be less reliable than White workers. Because of these perceptions, some employers recruit through high schools and newspapers that only reach White middle class neighborhoods (Kirschenman and Neckerman 1990) or relocate to areas where few African-Americans live (Blauner 1992). Even when African-Americans and Whites are matched with similar resumes and trained to behave comparably, Whites receive about 50 percent more job offers (Turner, Fix and Struyk 1991).

Using 1990 census data, Hacker (1992) shows that African-Americans who finish college have a jobless rate 2.24 times that of Whites with high school diplomas. The data also show substantial differences in income for college graduates for African-American and White men. African-American college men earn only slightly more than White men with high school diplomas and African-American men who finish graduate school earn $771 compared to $1,000 for their White counterparts (Hacker 1992). Although African-American women come closer to economic parity with White women (5+ years of college - $973 for every $1,000 earned by White women), the greater economic parity between African-American and White women results largely from the fact that few women of either race rise far in the occupational hierarchy (Hacker 1992).

## POLITICAL SUBORDINATION

The political power and participation of African-Americans has varied over the last two centuries. Although slaves were nonparticipants in the political system, a few free African-American male property owners in the New England states were able to vote in the early decades of political development (Walton 1972). Their impact upon the political process, however, was at best minuscule. At the end of the Civil War, legislation such as the Civil Rights Act of 1866, as well as the 13th, 14th and 15th amendments increased African-American participation in the electoral process.

The Reconstruction period brought about remarkable changes. Not only did African-American men have the right to vote, but southern state constitutional conventions often included African-American delegates. African-Americans served in the U.S. House of Representatives, in the United States Senate, and were lieutenant governors and governor of southern states. Although African-Americans enjoyed political participation, and, as a result, were able to promote a number of educational and political reforms, they never presented a challenge to the dominant White economic and political power structure.

The movement of African-Americans from a limited to somewhat moderate political participation was short-lived. The end of Reconstruction brought a gradual, although definite, change in the political participation of African-Americans and retarded their integration into the American political system. Once again, African-American political participation was reduced to a limited status. In the South, African-American voters were disenfranchised through such tactics as the poll tax, literacy tests, and the grandfather clause. Unlike southern African-Americans, African-Americans in the North were enfranchised but their political capabilities were truncated by the white-controlled political machines and gerrymandering. The first decade of the twentieth century was a low point for African-Americans politically in that the political exclusion of African-Americans was directly institutionalized.

The political experience of recent European immigrants during the nineteenth, and the first decades of the twentieth century, differed from that of African-Americans. For the most part, recent European immigrants were able to benefit from urban political machines which played an important role in penetrating discrimination barriers, providing jobs and in facilitating upward mobility (Feagin 1978; Vander Zanden 1983). By the time African-Americans had migrated in large numbers to northern urban centers, the urban political machines were being dismantled. As a result African-Americans were not able to fully benefit from the socio-political influence that had been provided to other groups.

Furthermore, no other immigrant group faced the degree of systematic exclusion from urban political machines as did African-Americans (Wilson 1980). African-Americans were excluded from meaningful participation in the White-controlled political machines by practices of gerrymandering and by assignment to positions within the political machine where the flow of power was unidirectional - from the party headquarters to the segregated African-American institutions. Consequently, African-Americans were deprived of the kind of political development enjoyed by European immigrants whose political success on the local level enabled them to integrate their interests into the wider politics of the state and nation (Wilson 1980).

However, the second part of the twentieth century reveals an encouraging trend in African-American political participation and political power. There has been a dramatic increase in the number of African-Americans being elected to local, state and federal offices. Although this is evidence of increased African-American political power, in comparison to Whites, African-Americans have not achieved full participation within the political process (Jaynes and Williams 1989). And, African-American priorities are not fully appreciated nor are they recognized by either major political party.

Part of this inability to affect public policy decisions is due to the fact that African-American political success has come primarily in cities where significant numbers of African-American voters reside. These cities have declining employment and tax revenue bases. They are characterized by overburdened schools, housing and health care systems. Large numbers of these urban populations receive public assistance, which limits African-American influence in the policy process (Jaynes and Williams 1989).

African-American voting and political power in urban centers has been further diluted by pressures for regional and metropolitan governments as well as by the privatization of previously provided public services. These governments have moved many of the patronage positions — planning, health, fire, sanitation, water — formerly run by the city to suburban areas. In the suburbs, they are more likely to be dominated by White suburbanites (Turner, Singleton and Musick 1990).

## SOCIAL SUBORDINATION

The historical, economic and political subordination of African-Americans is supplemented by a social system that serves to relegate them to a lower caste. American society labeled African slaves, as well as the emancipated freedmen, as "inferior beings." This perception proceeded into the first part of the twentieth century with African-

Americans being characterized as mentally, biologically and morally inferior.

Moreover, African-Americans have suffered from the intentional destruction of their original African culture. To maximize domination and control, Whites involved in the slave trade separated slaves from the same tribes, kingdoms and linguistic groups. This practice destroyed much of the integral culture of the diverse African people.

As a result, most present day African-Americans have little knowledge of their cultural heritage, languages, or religions. When one speaks of the African-American culture, he refers to the traditional forms of behavior, beliefs, values and styles that have grown out of the African-American sense of mental and social isolation (Frazier 1957). While White ethnic groups often have given up their traditional ways in order to assimilate into dominant society, there is no intentional action to destroy their cultural heritage, languages, religions or traits.

While Jim Crow laws have been abolished and racist ideologies are not openly proclaimed by community leaders, the social status of African-Americans for the most part remains lower than the social status of Whites. And the social system reserves certain statuses and privileges for Whites.

The dual stratification system to which African-Americans are subjected enables them to obtain status and privileges within the hierarchy of their caste, however, they are not able to alter their group or racial status. Race relegates African-Americans to a subordinate status within the larger society.

This is not to argue that the social status of African-Americans has not changed for the better for many African-Americans. Whether one uses pre-World War II or the mid 1960's as a baseline, African-American social status has dramatically improved (Jaynes and Williams 1989). African-Americans have experienced gains in incomes, levels of education, and skilled and white-collar occupations. However, increased social status has not eliminated the racial separation that still exists. There is still the tendency for African-Americans to be stereotyped as being inferior based upon racial group membership (Hacker 1992; Jaynes and Williams 1989) and to be excluded from various spheres of social participation (Jaynes and Williams 1989). Research shows that within desegregated settings throughout American society, African-Americans do not share equal authority and representation throughout an organization or institution and are noticeably absent from decision-making positions (Jaynes and Williams 1989). NORC data from 1958 to 1982 show that in practice many Whites refuse or are reluctant to participate in social settings (e.g., neighborhoods and schools) in which significant numbers of African-Americans are present (Jaynes and Williams 1989).

## BEHAVIORAL ADAPTATIONS TO STRUCTURAL CONDITIONS

The internal colonialism theory argues that African-Americans have suffered greater social, political and economic oppression than their White counterparts. This has been the case historically, and as a consequence of this history, racial inequality between African-Americans and White Americans is evident today. Structural oppression, however, has behavioral consequences. People live within a social context and react to their social environment. African-Americans are likely to perceive that they are racially oppressed and as a result of these perceptions develop feelings of alienation.

Alienation, in turn, leads to assimilation, crime and delinquency, or protest. If crime is the outcome of alienation, the victims of the violence are primarily other African-Americans. As in the colonial world, it is not uncommon for African-Americans to turn their frustration and aggression against themselves or against other African-Americans as exhibited in the form of high suicide rates, high rates of drug abuse and high rates of homicide.

## ADEQUACY IN EXPLAINING CRIME AND DELINQUENCY

Internal colonialism offers a different perspective of the relationship between race and crime in the United States. Internal colonialism shifts the focus of the study of crime from the victims of oppression to exploitative structural systems (Staples 1989). Crime and delinquency are the behavioral responses of African-American adults and adolescents to a social environment that subjects them to limited opportunities for subsistence and social rewards, and limited access to social power because of race.

Internal colonialism is also valuable in explaining the relationship between race and crime because it examines the historical process of structural oppression, which provides a fuller understanding of the current conditions and perceptions of African-Americans. Thus, it illuminates the relationship between structural oppression, alienation, crime and delinquency. The historical aspect of the internal colonialism theory as well as the model's conceptualization of alienation separates it from other structural models.

The model of internal colonialism, however, suffers from theoretical and empirical limitations. Presently, the model is not well-defined. The theory fails to clearly identify factors that may lead individuals to a behavioral response. Two individuals can be subjected to similar oppressive conditions, yet respond differently to their social environment. What factors cause some individuals to assimilate while others choose crime, delinquency or protest?

Second, the theory fails to address the relevancy of experiencing one or more aspects of alienation. Are individuals who experience only one type of alienation more alienated than individuals who experience several types of alienation? Furthermore, does more than one type of alienation effect the selection of a behavioral response?

A third theoretical shortcoming of the model involves the issue of race and class. Class differences among the colonized are not adequately addressed by the model. While internal colonialism stresses the importance of race, it is clear that structural oppression, as well as alienation, are likely to vary among the African-American population according to social class position. In particular, how do structural oppression and alienation vary by race and social class, and what effect do these variations have upon behavioral responses?

Fourth, the internal colonial model fails to address the issue of alienation or class differences among Whites. The model implies that the alienation of African-Americans and Whites differ but fails to delineate this difference. Furthermore, the model does not indicate how the alienation of Whites varies by social class or how African-American and White alienation differ by race and class.

Fifth, the model fails to account for variations in historical structural oppression of different racial minorities (e.g., African-Americans, Hispanics, Native Americans). The relationships of various racial groups to the White power structure bear similarities, but are not identical. Moreover, the model fails to account for variations in structural oppression and alienation that are the result of racial gradation (or differences in skin color) within the same racial group.

And sixth, other behavioral responses to a colonial environment are possible. African-Americans (and other racial minorities) may protest a colonial society without engaging in the type of revolutionary activity that is discussed by Fanon. Rather, African-Americans may seek to promote racial pride and to avoid racism by only participating in African-American social and economic institutions. This voluntary separation is an acknowledgement that they have given up on the American dream of inclusion and assimilation (Cohen 1993).

The theoretical limitations of the model have made it difficult to test its propositions. Most studies using the model have been analytical essays or qualitative pieces describing the existence of one or more of the model's propositions. Other than Austin's (1983) examination of the impact of decolonization upon intragroup violence in the Caribbean, no other study has utilized the model to empirically assess the relationship between colonization and crime.

Part of the difficulty in empirically testing the model is the transformation of variables that identify a colonial society into measures

(Chalout and Chalout 1979). Some of the components of the internal colonialism framework (e.g., alienation and institutional racism) are difficult to operationalize and empirically test.

In order to improve the model of internal colonialism, the theoretical and empirical limitations that are discussed above must be resolved. Some of the problems of the model are now being addressed by internal colonialism analysts. Only through further research can these limitations be corrected and the model fully tested.

## SUMMARY

According to Ohlin (1983), "many competing biological, psychological, social and cultural theories of criminality have emerged. Yet none are sufficient to account for the rates and forms of crime today." The vacuum that is created by the insufficiency of current mainstream theoretical explanations warrants the examination of theoretical models that to a large extent fall outside the paradigm of traditional criminological thought.

The model of internal colonialism explains the association between race and crime by examining the relationship between structural oppression and alienation. The model, however, needs to be subjected to rigorous examination. The full explanatory power of the model cannot be assessed until this is accomplished.

## REFERENCES

Austin, R. 1983. "The Colonial Model, Subcultural Theory and Intragroup Violence." *Journal of Criminal Justice* 11:93-104.

Blackwell, J. 1991. *The Black Community: Diversity and Unity* (3rd ed.). New York: Harper and Row Publishers.

_______. 1985. *The Black Community: Diversity and Unity* (2nd ed.). New York: Harper and Row Publishers.

Blauner, R. 1992. "The Ambiguities of Racial Change." In *Race, Class, and Gender: An Anthology,* edited by M. L. Andersen and P. H. Collins. Belmont, CA: Wadsworth Publishing Company.

_______. 1972. *Racial Oppression in America.* New York: Harper and Row.

_______. 1969. "Internal Colonialism and Ghetto Revolt." *Social Problems* 16:393-408.

Bulhan, H. A. 1985. *Frantz Fanon and the Psychology of Oppression.* New York: Plenum Publishing Corporation.

Carmichael, S. and C. V. Hamilton. 1967. *Black Power.* New York: Oxford University Press.

Chalout, N. and Y. Chalout. 1979. "The Internal Colonialism Concept: Methodological Considerations." *Social and Economic Studies* 28:85-99.

Cohen, S. July 25, 1993. "Blacks Reject Integrated Lifestyles By Choice." *The Herald Sun*, p. A1.

Davidson, D. V. 1976. "The Sociology of Oppressed Cultures: An Analysis of the Socio-Cultural Dynamics of Colonialism." *The Review of the Black Political Economy* 6:421-437.

Dessous, N. 1987. "Fanon and the Problem of Alienation." *The Western Journal of Black Studies* 11:80-91.

Dubois, W. E.B. 1962. *Black Reconstruction in America: 1860-1880.* New York: Maxwell McMillian International.

Elliott, K. S. and S. Ageton. 1980. "Reconciling Race and Class Differences in Self-Reported and Official Estimates of Delinquency." *American Sociological Review* 45:95-110.

Fanon, F. 1967a. *Black Skin, White Masks.* New York: Grove Weidenfeld.

_______. 1967b. *A Dying Colonialism.* New York: Grove Press.

_______. 1963. *The Wretched of the Earth.* New York: Grove Press.

Feagin, J. R. 1978. *Racial and Ethnic Relations.* New York: Prentice-Hall.

Federal Bureau of Investigation. 1992. *Crime in the United States.* Washington, D.C.: U.S. Government Printing Office.

Frazier, E. F. 1957. *Race and Culture Contacts in the Modern World.* Boston: Beacon Press.

Hacker, A. 1992. *Two Nations: Black and White, Separate, Hostile, Unequal.* New York: Charles Scribner and Sons.

Hansen, E. 1977. *Frantz Fanon: Social and Political Thought.* Columbus: Ohio State University Press.

Jinadu, L. A. 1986. *Fanon: In Search of the African Revolution.* London: KPI.

Jaynes, G. D. and R. M. Williams, eds. 1989. *A Common Destiny: Blacks and American Society.* Washington, D.C.: National Academy Press.

Kirschenman, J. and K. Neckerman. 1990. *Hiring Strategies, Racial Bias, and Inner-City Workers.* Mimeo. University of Chicago.

Memmi, A. 1968. *Dominated Man.* New York: Orion Press.

Ohlin, L. 1983. "The Future of Juvenile Justice Policy and Research." *Crime and Delinquency* 29:463-472.

Sigmon, S. B. 1987. "An Existential Psychohistory of Frantz Fanon." *The Western Journal of Black Studies* 11:76-79.

Staples, R. 1989. *The Urban Plantation.* Oakland: The Black Scholar Press.

_______. 1975. "White Racism, Black Crime and American Justice: An Application of the Colonial Model to Explain Race and Crime." *Phylon* 36:14-22.

_______. 1974. "Internal Colonialism and Black Violence." *Black World* 23:16-34.

Turner, J. H., R. Singleton and D. Musick. 1990. *Oppression: A Socio-History of Black-White Relations in America.* Chicago: Nelson-Hall.

Turner, M. A., M. Fix and R. J. Struyk. 1991. *Opportunities Denied, Opportunities Diminished: Discrimination in Hiring.* Washington, D.C.: Urban Institute.

U. S. Bureau of Census. 1992. *The Black Population in the United States: March 1991.* Washington, D.C.: U.S. Government Printing Office.

U.S. Department of Justice. 1992. *Criminal Victimizations in the United States, 1991.* Washington, D.C: Bureau of Justice Statistics.

Vander Zanden, J. W. 1983. *American Minority Relations* (4th ed.). New York: McGraw-Hill, Inc.

Walton, H. Jr. 1972. *Black Politics.* Philadelphia: J. P. Lippincott Press.

Wilson, A. 1990. *Black on Black Violence: The Psychodynamics of Black Self-Annihilation in Service of White Domination.* New York: Afrikan World Infosystems.

Wilson, W. J. 1987. *The Truly Disadvantaged: The Inner City, the Underclass, and Public Policy.* Chicago: University of Chicago Press.

_______. 1980. *The Declining Significance of Race: Blacks and Changing American Institutions.* Chicago: University of Chicago Press.

_______. 1973. *Power, Racism and Privilege: Race Relations in Theoretical and Sociohistorical Perspectives.* Chicago: University of Chicago Press.

Zahar, R. 1974. *Frantz Fanon: Colonialism and Alienation.* New York: Monthly Review Press.

# BLACKS, SELF-ESTEEM, AND DELINQUENCY: IT'S TIME FOR A NEW APPROACH

*Lee Elbert Ross is an assistant professor. He teaches criminology and criminal justice courses at the University of Wisconsin in Milwaukee. Ross received his doctorate degree in criminal justice from Rutgers, the State University at Newark.*

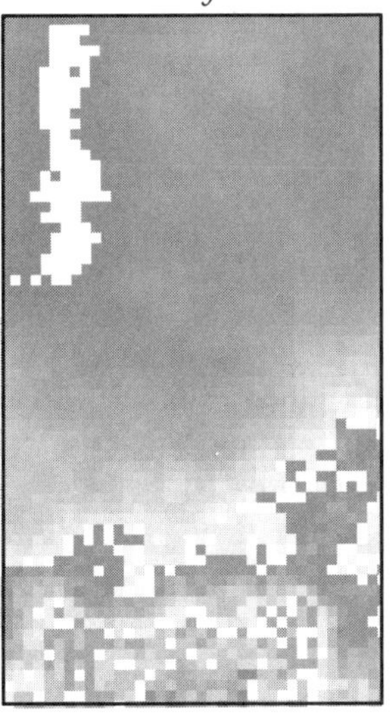

For several decades social scientists have shown enormous interest in the relationship between self-esteem and delinquency. Investigations have examined whether one's level of self-esteem is both related to and predictive of delinquency. Some studies have shown this relationship; others have failed to sustain it. More recently, researchers have tried to determine whether "race" affects this relationship, but the findings have been mixed.

This article extends the exploration of self-esteem and delinquency by considering the relative importance of race as an explanatory factor. First, we will explore whether racial differences exist in the development of self-esteem and delinquency by considering the relative importance of race as an explanatory factor. Then we will assess the impact of those differences on human behavior, particularly delinquent or criminal behavior.

This paper assumes that the manner in which we regard ourselves indicates the manner in which we behave. Before we can test this assumption, however, it is critical that we recognize and distinguish among different measures of self-esteem for persons of different racial backgrounds.

The purpose in writing this article is twofold: 1) to identify various conceptual and methodological problems encountered in studies of race, self-esteem, and delinquency; and 2) to distinguish personal identity measures from group identity measures of self-esteem. This article questions the validity of prior measures of self-esteem, especially when racial comparisons are involved.

## PROBLEMS AND CONCERNS

Most researchers offer no theoretical perspective for understanding the relationship between race, self-esteem, and delinquency. One notable exception is the work of Reckless and Dinitz (1967) on containment theory. A basic premise of containment theory is that behavior has both internal and external controls. Reckless and Dinitz suggest that inner containment is the more important in our society because individuals spend much of their time away from family and other supportive groups.

A fundamental problem in research on race, self-esteem, and delinquency is the lack of consensus regarding the conceptualization of "self-esteem." Researchers have used the concept of self-esteem in different ways. Some studies use the following terms interchangeably: self-esteem, self-concept, self-actualization, self-worth, self-realization, self-perception, and self-enhancement. In view of the broad use of this concept, ambiguity is inevitable. Yet, no standard theoretical or operational definition exists.

The psychological literature reveals well over 200 different measures of self-esteem. In some studies the chosen scale of measurement coincides with the strengths and weaknesses of a particular research design. That is, researchers tend to choose measurement scales that focus on the dimensions or aspects of self-esteem which interest them. The problem with this tendency is that it gives little assurance the dimensions measured are present equally among different races. For much of the research under review, this matter remains unresolved.

Definitional problems exist as well. For many researchers, self-esteem is a symbol representing varied perceptions, memories, and meaningful experiences in one's life. It enables persons to determine their character, beliefs, values, and personality traits. To paraphrase Coopersmith (1967), these resultant concepts lead to the development of certain mental images and evaluative sentiments known as "self-esteem."

Most definitions of self-esteem are actually personal identity measures that have guided current research in psychology, sociology, and criminology. The result has been an overreliance on personal identity measures with little regard shown for group identity measures. Consequently, in studies of blacks, some scholars claim "self-esteem" is confused with racial identity (Cross 1991; Erickson 1968; Jackson, McCullough and Gurin 1988). Any comparative study that fails to distinguish between personal and group measures of self-esteem leads to confusing findings.

Moreover, such studies reflect a basic disregard for the axiological differences between black and white definitions of self-esteem; these definitions are shaped by forces unique to each race. In the development and formation of racial personalities in general, for instance, the white approach places heavy emphasis on individuality, whereas the black approach reflects the degree to which one is conscious of shared oppression (See Akbar 1976; Carter and Helms 1987; Katz and Ivey 1977). This "failure to distinguish" is pervasive in research involving race, self-esteem, and delinquency.

Equally problematic is the uncertainty as to whether self-esteem is a multidimensional or a unidimensional concept. At times different measures of self-esteem reflect different underlying dimensions; thus it is difficult to achieve consistency. Theoretically, dimensions of self-esteem emerge when people are asked about their responses to different aspects of themselves (e.g., academic or social). Because different people derive self-esteem from different sources, scales must include the dimensions that are important for each individual (See Shaver 1973). Given the enormity of the task, few researchers have attempted to do this.

Other research problems in the study of self-esteem and delinquency stem from an apparent preoccupation with certain variables (e.g., gender). Such variables are thought to influence the relationship; meanwhile, little regard is shown for "racial identity" as a factor that also might influence the relationship. Most research has proceeded from the premise that self-esteem is correlated highly with one's racial identity. Various authors however have convincingly contradicted this assumption (Casas 1984; Cross 1991; Erickson 1963, 1968; Jackson et al. 1988).

Thus, if we accept the notion that self-esteem generally is ill-defined and conceptually misunderstood, it is quite possible that its role is misinterpreted in studies of race, self-esteem, and delinquency. Therefore, studies that fail to distinguish among conceptual dimensions of self-esteem require a cautious interpretation.

## RESEARCH ON RACE AND SELF-ESTEEM

Research studies on self-esteem and race were conducted by an impressive list of pioneers (e.g.,Clark and Clark 1947; Horowitz and Horowitz 1938; Kardiner and Ovesey 1951; Lewin 1941; Lind 1913). Perhaps the most renowned and most controversial of these studies are those of Kenneth and Mamie Clark (1947) concerning racial identification. Clark and Clark maintained that even when age and skin color were considered, children preferred white dolls to black dolls. They concluded that this finding suggested low levels of self-esteem (and possibly self-hatred) among black children. The Clark findings were replicated twice (Goodman 1952; Morland 1969). These studies also found that black children under age 5 frequently manifested uneasiness because of their awareness of skin color.

Despite considerable disagreement about the proper interpretation of the black children's "preference," most researchers agreed that the choice suggested some type of identity crisis among black children, fostered in part by low levels of self-esteem. As a partial explanation, one researcher claimed that "they learned that the world is white and they are black...that beauty, success and status all wear a white skin" (Kvaraceus 1965, p. 154). According to Kunjufu (1984), the finding probably meant that preference for whites by children of both races developed early, even before racial differences could be communicated.

These early findings stimulated interest in determining additional factors that damage blacks' self-esteem, as well as in examining the consequences of having low self-esteem. One immediate effect on the black community was to "overvalue all those traits of appearance that are most Caucasian" (Grambs 1965, p.155). Moreover, the impact of showing preference for Caucasian appearances led some black parents to show similar preferences for their lighter-skinned children while sadly neglecting some of their darker-skinned children (Grambs 1965).

Generally, when research studies consider racial differences in self-esteem, it is suggested that blacks have lower levels of self-esteem than whites. In view of black experiences with slavery, segregation, and economic struggles in American society, it is easy to understand why blacks might differ from whites in self-esteem (See Clark and Clark 1947; Kardiner and Ovesey 1951; Nobles 1973). Taylor and Walsh (1979) suggest that "until the late 1960's it was an axiom of social science that white discrimination depressed and debilitated the psyche of the average black person in this country" (p. 242). Such assertions carry serious implications for blacks in general because they shape self-esteem, which is critical in many respects—educational, social, and psychological. On the importance of self-esteem in shaping behavior, Kunjufu (1984) commented:

> Self-esteem is one of the most important possessions a person can have. We often hear people wishing they had a job, clothes, car, money, spouse, or children, but seldom do you hear people talking about themselves. The best way to solve any problem is to admit you have one. Very few people admit they have low self-esteem and fewer develop strategies to improve. (p. 17)

According to some scholars (Akbar 1976; Cross 1991; Helms 1987), many prior researchers in this area assumed erroneously that measures of personal identity (i.e., self-esteem) and measures of group identity (i.e., racial self-identification) are highly correlated. Cross (1991) in particular, however, argues that these two factors are independent; when combined, they equal one's self-concept. In studies employing similar measures, some scholars (e.g., Klein 1974; McAdoo 1970; Spivey 1976) maintain that no racial differences in self-esteem exist. In fact, some studies purport differences favoring blacks over whites (See Baughman and Dahlstrom 1968; Rosenberg and Simmons 1972). Powell and Fuller (1973) suggest that increases in black nationalism, with its emphasis on black pride, translated into higher self-esteem among blacks.

Many researchers explain high levels of self-esteem among blacks as the result of academic curricula designed around (and in deference to) black history. Alternative explanations center around the "games" blacks play that are designed to lessen the impact of white racism. Coopersmith (1965) claims that blacks actually "derive self-esteem in the white community by being agreeable, virtuous and capable, rather than being powerful, independent and assertive" (p. 160). Although Nobles (1973) supports this notion, he cautions that blacks derive self-esteem from various sources. Often, however, these sources are overlooked by researchers failing to distinguish between blacks' self-perceptions and whites' perceptions of blacks.

Other theories regarding comparable levels of self-esteem among blacks were offered by Myrdal (1944), who claimed that some blacks have blamed the "system" for their personal failures. This "blaming" enabled many black persons to escape the negative self-evaluations that could result. In keeping with this notion, Taylor and Walsh (1979) asserted that "systemblaming" acted as a buffer to protect the self-esteem of the most vulnerable blacks.

Clearly, a great deal of research documents the critical importance of self-esteem in shaping behavior. Some researchers suggest that societal discrimination and racism may have harmed blacks' self-esteem. Other authors, however, maintain that these effects have been minimized by various adjustments and coping strategies. Nonetheless, we must acknowledge that there are differences between personal and group identity measures of self-esteem as defined by Cross and others.

## RESEARCH ON SELF-ESTEEM AND DELINQUENCY

The "general" relationship between self-esteem and delinquency has been well documented. As early as 1957, theories of self-esteem and delinquency were advanced by Reiss, who suggested that delinquents had weak "ego ideals" and lacked the personal controls to produce conforming behavior. Similarly, Briar and Piliavin (1965) described delinquents' weak commitment to conformity. In their view, conformity to social expectations was most prevalent among youths who feared that apprehension for criminality would damage their "self-image" and their relationships with others. From these early findings, interest in the theoretical merit of self-esteem began to take shape. As a result, subsequent researchers examined these hypothesized relationships from a variety of perspectives, using different subjects in a variety of social conditions.

To discover factors that steer youths in high-delinquency areas of large cities away from delinquency, Reckless and Dinitz (1967) pioneered the evaluation of "self-concept" as one possible factor. Their evidence, based on studies of juveniles in Columbus, Ohio, demonstrated that "predicted delinquents" (bad boys) had lower "self-concepts" than "predicted nondelinquents" (good boys), as measured by official records (Shoemaker 1984). Reckless asked teachers to predict whether certain boys in their classes were "good" or "bad." Measures of the boys' self-concept were cross-validated by their teachers' and their mothers' appraisals. On the basis of these findings, these researchers believed they had made an important discovery, namely that self-concept in early adolescence might be one of the factors of self that determined subsequent behavior (Reckless and Dinitz 1967). Specifically, "good boys" showing strong self-concepts avoided trouble, while "bad boys" showing weaker self-concepts got into trouble.

Earlier studies (Dinitz, Scarpitti, and Reckless, 1962; Scarpitti et al. 1960) declared that "good boys" not only remained free from official contacts with police, but also consistently demonstrated higher levels of self-concept from younger ages well into adolescence (Shoemaker 1984). Although Reckless and Dinitz (1967) received favorable reviews in the research community, their methods were heavily criticized. Some researchers (Orcutt 1970; Schwartz and Tangri 1965) contended that it was improper to measures one's self-concept from the judgments of others (e.g., teachers and mothers). Such judgments, it was claimed, caused confusion between what a person thinks of himself and what he thinks others think or expect of him. Orcutt (1970) also questioned the reliability and validity of teachers' predictions because some of the predictions were inaccurate. Nonetheless, Reckless and Denitz stimulated further research on the relationship of self-concepts of black children relative to delinquency by improving the methods of studying this relationship.

In response to problems associated with the concept and measurement of self-esteem, some scholars (Gold and Mann 1972) felt an obligation to distinguish between conscious and unconscious levels of self-esteem. Their study discovered that "no significant differences in conscious self-esteem existed between highly delinquent high achievers and highly delinquent low achievers, although there were differences between high achievers, and low achievers among boys who were not highly delinquent" (Gold 1978, p. 297). Also, highly delinquent low achievers registered the lowest unconscious self-esteem, significantly different from that of the high achievers. The authors interpreted this finding to mean that delinquent behavior served a defensive function, elevating the boys' conscious but not their unconscious level of self-esteem.

Although the evidence suggests positive self-esteem reduces the likelihood of involvement in delinquent behavior, studies that use causal models present findings to the contrary. Generally these studies tend to employ more advanced and more sophisticated research methodologies and statistical techniques such as LISREL or path analysis. Perhaps the most influential of these studies was Kaplan's (1978, 1980) "esteem enhancement model." Previous researchers had yet to determine whether high self-esteem prevented delinquency or led to delinquency. Therefore, Kaplan's study was designed to clarify the direction and form of the relationship by attempting to causally link low self-esteem with delinquent and disruptive behavior. He found that more of those who had given evidence of low self-esteem at the start of the year reported having committed certain delinquent acts during that year than did those who had indicated high self-esteem.

Similar studies (Wells and Rankin 1983) used a path-analytic technique. They concluded that self-esteem had little effect on subsequent delinquency and did not increase by engaging in delinquent behavior. According to McCarthy and Hoge (1984), regardless of the type of analysis—measures of self-esteem or measures of delinquent behavior—"the effect of self-esteem on delinquent behavior is negligible" (p. 407). In their examination, "causation [was] mostly in the opposite direction, from delinquent behavior to subsequent self-esteem—the more delinquent the behavior, the lower the self-esteem." Furthermore, the strength of the relationship was only modest. McCarthy and Hoge (1984) explained that "certain forms of delinquent behavior enhance an adolescent's esteem among peers, thus counteracting other mechanisms which link delinquency to depressed self-esteem" (p. 408).

These studies are not exhaustive, but they represent the mixture of findings in self-esteem and delinquency research. Some of the findings are counter-intuitive; others reflect conventional wisdom. It is difficult to say whether these findings are artifacts of research strategies, of sample sizes, or of operational definitions. While these studies demonstrated tremendous concern for the issues, specific racial comparisons along these lines were neglected. Although some of the studies involved subjects from different racial backgrounds, attempts at racial comparisons were merely incidental and beyond the intent of the studies.

Similar charges can be leveled against more recent theories of crime causation, in which the relationship among race, self-esteem, and delinquency has gone relatively unnoticed (e.g., Gottfredson and Hirschi 1990; Thornberry, Moore, and Christenson 1985; Wilson and Hernstein 1985). The reasons for this failure to consider the critical importance of self-esteem are not clear. Nonetheless, the lack of attention to racial differences in the relationship between self-esteem and delinquency mandates further research.

## RESEARCH ON RACE, SELF-ESTEEM, AND DELINQUENCY

Various studies (Deutsch 1960; Erickson 1959; Lefevre 1966; Schwartz and Tangri 1965) suggest that some differences in self-esteem might be found in comparisons between black and white adolescents. Schwartz and Tangri (1965) conducted a study of 101 school-nominated "good" and "bad" sixth-grade boys in an all-black school in a high-delinquency area of Detroit. They examined self-esteem by using a semantic differential test, whereby juveniles were asked to rate themselves on a "good-bad" continuum along several dimensions. Later, these perceptions were correlated with respondents' judgments of how mothers, friends, and teachers regarded them. Like the work of Reckless and Dinitz (1967), this study found that "good boys" had higher personal self-concepts than those who were thought to be "bad boys." Interestingly, comparisons of self-concept with perceptions of other people's opinions showed that self-image was correlated with the perceived views of significant others, which varied between "good" and "bad."

In 1972, Wax studied 55 institutionalized boys between the ages of seven and 12 to learn more about preadolescent delinquents. He made comparisons in terms of age, socioeconomic status, class, race, and physical and mental health. Wax (1972) found significant differences on one concept in particular, "boys who get into trouble" (p. 168). The white group appeared to have a lower self-concept of boys who get into trouble than did the black group. Apparently among blacks, boys who got into trouble were perceived to be stronger, smarter, tougher, and generally more positively endowed than boys who did not do so, a notion consistent with prior studies (See Erickson 1959; Miller 1958; Pettigrew 1964).

Jensen (1972) examined the association between delinquency and adolescent self-concept among high school students in terms of race and status. His study was based on a secondary analysis of data (gathered at one point in time) from an in-school population consisting of juniors and seniors from 11 high schools in California. Although data were available on females, Jensen restricted the analysis to a subsample of black and white males. Self-esteem was measured on the basis of agreement or disagreement with items such as "At times I think I am no good at all."

In addition to comparisons of self-esteem, Jensen tested the hypothesis that self-reported delinquency and official delinquency were more strongly related for white than for black adolescents. His findings were as follows: 1) positive correlations existed between official delinquent evaluations and personal delinquent evaluations; 2) delinquents tended to exhibit lower self-esteem than nondelinquents; and 3) delinquents differed most from nondelinquents among middle and upper class blacks and least among lower class blacks. In defense of these findings, Jensen (1972) relied on the same reasoning as Hewitt (1970) in stating that "lower stratum delinquency feeds on official definitions while middle status boys are insulated from such experiences and resulting self-definitions" (p. 90).

Emms, Povey, and Swift (1986) reported a British comparative study of self-esteem levels among young black and white offenders incarcerated in a youth custody center. Some prior researchers, mainly Louden (1981), found that West Indian blacks showed a propensity for delinquency while simultaneously exhibiting high levels of self-esteem. These findings ran counter to earlier British research, in which low levels of self-esteem in blacks were commonly reported (See Bagley, Mallick and Verma 1979).

The Emms et al. study (1986) was based on a small sample of 20 black and 20 white delinquents, all of whom had been incarcerated at least four months before the study. Berger's (1952) scale of "self and others" also was used to measure self-esteem, though it employed only attitudinal items. Findings revealed no significant racial differences in mean levels of self-esteem. In other respects, black delinquents had slightly higher scores than a matched group of white delinquents. Although this finding conflicted with previous British research in this area, it supported expectations for delinquents in institutions. Moreover, Emms et al. (1986, p.391) suggested that within the delinquent subculture, a movement was afoot in blacks' levels of self-concept, analogous to that in the United States. Even so, they thought these findings were mere artifacts of custodial settings or of the tendency of delinquency to be a potent source of status for the most marginal and most discriminated-against groups in society.

Leung and Drasgow (1986) examined whether low levels of self-esteem were related to high frequencies of delinquent behavior. Their study used only males representing three ethnic groups. The samples consisted of 1,241 blacks, 2,690 whites, and 678 Hispanics. The findings showed Hispanics had significantly lower levels of self-esteem than blacks and whites. Differences between blacks' and whites' levels of self-esteem were small and insignificant. As for delinquency, whites reported higher frequencies than did blacks and Hispanics. Differences in delinquency between blacks and Hispanics were not significant. These authors concluded that Kaplan's theory may not hold for the blacks and Hispanics interviewed in their study.

## DISCUSSION

It is clear that research in this area is filled with inconsistent findings. In regard to racial comparisons, all arguments for and against the critical importance of self-esteem in explaining delinquency are based on studies that fail to distinguish between personal and group measures of self-esteem. Some researchers assumed that one's racial identity and personal identity were the same. As a result, many proceeded to make racial comparisons about the relative importance of self-esteem. Interestingly, contemporary theories of crime and delinquency neglect to consider "race" as a component of self-esteem but rarely hesitate to include other variables (e.g., sex) thought to be relevant. Surely, however, our feelings about ourselves are determined partially by our racial identity.

Inconsistent research methodologies, inadequate methods, and unusually small samples are common in these studies. Moreover, some studies found blacks' levels of self-esteem to be equal to or greater than those of their white counterparts. Yet, few differences in delinquency involvement were found. Such findings are at best inconclusive. Perhaps the most methodologically sound approach to the relationship between race, self-esteem, and delinquency was advanced by Leung and Drasgow (1986), whose use of item response theory demonstrated great concern for issues of reliability and validity.

In these studies, operational definitions of self-esteem often competed with comparable terms such as "self-concept" and "self-evaluation" in the midst of numerous other scales designed to measure self-esteem. At times the choice of scales appeared to be a matter of convenience. In addition, studies involving adjudicated delinquents (Emms et al. 1986), adult criminals (Redfering 1971), and preadolescents (Wax 1972) failed to consider the causal order of variables for a given relationship. Some studies simply looked at the relationship between two variables (e.g., correlating some measure of self-esteem with some measure of delinquency or crime). In short, these studies often reflected more confusion than understanding.

## CONCLUSIONS

The question of race, self-esteem, and delinquency continues to fascinate researchers because of its potential to theoretically discern and explain racial differences in crime and delinquency. At the present, we must address the theoretical inadequacies and methodological inconsistencies that often are viewed as responsible for certain outcomes. Many of the studies under review here contain all of the elements needed to study race, self-esteem, and delinquency. These elements, however, are scattered widely and need to be incorporated into one research design. Therefore, it appears future research would benefit tremendously from a consideration of the following points.

Because self-esteem has different meanings for persons of different races, it should be accordingly conceptualized. Efforts are needed to ensure that cultural experiences which shape the self-esteem of blacks and other racial groups are reflected in these various dimensions. All of us could benefit greatly from the advice of Cross (1991) and others by employing two measures of self-esteem, one of personal identity and one of group identity. In addition, we should consider research methodologies capable of determining whether low self-esteem leads to crime or whether crime causes low self-esteem (See Wells and Rankin 1983). Also, we must insure that items chosen to measure self-esteem are valued among all races and cultures (See Leung and Drasgow 1986). Finally, we need to discern the underlying dimension of the chosen scale so that we are certain of what is being measured. In doing so, we should: 1) specify the direction of the relationship; 2) ensure measurement equivalence; and 3) reveal factorially distinct dimensions of self-esteem, both personal and racial. This would make possible a more valid discussion of the comparative aspects of race, self-esteem, and delinquency.

At present, we cannot specify any causal relationship between self-esteem and delinquency. Some researchers suggest that certain delinquent acts raise levels of self-esteem (e.g., selling illegal narcotics). Selling drugs initially might reflect low self-esteem. As profits accumulate, however, enabling sellers and dealers to acquire certain status symbols (e.g., owning BMWs or gold chains), these persons might begin to feel higher self-esteem. This scenario complicates matters because it suggests that some sources of self-esteem (e.g., courage) enhance crime and delinquency. Furthermore, confusion is increased by not knowing the temporal sequence of the relationship. This lack of knowledge highlights the need for improved research designs.

It is more often maintained that any single theoretical perspective will explain only a small amount of the variance in delinquency. Efforts might be spent more usefully in incorporating additional theoretical perspectives. Of all existing theoretical perspectives, however, this relationship is most clearly understood from a social control perspective. This paper assumes that high levels of self-esteem act as social controls on delinquent behavior, whereas low levels of self-esteem partially explain delinquent involvement. Moreover, if self-esteem represents a form of "inner containment," it probably also controls social behavior. Conceivably the incorporation of self-esteem into social control theory might result in a more useful theoretical model.

## REFERENCES

Akbar, N. 1976. *Natural Psychology and Human Transformation.* Chicago: World Community of Islam in the West.

Bagley, C., K. Mallick, and G. K. Verma. 1979. "Pupil Self-Esteem: A Study of Black and White Teen-Agers in British Schools." In *Race, Education, and Identity,* edited by G. K. Verma and C. Bagley. London: MacMillan.

Baughman, E. and W. G. Dahlstron. 1968. *Negro and White Children: A Psychological Study in the Rural South.* New York: Academic Press.

Berger, E. 1952. "The Relations Between Expressed Acceptance of Self and Expressed Acceptance of Others." *Journal of Abnormal Psychology* 47: 778-82.

Briar, S. and I. Piliavin. 1965. "Delinquency: Situational Inducements and Commitment to Conformity." *Social Problems* 13:35-45.

Carter, R. T. and J. E. Helms. 1987. "The Relationship Between Black Value Orientations and Racial Identity Attitudes." *Measurement and Evaluation in Counseling and Development* 19:185-95.

Casas, J. M. 1984. "Policy, Training, and Research in Counseling Psychology: The Racial/Ethnic Minority Perspective." In *Handbook of Counseling Psychology,* edited by S. D. Brown and R. W. Lent. New York: Wiley.

Clark, K. B. and M. N. Clark. 1947. "Racial Identification and Preference in Negro Children." In *Readings in Social Psychology,* edited by T. Newcomb and E. Hartley. New York: Holt.

Coopersmith, S. 1965. "Self-Concept, Race and Education." In *Race and Education Across Cultures,* edited by G. K. Verma and C. M. Bagley. London: Heinemann.

_______. 1967. *The Antecedents of Self-Esteem.* San Francisco: Freeman.

Cross, W. E. 1991. *Shades of Black: Diversity in Blacks Identity.* Philadelphia: Temple University Press.

Deutsch, M. 1960. *Minority Group and Class Status as Related to Social and Personality Factors in Scholastic Achievement.* Albany: New York Society of Applied Anthropology.

Dinitz, S., R. Frank, C. Scarpitti, and W. C. Reckless. 1962. "Delinquency Vulnerability: A Cross Group and Longitudinal Analysis." *American Sociological Review* 27:515-17.

Emms, T. W., R. M. Povey, and S. M. Swift. 1986. "The Self-Concept of Black and White Delinquents." *British Journal of Criminology* 26:385-93.

Erickson, E. H. 1959. "Ego Development and Historical Change." *Psychological Issues* 1:18-49.

_______. 1963. *Youth: Change and Challenge*. New York: Basic Books.

_______. 1968. *Identity: Youth and Crisis*. New York: Norton.

Gold, M. 1978. "School Experience, Self-Esteem, and Delinquent Behavior: A Theory of Alternative Schools." *Crime and Delinquency* 24:294-95.

Gold, M. and D. Mann. 1972. "Delinquency as Self-Defense." *American Journal of Orthopsychiatry* (April):463-79.

Goodman, M. 1952. *Race Awareness in Young Children*. Cambridge, MA: Addison-Wesley.

Gottfredson, M. R. and T. Hirschi. 1990. *A General Theory of Crime*. Stanford, CA: Stanford University Press.

Grambs, J. D. 1965. "The Self-Concept: Basis for Education of the Negro Youth." In *The Negro Self-Concept: Implications for School and Citizenship*, edited by W. C. Kvaraceus. New York: McGraw-Hill.

Helms, J. E. 1987. "Cultural Identity in the Treatment Process." In *Handbook of Cross-Cultural Counseling and Psychotherapy*, edited by P. B. Pedersen. Westport, CT: Greenwood Press.

_______. 1989. "Considering Some Methodological Issues in Racial Identity Counseling Research." *The Counseling Psychologist* 17:227-52.

Hewitt, J. P. 1970. *Social Stratification and Deviant Behavior*. New York: Random House.

Horowitz, E. L. and R. E. Horowitz. 1938. "Development of Social Attitudes in Children." *Sociometry* 1:301-38.

Jackson, J. S., W. R. McCullough, and G. Gurin. 1988. "Family, Socialization Environment and Identity Development in Black Americans." In *Black Families*, edited by H. P. McAdoo. Newbury Park, CA: Sage.

Jensen, G.F. 1972. "Delinquency and Adolescent Self-Conceptions: A Study of the Personal Relevance of Infraction." *Social Problems* 20:84-103.

Kaplan, H. B. 1978. *Deviant Behavior in Defense of Self*. New York: Academic Press.

_______. 1980. "Self-Attitudes and Deviant Response." *Social Forces* 54:788-801.

Kaplan, H. B. and C. Robbins. 1983. "Testing a General Theory of Deviance Behavior in Longitudinal Perspective." In *Perspective Studies in Crime and Delinquency*, edited by K. T. Van Dusen and S. A. Mednich. Boston: Kluwer-Nijhoff.

Kardiner, A. and L. Ovesey. 1951. *The Mark of Oppression*. New York: Norton.

Katz, J. H., A. E. Ivey. 1977. "White Awareness: The Frontier of Racism Awareness Training." *Personnel and Guidance Journal* 55:485-88.

Klein, B. L. 1974. "Development, Validation, and Experimental Application of an Instrument to Assess Self-Concept." Doctoral Dissertation, University of Texas at Austin.

Kunjufu, J. 1984. *Developing Positive Self-Images and Discipline in Black Children*. Chicago: Blacks Images.

Kvaraceus, W. C. 1965. *The Negro Self-Concept: Implications for School and Citizenship*. New York: McGraw-Hill.

Lefevre, C. 1966. "Inner City School: As the Children See It." *Elementary School Journal* 67:8-15.

Lewin, K. 1941. "Jewish Self-Hatred." *Contemporary Jewish Record* 4:219-32.

Leung, K. and F. Drasgow. 1986. "Relations Between Self-Esteem and Delinquent Behavior in Three Different Groups: An Application of Item Response Theory." *Journal of Cross Cultural Psychology* 17:151-67.

Lind, J. E. 1913. "The Dream as Simple Wish-Fulfillment in the Negro." *Psychoanalytic Review* 1:295-300.

Louden, D. M. 1981. "Toward a Typology of Behavior Patterns Among West Indian Adolescents." *Journal of Adolescence* 4:321-88.

McAdoo, H. P. 1970. "Racial Attitudes and Self-Concepts of Black Pre-School Children." Doctoral Dissertation, University of Michigan.

McCarthy, J. and D. Hoge. 1984. "The Dynamics of Self-Esteem and Delinquency." *American Journal of Sociology* 90:396-410.

Miller, W. E. 1958. "Lower Class Culture as the Milieu for Gang Delinquency." *Journal of Social Issues* 14:5-19.

Morland, J. 1969. "Race Awareness Among American and Hong Kong Chinese Children." *American Journal of Sociology* 75:360-74.

Myrdal, G. 1944. *An American Dilemma*. New York: Harper and Row.

Nobles, W. W. 1973. "Psychological Research and the Black Self-Concept: A Critical Review." *Journal of Social Issues* 29:11-31.

Orcutt, J.D. 1970. "Self-Concept and Insulation Against Delinquency: Some Critical Notes." *Sociological Quarterly* 2:381-90.

Pettigrew, T. F. 1964. *A Profile of the American Negro*. Princeton: Van Nostrand.

Powell, G.J. and M. Fuller. 1973. *Black Monday's Children: A Study of the Effects of School Desegregation on Self-Concepts of Southern Children*. New York: Appleton-Century-Croft.

Reckless, W.C. and S. Dinitz. 1967. "Pioneering with the Self-Concept as a Vulnerability Factor in Delinquency." *Journal of Criminal Law, Criminology and Police Science* 58:515-23.

Redfering, D.L. 1975. "Differential Effects of Group Counseling with Black and White Females." *Corrective Psychiatry and Journal of Social Therapy* 18:29-34.

Reiss, A. 1957. "Delinquency as a Failure of Personal and Social Controls." *American Sociological Review* 16:196-207.

Rosenberg, M. and R. G. Simmons. 1972. *Black and White Self-Esteem: The Urban School Child.* Washington, DC: American Sociological Association.

Scarpitti, F. R., E. Murray, S. Dinitz, and W. C. Reckless. 1960. "The Good Boy in High Delinquency Areas: Four Years Later." *American Sociological Review* 25:555-58.

Shaver, P. R. 1973. "Measurement of Self-Esteem and Related Constructs." In *Measures of Social Psychological Attitudes,* edited by J. P. Robinson and P. R. Shaver. Ann Arbor: Institute for Social Research, University of Michigan.

Shoemaker, D. J. 1984. *Theories of Delinquency: An Examination of Delinquent Behavior*. Oxford: Oxford University Press.

Spivey, W. L. 1976. "A Study of the Self-Concept and Achievement Motivation of Black Versus White High School Male Achievers." Doctoral Dissertation, California School of Professional Psychology at San Francisco.

Taylor, M. C. and J. E. Walsh. 1979. "Explanations of Black Self-Esteem: Some Empirical Tests." *Social Psychology Quarterly* 42:242-53.

Thornberry, T. P., M. Moore, and R. L. Christenson. 1985. "The Effect of Dropping Out of High School on Subsequent Criminal Behavior." *Criminology* 23:3-18.

Wax, D. E. 1970. "Self-Concept in Negro and White Pre-Adolescent Delinquent Boys." *Child Study Journal* 2:165-71.

Wells, E. and J. Rankin. 1983. "Self-Concept as a Mediating Concept in Delinquency." *Social Psychology Quarterly* 46:11-22.

Wilson, R. C. and R. J. Hernstein. 1985. *Crime and Human Nature* New York: Simon and Schuster.

# THE POLITICS OF DISPROPORTIONALITY

*Vernetta Young is a tenured professor. She teaches criminology and criminal justice courses at Howard University. Young received her doctorate degree in criminal justice from the State University of New York in Albany.*

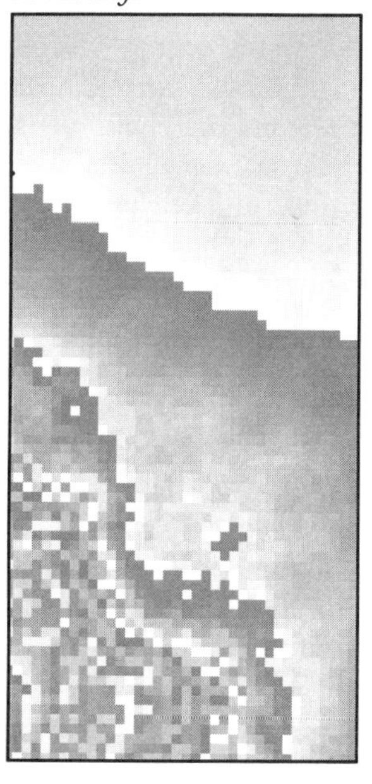

## INTRODUCTION

There is a long and varied history of the counting of Blacks in America. Over the last two hundred years the nature and objectives of these approaches to the counting of Blacks have been novel. The purposes of this paper are to examine these approaches and to determine the functions they have served in the measurement of Blacks in America. The central objective of this paper is to explore the use of the concept of disproportionality as it relates to race and crime.

Disproportionality has been used primarily as a tool to identify Blacks as criminals. More importantly, disproportionality has been used to identify Blacks as the more serious, dangerous criminals. Although great pains are taken to make measurement appear objective and apolitical, the nature of measurement is a political issue.

## EARLY HISTORY OF ATTEMPTS TO COUNT BLACKS

Over two hundred years ago the importance of counting Blacks in America became evident. The number of Blacks in southern states had an impact upon "the allocation and transfer of power and resources among the states" as well as the formula for assessing taxes to pay for war debts (Anderson 1988, p. 158). Of course, the institution of slavery played a central role in this controversy.

Prior to the Revolutionary War, slaves were not counted by the southern states for legislative apportionment (Anderson 1988, p.12). It was clear, however, that continuing this practice of excluding the counting of slaves as property for the apportionment of taxes would put an unfair financial burden on the nonslave states. On the other hand, allowing the slave states to count slaves as they would free men would give them an unfair advantage with respect to representation. A vigorous debate was waged which led to what was called the three-fifths compromise. According to Article I, Section 2, Paragraph 3 of the United States Constitution:

> Representatives and direct taxes shall be apportioned among the several States which may be included within this Union, according to their respective numbers, which shall be determined by adding to the whole number of free persons, including those bound to service for a term of years, and excluding Indians not taxed, three fifths of all other persons.

Meier and Rudwick (1966) noted that this provision:

> clearly recognized and legitimized the existence of slavery. It provided that for purposes of direct taxes and apportioning representation in the House of Representatives, each slave would count as three-fifths of a person. (p. 47)

The next stage in the war of numbers began just prior to the advent of the Civil War and lasted throughout the course of the war. Having already established how Blacks would be counted, the focus during this time period was on how the numbers would be interpreted. Prior to the war, there were several proposals aimed at soliciting information about the slave population. These proposals generated much debate in Congress. Sectional rivalries were re-ignited over the possible uses of these data. For example, William Seward, a Whig from New York, argued that these data would provide information on the "progress" of Blacks in the United States and asserted that if improvement was indicated there would be no bases for continuing to hold Blacks in servitude (Anderson 1988, p. 41). Nevertheless, measures were passed to begin the data collection.

Not surprisingly, these data were used to "statistically" defend *AND* attack slavery. The key issue was the operation of the labor systems in the North and the South. Abolitionist forces argued the data indicated production in nonslave states was thriving, whereas the peculiar institution of slavery had killed the productive spirit of whites in slave states, thereby, taking its toll on the southern economy (Helper 1857, p. 25). Proslavery forces countered with the charge that laborers in the

North were subject to both poorer labor conditions and poorer living conditions than slaves and poor whites in the South and that this resulted in the statistically supported finding of a much larger number of paupers living in the North than in the South (McPherson 1982, pp. 110-113).

During the War, the focus of the debate changed. The statistical data were used mainly to bolster the Union forces and supporters. More specifically, these data were used to help convince those fighting for the abolition of slavery that the emancipation of Blacks would not lead to the destruction of the Union but that the Union would become stronger as a result of the abolition of slavery. As Anderson (1988, pp. 68-69) reported, Joseph Kennedy, the Superintendent of the Census, argued that the introduction of Blacks among the general population would not negatively affect progress. Moreover, Kennedy felt that Blacks were demographically inferior to whites and as a result they would be "doomed" to extinction.

Finally, during Reconstruction, the concern was with the impact that the abolition of the three-fifth's compromise would have on reapportionment. If political reapportionment was based solely on population, then the inclusion of Blacks as equals in terms of numbers would significantly increase the number of southern seats in the House of Representatives and shift the balance of power in favor of the South. This led to a battle waged over changing the basis of reapportionment from total population to total voting population and to the controversy over the right to suffrage for freed Blacks. It was argued that if political reapportionment was based on a voting population which included freed Blacks then the North would have the advantage because freed Blacks would align themselves with northern candidates and causes. However, if freed Blacks were denied the right to vote, then the South would have the advantage. By 1870, it appeared that the inclusion of Blacks in the counting of the voting population only served to maintain the status quo. But Walker (1899), the new Census Superintendent, reported that this had more to do with geographic population growth and loss, the population losses of the South due to the war, and the undercounting of the southern population by the census.

It is important to note that during this entire one hundred year period the counting of Blacks was not used for the benefit of Blacks but for the benefit of those in power or those vying for power. This concern with the counting of Blacks continued with the systematic restriction of Black suffrage in the South and the imputation of the "symbiosis of race and crime" (Gomes and Williams 1990, p. 61) through the use of the concept of disproportionality.

## THE COUNTING OF BLACKS BY THE CRIMINAL JUSTICE SYSTEM

Prior to the Civil War, Blacks were underrepresented in the crime statistics. Work (1913) and others attributed this to the system of social control exhibited by the institution of slavery. However, after the War other mechanisms of social control, such as penitentiaries and reformatories and chain gangs, were introduced to control the Black population. The result was that the criminal justice system was composed of increasingly larger numbers of Blacks.

A review of the work of early Black scholars on the issue of race and crime indicates that these scholars were more intent on explaining why the criminal justice system was so Black rather than why Blacks were criminal (Myers 1989). A number of major themes run through the works of these scholars. Two themes of special interest here include the subject of the use and misuse of statistics and the discriminatory manner in which the administration of justice operated (Young and Sulton 1991).

At the turn of the century, DuBois (1899) and Work (1913) stressed the importance of being aware of the impact of discrimination on the numbers of Blacks in the criminal justice system. DuBois (1899, p. 19) implored his readers to remember that Blacks were arrested for less cause and sentenced for longer periods than whites. Work (1913, p. 69) adds that the policy was to sentence Blacks for more trivial kinds of acts. Both authors emphasized the significance of looking at the number of prisoners received at different institutions during the year of interest rather than the total prison population at particular times because the latter was confounded by the policy of differential sentencing of Blacks.

DuBois (1899) made the connection to disproportionality by reporting that:

> in Philadelphia from 1830 to 1850...less than one-fourteenth of the population was responsible for nearly a third of the serious crimes committed.

Work (1913) argued that the increase in crime among Blacks after the war was largely attributed to concerns about social control, "punishment and restraint rather than protection."

A second group of Black scholars, writing after World War I, also criticized available criminal statistics. Cantor (1930) and Johnson (1941) reiterated the problem with using the number of inmates institutionalized as opposed to using the number of inmates committed for the year. Cantor (1930) addressed the impact that the disparity in sentences for Blacks and Whites, especially the discriminatory manner in which alternative sentences were imposed, had on commitment rates. Johnson

(1941) framed his discussion of discrimination in terms of caste barriers and designated the administration of justice as "a direct and indirect causative factor in the production of Negro crime" (p. 104).

Black scholars writing during the 1950s and early 1960s focused primarily on theory testing. Blue (1948) and Hill (1959) argued that delinquency among Blacks was not caused by racial factors. Blue (1948) examined delinquency rates in Detroit and concluded that delinquency was more closely related to economic status than to race. Hill (1959) tested the applicability of anomie and social disorganization theories and concluded that delinquency was caused by a lack of integration into society rather than social disorganization. Vontress (1962) presented a two fold argument. First, he argued that patterns of segregation and discrimination contributed to crime among Blacks. He then added that statistics were used to substantiate racial differences in crime rates.

The most recent group of Black scholars, publishing during the last three decades, still voice concern about why the criminal justice system is so Black. This body of work has taken at least three routes.

First, much of the discussion from the late 1960s and 1970s centered around institutional racism and its impact on the administration of justice (Peirson 1977; Debro 1977). Peirson (1977) contended that crime statistics were used to "prove" that Blacks were disproportionately involved in crime. He noted that this belief was bolstered by the failure to measure disposition by race past the point of arrest where many arrestees were either released or convicted of a lesser charge.

Debro (1977) argues that the shift in the prison population from predominately white to predominately Black has prompted a corresponding shift in the handling of inmates from an emphasis on rehabilitation to one of punishment. According to Debro (1977) this shift:

> is a form of institutional racism designed to insure that when the black offender returns to the community he is worse than when he was committed. (p. 145)

A second concern prominent in the 1980s and early 1990s is challenge of theories purporting to explain race and crime. These theories are based upon cultural and social factors normed upon a non-Black population without reference to racial and ethnic differences (Austin 1989; Covington 1984).

For example, Covington (1984) provided fuel for the reassessment of the importance of self-esteem on behavior when she examined the effect of employment on the self-esteem of Black and white, male and female addicts and found that only for white male addicts was the effect positive. According to Covington (1984), employment did not effect the self-esteem of the other groups (Black male addicts, Black female addicts, and white female addicts) because they were normally subjected to less stable working conditions.

Similarly, Austin (1989) challenged the popular view that father-absence, or more specifically female-based households, were positively related to delinquency. Austin (1989) reports that if father-absence was not strongly condemned by the culture it would not be harmful to the juvenile.

Black scholars are involved in attempting to understand the nature, extent and causes of the involvement of Blacks in crime. This is occurring in an environment that has popularized "the validity of the relationship between race and crime" through all forms of media and even in our social context (Gomes and Williams 1990, p. 59) The one concept that seems to carry much of the onus is disproportionality.

## THE MEANING OF DISPROPORTIONALITY

The concept of disproportionality has become the mainstay of discussions on race and crime. A review of current undergraduate textbooks indicate that when authors review trends and patterns of crime and introduce the "variable" race the comparisons are between Blacks, whites, and others and the emphasis is on the disproportionate involvement of nonwhites, in particular Blacks.

What does this mean? A rather simplistic definition of the word disproportionate is found in Webster's New World Dictionary (1972): "not proportionate, not in proportion." Generally, this suggests that one is looking at something as a part, share, or portion, especially, in its relation to the whole. It is the comparative relation between parts, things or elements with respect to size, amount, or degree. It is with reference to two things which have a reciprocal relationship to each other.

If the whole is total population then one can talk about the population being disproportionately white. What is the whole when we talk about disproportionate involvement of Blacks in crime? Is it all crime? No, current usage is a statement of relativity based on the racial composition of the total United States population.

### *How has disproportionality been used?*

The concept of disproportionality has been used almost exclusively to discuss race and crime in the United States. More specifically, this concept has been used to discuss the involvement of Blacks in crime. Given that Blacks account for about 12 percent of the total population, any contribution that they make to total arrests that is significantly greater than 12 percent is characterized as disproportionate involvement.

In 1991, Blacks were disproportionately arrested or involved in crime because they accounted for 29 percent of all arrests. Moreover, Blacks were disproportionately involved in violent index crimes because they accounted for 44.8 percent of all arrests for violent index crimes and disproportionately involved in property index crimes because they accounted for 31.3 percent of all arrests for these crimes.

*Meaningfulness and usefulness:*

The relative involvement of Blacks in crime may be better explained by their ranking on what some have called the "misery index." One's ranking is determined by income, employment, and access to adequate housing, educational opportunities, and health care. Exploring these factors *COULD* be both meaningful and useful.

Much of the theory in criminology suggests that there is a relationship between involvement in crime and poverty, unemployment, class, education, and housing. Systematically addressing these issues may lead us to a better understanding of what needs to be done to reduce crime. Such an undertaking would be useful because it may help to depolarize — move us away from equating race, in particular Blacks, with crime. On the other hand, addressing these issues may lead to a questioning of the social and economic foundation of a society in which an easily identifiable racial group is also "disproportionately" represented among the dispossessed of that society.

*When is more not so bad:*

Although Blacks in 1991 were disproportionately arrested for all crimes, they did not account for the largest share of these arrests. In fact, whites accounted for 69 percent of all arrests in 1991, 53.6 percent of all arrests for violent index crimes and 66.4 percent of all arrests for property index crimes. In other words, whites accounted for the largest number of arrests, far more arrests than Blacks. But the relative comparison between Blacks and whites is underplayed and the emphasis is on Black involvement relative to Black population. What comes through is the idea that more, meaning more arrests of whites, is not so bad, because the less, meaning the arrests of Blacks, is disproportionate to the proportion of Blacks in the population.

*Consequences of overemphasis on disproportionality:*

Using the contribution of Blacks to the total population as a basis for discussing the disproportionate involvement of Blacks in crime serves a political purpose. It presents:

> the Typical Criminal, the one whose portrait President Reagan has described as "that of a stark, staring face, a face that belongs to a frightening reality of our time—the face of a human predator, the face of the habitual criminal. Nothing in nature is more cruel and more dangerous." (Reiman 1984, p.38)

The use of the involvement of Blacks in crime relative to their minor contribution to the total population identifies them as this typical criminal. Reiman made the above statement nine years age but it has come back to haunt us many times.

This tendency to define Blacks as the typical criminal has led to increased racial tension during the last decade. We could start with Bernard Goetz in 1984 and move most dramatically to the 1989 shooting death of Carol Stuart in Boston, Massachusetts, the 1989 shooting death of Yusuf Hawkins in the Bensonhurst section of Brooklyn, New York, the 1991 beating of Rodney King in Los Angeles and the 1992 beating death of Malice Green in Detroit. This is just a beginning of the litany but it shows that the presentation of crime fostered by the overemphasis on disproportionality has led to an environment in which false images of Black males have influenced their treatment as offenders and victims, not only by the criminal justice system, but by some segments of white and Black America.

The Bernard Goetz case provides an interesting starting point. Chambliss and Courtless (1992) suggest that the "general public saw this as simply a question of a man's right to defend himself against would-be attackers," whereas the legal issues were much more complicated (pp. 3-4). They argue that the judge created a legal fiction with respect to the self-defense instruction which then allowed the jury to return a verdict of not guilty which was in keeping with the social climate of the time.

But in the Goetz case there was no "general public." There were significant disagreements about characterization of this as a case of self-defense, with positions often differing based upon one's race. It is of great concern that a segment of the public looked at this case and saw a "potential" victim responding to an image of young Black males as dangerous, armed thugs and used this image to justify action that absent the image probably would have been declared criminal.

It was also painfully evident in the killing of Yusuf Hawkins that young whites responded to attitudes which hold that Blacks do not belong in that neighborhood and that Blacks were "human predators" against whom they had to defend. Consequently, the offenders were "justified" in driving Hawkins out of "their" neighborhood. The result was death for Mr. Hawkins.

The 1989 shooting death of Carol Stuart began as a fabricated story about a Black assailant killing Mrs. Stuart and wounding her husband Charles. This story was readily accepted by the police and the news media. Charles Stuart, the author of that fabrication, played upon the image projected in this society of the typical criminal as a Black male. The police were driven by this picture of the criminal. Once it was discovered that the story had been used to divert police attention away from the husband, the pattern of police abuse against blacks was exposed:

> Boston police resorted to threatening and coaching witnesses, cursing and intimidating civilians and planting drugs on potential witnesses as they hunted a suspect. (Daly 1991, p. A3)

The "carnival-mirror image" of the criminal (Reiman 1979), which is based on the concept of disproportionality, led to a carnival like atmosphere for solving this case.

The first Rodney King verdict and its attendant circumstances provides yet another brutal example of the role of race in issues of crime and justice. The characterizations of the Black male presented by the defense in the first King trial, and evidently accepted by many members of the jury, as well as its impact on the response of white America to the Black male, should be examined. The defense argued that their clients were standing between law abiding citizens and the "jungle" of Los Angeles. They further implored the all white jury to see events as the police, also all white, did. The defense encouraged the jurors to see themselves confronted by a 250 pound "Black" man with "very powerful arms." The not so subtle message was that crime and criminals in America have a black face and that Black men are dangerous and should be feared.

Are the serious crimes perpetrated by Blacks more heinous than those perpetrated by whites? In other words, is there any empirical basis to fear Black male offenders more than white male offenders? Reviewing homicide data, because it is the most serious crime, may be useful in making a determination about the "dangerousness" of Black offenders vis-a-vis white offenders.

It is readily apparent that research on homicide in the United States has focused on homicidal violence among Blacks almost to the exclusion of the violence by and among other groups. Of course, this is attributed to the high reported rates among Blacks. But there have been a few attempts to look at white violence. Gary (1986) reported that homicides among middle and upper income groups were committed mainly by white males. Humphrey and Palmer (1987) reported that whites victimize families more than Blacks. The body of literature on serial murders and on mass murders indicate that serial murderers and mass murderers seem to be primarily white.

Victims of serial murderers and mass murderers generally are vulnerable targets such as runaways, prostitutes or the homeless (Holmes and DeBurger 1988). Holmes and DeBurger (1988, p.19) estimate that between 3,500 and 5,000 persons are slain per year by these murderers (17 to 24 percent of the total murders for 1988). But these murders are written off as rare and dramatic.

Unfortunately, there have been few attempts to compare the homicides involving Blacks as offenders with those involving whites as offenders. When looking at the Uniform Crime Reports supplemental homicide data from 1990, we find that the two groups differed with respect to age and sex. White offenders were older than Black offenders. White offenders as a group included significantly fewer female offenders than did Black offenders. And, there was no significant difference in the number of offenders involved. For both whites and Blacks, criminal homicides were more likely to involve single offenders.

Although all criminal homicides were more likely to be intraracial than interracial, this was significantly more likely with white offenders than with Black offenders. Criminal homicides involving white offenders were significantly more likely than those involving Black offenders to have female victims. The victims of white offenders were more likely than those of Black offenders to be family members. In addition, victims in criminal homicides perpetrated by whites were older than those in criminal homicides perpetrated by Blacks.

A gun was the weapon of choice for both white and Black offenders. But the two groups differ with respect to the type of gun used. White offenders were more likely to use a rifle or shotgun, whereas Black offenders were more likely to use a handgun. There are also some differences between the two racial groups in the subcircum-stances of criminal homicides. White offenders were more likely than Black offenders to be involved in felonious attacks on police. On the other hand, Black offenders were more likely to be involved in felony homicides, and felonious attacks on other civilians.

Unfortunately, a review of the Uniform Crime Report data is of limited utility. White offenders are older and more likely to be male. But it is not clear that these characteristics define a more or less dangerous type of offender. Victims of white offenders were more likely to be older, female and family members than those of Black offenders. Is a criminal homicide that targets this group any more heinous or dangerous than one targeting younger, male, non-family members? With respect to the incident characteristics, one group uses a rifle, the other a handgun.

It is apparent that a much closer look at homicides perpetrated by white and Black offenders is needed before any conclusions can be reached about which is more contemptible. However, at this point it appears that the concept of disproportionality has been used to "criminalize" Black people, especially Black males. Overreliance on this concept in our discussions of race and crime intimate that the crimes of Blacks are the crimes that we should be most concerned with and that Black criminals are the criminals to be feared. The fact that most or just as many whites are arrested for offenses of criminal homicide and aggravated assault is ignored.

The image of the criminal thus presented has encouraged researchers and policy makers alike to approach the problem of crime in America by focusing on the Black community. This counting of Blacks as criminals, as a problem segment of the population, makes it possible to continue the business of crime fighting without any fundamental questioning of our social and economic institutions. So again the counting of Blacks has served a political end not for the benefit of Blacks but for the benefit of those in power or those vying for power.

## SUMMARY

The counting of Blacks in the United States has served many different purposes over the last two hundred years. It is clear that during the first of these two centuries the counting of Blacks had obvious political objectives — apportionment for purposes of representation and tax. During the last century, counting has had political purposes as it relates to crime.

Black scholars have long been skeptical of the use of statistics on crime in discussions on race. The counting of Blacks in the United States has continued through the use of the concept of disproportionality. Although there are ways in which the concept could be used beneficially, it has primarily been used to identify Black males as "typical criminals." It has served to divert attention away from looking at non-Black offenders involved in serious crimes. It has functioned to deflect concern from other types of crimes, for example corporate and white collar crime. It has also operated as a justification for the discriminatory treatment accorded Black offenders.

There must be an open dialogue on race and crime. However, this dialogue should go beyond identifying a trend, a pattern, or an overrepresentation. It must consider the contributions of all racial and ethnic groups to the "crime" problem. The definition of crime must be extended beyond that of "street crime." Most importantly, it is incumbent upon scholars to cautiously view the use and abuse of the concept of disproportionality.

**REFERENCES**


Anderson, M. 1988. *The American Census: A Social History.* New Haven: Yale University Press.

Austin, R. 1989. "Family Environment, Educational Aspiration and Performance in St. Vincent." *The Review of Black Political Economy* 17 (3):101-22.

Blue, J. 1948. "The Relationship of Juvenile Delinquency, Race, and Economic Status." *The Journal of Negro Education* 17:469-77.

Cantor, N. 1931. "Crime and the Negro." *Journal of Negro History* 16:61-66.

Chambliss, W. and T. Courtless. 1992. *Criminal Law, Criminology and Criminal Justice.* California: Brooks/Cole Publishing.

Covington, J. 1986. "Self-Esteem and Deviance: The Effects of Race and Gender." *Criminology* 24 (1): 105-36.

Daly, C. 1991. "Pattern of Police Abuses Reported in Boston Case." *The Washington Post.* Friday, July 12, p.Ae:5.

Debro, J. 1977. "Institutional Racism Within the Structure of American Prisons." In *Black Perspectives on Crime and the Criminal Justice System,* edited by R. Woodson. Boston: Hall.

DuBois, W. 1899. "The Negro Criminal." In *Review of Black Political Economy.*

Gary, L. 1986. "Drinking, Homicide and the Black." *Journal of Black Studies* 17:15-31.

Gomes, R. and L. Williams 1990. "Race and Crime: the Role of the Media in Perpetuating Racism and Classism in America." *The Urban League Review* 57-69.

Helper, H. 1857. *The Impending Crisis of the South.* New York: Burdick Brothers.

Hill, M. 1959. "The Metropolis and Juvenile Delinquency Among Negroes." *Journal Of Negro Education* 28:277-285.

Holmes, R. and J. de Burger. 1988. *Serial Murder.* San Diego, CA: Sage.

Humphrey, J. and S. Palmer. 1987. "Stressful Life Events and Criminal Homicide." *Omega* 17:299-308.

Johnson, G. 1941. "The Negro and Crime." *The Annals of the American Academy of Political and Social Science* 271:93-104.

McPherson, J. 1982. *Ordeal by Fire: The Civil War and Reconstruction.* New York: Knopf.

Meier, A. and E. Rudwick 1966. *From Plantation to Ghetto.* New York: Hill and Wang.

Myers, S. 1989. "Introduction." In *Review of Black Political Economy* 16.

Peirson, G. 1977. "Institutional Racism and Crime Clearance." In *Black Perspectives on Crime and the Criminal Justice System,* edited by R. Woodson. Boston: Hall.

Reiman, J. 1979. *The Rich Get Richer and the Poor Get Prison: Ideology, Class, and Criminal Justice*. New York: John Wiley & Sons.

Vontress, C. 1962. "Patterns of Segregation and Discrimination: Contributing Factors to Crime Among Negroes." *Journal of Negro Education* 31:108-116.

Walker, F. 1899. "The Colored Race in the United States." In *Discussions in Economics and Statistics,* edited by D. Dewey. New York: Burt Franklin.

Work, M. 1913. "Negro Criminality in the South." In *Review of Black Political Economy.*

Young, V. 1986. "Gender Expectations and Their Impact on Black Female Offenders and Victims." *Justice Quarterly* 3(3):305-27.

Young, V. and A. Sulton. 1991. "Excluded: The Current Status of African-American Scholars in the Field of Criminology and Criminal Justice." *Journal of Research in Crime and Delinquency* 28(1):101-16.

# FEAR OF CRIME AMONG FOREIGN STUDENTS IN THE UNITED STATES

*Charisse Coston is an assistant professor. She teaches criminology and criminal justice courses at the University of North Carolina. Coston received her doctorate degree in criminal justice from Rutgers, the State University of New Jersey.*

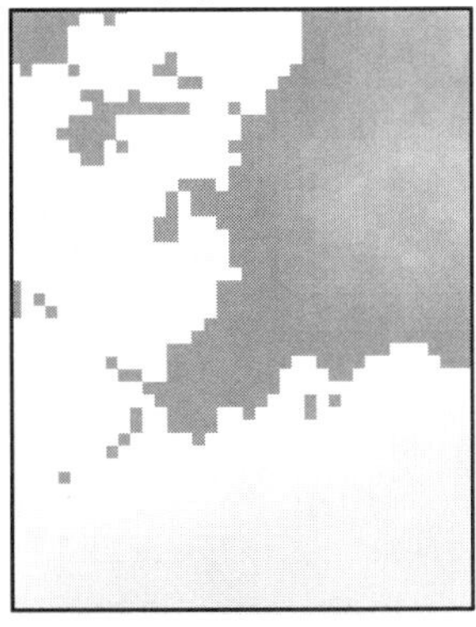

The author would like to acknowledge the support of Adel Ali Helal (employed by The Arab Security Studies and Training Center, in Riyadh, Saudi Arabia) who assisted with the interviews of the subjects in this study and Robert M. Bohm who edited drafts of this manuscript.

Little has been written about the concerns of foreign students studying outside their native countries. Spaulding and Flack (1976) and Brown (1980) have mentioned that foreign students are worried about loved ones back home or are homesick. They are concerned about economic well-being, as well as the physical health condition of parents, other relatives, spouses and their own children left behind in their home country.

Another worry of foreign students is their ability to read, write, speak and comprehend the host country's language (Moumen 1985). Moumen (1985) states that the learner, in a foreign environment, needs and depends on the English language more than anything else to communicate to the people of that foreign culture his or her views about himself or herself, his or her identity, the world, and his or her feelings or thoughts.

Failing in school has been mentioned by Brown (1980) as a constant worry of foreign students. Brown (1980) and Hossain (1983) believe that foreign students studying abroad are at times worried about their legal obligations to return to their native country. Many foreign students, according to Hossain (1983), have signed agreements promising to return to the home country or previous job after school.

There also is the worry about returning to a new job that is waiting for the foreign student after finishing school. Another worry of some foreign students is the political instability in their native country (Spaulding and Falk 1976). Other worries briefly mentioned by researchers are: continuing to be morally right, practicing their religion, not having enough money, finding friends who are morally right, and finding romantic love (Spaulding and Falk 1976; Brown 1980; Hossain 1983; Moumen 1985). Conspicuously absent from this literature is research which focuses on foreign students' worries about being victimized by crime.

This exploratory and descriptive study examines the salience of the role that worries about crime occupy in the lives of foreign students studying in the United States. Two groups of foreign students were interviewed and compared: one group from an urban campus on the east coast and one from a rural campus in the midwest. Additionally, those factors that might influence foreign students' worries about criminal victimization were assessed.

Broad generalizations about the worries of all foreign students studying at all universities in the United States cannot be made from any single study. However, this study may be useful to victimologists and those working with foreign students. This study is undertaken in order to extend the literature on worries about crime and victimization experiences to a little studied and an apparently susceptible sub-group for criminal victimization in the United States.

## BACKGROUND

Potentially, foreign students may be a group that is especially susceptible to criminal victimization because they may not be well versed in the English language or assimilated into the American culture. Difficulties of coping with an alien, culturally-different population and a general fear of strangers can make foreign students feel helpless and especially vulnerable to crime, making them worry about the possibility of crime happening to them. Worrying about crime results from the experience of helplessness in the face of harm (Merry 1981; Coston 1992).

Researchers have noted that acts of criminal victimization are not random (Hindelang et al. 1978; Sparks 1982; Garofalo 1987). There are certain attributes of victims and the situations in which they are involved that make them high-risk targets for criminal victimization. In short, there are high-risk persons, high-risk locations, and high-risk time periods.

Researchers suggest that an individual's perception of danger in a community is really a fear of strangers (Merry 1981; Lewis and Tilly 1982; Lodhi 1983; Roberts 1989; Lynch 1990; Wirth 1991). Merry (1981) defines strangers as "persons who are potentially harmful, and whose behavior seems unpredictable and beyond control" (p. 125). Foreign students would appear to have the potential of being exceptionally worried about crime victimization because so many more people are strangers to them.

They are, as Merry (1981) describes, foreign immigrants "lost in a sea of strangers" (p. 125).

Merry (1981) describes two types of strangers that typically are encountered. The first is those passing by "who appear fleetingly, but never participate in the social life of the community" (p. 94). Simmel (1950) refers to this type of stranger as "those who come today and go tomorrow" (p. 402). The second type is long-term, near-by residents but still unknown as persons with names or personal histories. They remain anonymous. This kind of stranger has been described by Simmel (1950) as the "person who comes today and stays tomorrow, but never becomes part of a social system" (p. 403). Foreign students are more likely to encounter strangers of Merry's (1981) first type at an urban university due to the transient nature of large urban centers. Foreign students are more likely to meet strangers of the second type at a rural university. Thus, foreign students in an urban setting are more likely to feel more vulnerable and more worried about becoming the victim of a crime than those studying in a rural setting.

Foreign students on an urban campus on the east coast (a high crime environment) would appear to be at a higher risk for criminal victimization when compared to those foreign students on a rural campus in the midwest (a low crime environment). People living in large urban cities may live next door to others and still remain strangers, even though they use the same laundromat and walkways. They cross paths without ever touching (Merry 1981). People living in small towns with large universities still have a "sense of a cohesive local social unit to which residents feel identification and belonging" (Merry 1981, p. 94).

Most research in the area of concern, worries, or fears about crime have analyzed the causes of these emotions among segments of the general population, e.g., females, the elderly, racial minorities, urban residents (Meerlo 1950; Biderman 1967; Ennis 1967; Kleinman and David 1973; Bishop 1978; Yin 1980; Lewis 1989; Meithe 1984; Stafford and Galle 1984). Recent studies suggest that the rank-ordering of fears, worries and concerns about crime in relation to other fears, worries, or concerns should be the initial direction of research prior to any assessment of the causes of these emotions (Yin 1982; Stein et al. 1984; Gibbs 1986; Hanrahan 1990; Coston 1992). For example, Yin (1982) found the elderly were not fearful of crime to the point of being prisoners in their own homes. He also found lack of money and poor health were greater concerns than crime for the elderly.

A secondary goal of the present research was to explore the correlates of foreign students' worries about crime. A review of the results of past research on the correlates of the general population's worries and fears about crime has shown that urban residents are more fearful of crime than rural or suburban residents (Sundeen 1976; Wiltz 1982; Stein et al. 1984; Gordon and Riger 1989). Diverse samples of people who were living in large urban cities (cities having a population of over one million) have revealed they are afraid of walking alone in their neighborhoods at night and during the day (Hindelang 1974; Garofalo 1987). Those people (females and the elderly) most afraid of crime are not those people most victimized by crime (Conklin 1975; Yin 1980; Riger 1983; Gordon and Riger 1989).

The fear of crime literature does not reveal the impact of marital status, having children living in the household, or self-perceived abilities to speak, read, write and comprehend the English language on fear of crime. Foreign students are not mentioned by past researchers having studied the causes of worries or fears about crime. The purpose of this study is to examine foreign students' worries about crime. It compares foreign students living in urban and rural settings.

## METHODOLOGY

The terms foreign students, international students, and non-native students are used interchangeably to refer to those pupils from another country enrolled in an institution of higher education in the United States. They are not United States natives nor United States citizens.

The sites selected were two universities, one in the midwest and one on the east coast. The two universities had nearly equal numbers of total students and foreign students in 1990 (the year data were collected). The midwestern university, located in a rural setting in Indiana, had approximately 34,000 total students and 1,727 foreign students registered in 1990. The east coast university, located in an urban setting in New York state, had approximately 40,000 total students and 1,940 foreign students registered in the same year.

The Registrar at the midwestern university generated a random sample of 200 from the 1,727 full-time foreign students who were registered for the spring semester of 1990. Packets of materials containing the survey instrument and instructions were sent to the 200 foreign students selected. These 200 students were advised to call and schedule a meeting with researchers if they wanted to have each question read and explained to them. Twenty respondents availed themselves of this service. Students were read the question in their native language if they requested.

Thirty-seven sample respondents returned the original questionnaire through the mail. Three follow-up mailings resulted in 10 more completed surveys. Six of these respondents attended another meeting to have the questionnaire explained to them; four of these latter respondents mailed in the completed questionnaire. The total number of respondents in the sample from the rural university was 67, a 33.3 percent response rate.

Likewise, a random sample of 200 foreign students registered full-time during the spring semester of 1990 was generated by the Registrar at the urban university. The 200 foreign students were mailed copies of the questionnaire, instructions, and a list of meeting times from which to choose to meet with researchers and have the survey read to them. A total of 77 respondents in the sample came to three group meetings and had the survey read and explained to them. Their native languages were used to explain questions and provide English responses when the subjects requested. Several follow-up mailings resulted in one additional group meeting which yielded five additional completed interviews. The total sample size of foreign students at the urban university was 82, a 41 percent response rate.

## THE SURVEY INSTRUMENT

### *Personal characteristics*

Respondents were asked their age, sex, region of the world from which they came, and length of time spent in the United States. If all of their time spent in the United States was not spent at the university in which they were currently enrolled, they were asked where else they had lived or visited, the length of time they spent at each one of the locations they listed, and the purpose of their residence or visit.

Respondents also were asked if they were married and if their spouse and any children were living with them. They were asked about their primary source(s) of income, their year in school, and major area of study. They also were asked to indicate the type of neighborhood in which they lived in the United States (urban, suburban or rural).

Subjects were asked about their ability to read, write, comprehend, and speak the English language. The wording of the question was: On a scale of 1 (not fluent) to 5 (fluent), how would you rate your abilities in the following four areas of English language: speaking, reading, writing, and comprehension. Results of this question were aggregated into an index. The index for samples of subjects at both universities showed a high degree of reliability (a=.90). In other words, there was no difference within either sample in the ability to speak, read, write and comprehend the English language. Therefore, each foreign student in both samples was given an average self-perceived ability in the English language score. The mean for all foreign students at the midwestern university was 4. The mean for all foreign students at the urban university was 3. The urban group believed they were less fluent in the English language than the rural group, but both groups reported fluency in English.

*Crime-related variables*

Foreign students were asked if they had ever been the victim of a crime while in the United States or in any other country in which they lived or visited. If they had been victimized, they were asked about the nature and extent of their past victimization experiences (including attempts). Respondents also were asked about the nature of their vicarious victimization experiences, i.e., only hearing about the victimization experiences of other foreign students.

*Perceptual variables*

The foreign students were asked about their perceptions of vulnerability. The two specific questions were: How likely do you think it is that you could be the victim of (1) a property offense (theft, burglary) and (2) a personal crime (rape, robbery, murder) while studying in the United States? Response categories ranged from 1 (not likely) to 7 (extremely likely). Results for the two questions were aggregated into an index. The reliability for this index was high for subjects at each university (a=.81 for the rural university and .96 for the urban university). Foreign students in both samples made no distinction between the likelihood of personal or property victimization. The index was then collapsed for both samples and each foreign student was given an average vulnerability to criminal victimization score. The means, for foreign students at the rural university (4) and at the urban university (5), show that subjects at the rural university felt less vulnerable than subjects attending the urban university. However, both groups felt vulnerable.

*Anticipatory variables*

Foreign students were asked about their use of protective behaviors. Specifically, they were asked whether they avoided certain places, what types of places they avoided and why. They also were asked whether they carried anything to protect themselves and what they carried.

*Identifying and rank-ordering worries*

Each person in the sample was asked to list the five biggest worries they have in their lives while living in the United States. After giving them time to list their worries, they were asked to rank-order the worries they had listed, ranging from 1 (the biggest worry) to 5. This initial list of worries was generated by the foreign students, i.e., they were not given a prepared list from which to choose.

*Worries about crime*

The last question on the survey instrument asked foreign students to indicate on a five-point Likert-type scale, the degree to which they worry about becoming the victim of (1) a property offense and (2) a personal crime while studying in the United States. For both samples of students, there was high reliability among these two variables (a=.88 for the rural sample and .97 for the urban sample).

Next, each foreign student in each of the two groups was given an average worry about criminal victimization score. The mean scores for each group, the rural university and urban university foreign students, were 2.2 and 3.4, respectively. There was no difference in worries about property or personal victimization for subjects in these samples. Subjects attending the urban university worried more about becoming the victim of both personal and property crime than subjects at the rural university. This variable was the dependent variable in the regression analyses.

## DEMOGRAPHIC CHARACTERISTICS OF THE SAMPLE

Of those interviewed, the average age of a foreign student at the rural university was 28 while the average age of a foreign student at the urban university was 25. The students from the rural campus reported having been in the United States an average of 24 months, while students at the urban university reported a shorter stay of 13 months. Most of the respondents at the rural university were male (56 percent); most of the respondents at the urban university were female (55 percent).

Students reported their native countries. Students in the sample from the rural campus were most often from the Far East, followed by the Middle East and Africa, respectively. Foreign students in the sample from the urban university were represented most often by the Far East followed by Europe and South America. Most of the foreign students attending school on both campuses reported being single, although many of them were married (37 percent in both samples). Most of those subjects who were married reported living with their spouse while here in the United States. Thirty one percent of the married students did not have children living with them in their households.

Most foreign students from both samples reported their primary income source while studying in the United States came from their family and relatives in their native country. Twenty four percent of foreign students from the urban university reported they were working and that this was their primary income source.

The educational objective reported most often by foreign students in both groups was the undergraduate degree, but the Master's degree closely followed as second. Other educational goals included legal, medical, and Ph.D. degrees; two students mentioned a double major in law and psychology and law and sociology. Respondents majored in the social sciences area more often than the humanities or natural sciences.

Most foreign students had not spent time in any other city in the United States or its territories. Foreign students, having stayed in other locales, stayed a few days for a short vacation.

## VICTIMIZATION AND WORRIES

Most foreign students on both campuses reported not having been the victim of a crime while in the United States. Thirty seven percent of the foreign students on the rural campus and 28 percent of the foreign students on the urban campus reported being the victim of a crime. No foreign students in either sample reported more than four victimization experiences.

Of those reporting being victimized while attending the rural university, 56 percent reported being victimized once; 20 percent twice; 16 percent three times; and eight percent four times. Of these students, burglaries and thefts most often were the victimization experiences.

Foreign students attending the urban university also reported being crime victims. The type of crime they most often reported was robbery. Theft, burglary and assault also were reported.

Most foreign students reported no past victimization experiences. Of those reporting past victimization experiences, 34 percent of foreign students at the rural university reported incidents, while 23 percent of foreign students on the urban campus reported incidents. The types of victimization experiences included theft, burglary, assault, and robbery.

Five percent of the foreign students who had been victimized while attending the rural university also had been the victim of a crime in their native country. Eleven percent of the urban university's foreign students having been victimized in the United States also had been victimized in their native country.

The urban university foreign students' prediction of future victimization was slightly higher than were students at the rural university. As discussed earlier, the results show that foreign students attending the rural university are less worried about victimization than their urban counterparts.

Table 1 shows the behaviors used by foreign students to insulate themselves from criminal victimization. Of those students attending the rural university who reported avoiding situations, most reported avoiding ghettos. The second and third types of situations avoided by foreign students at the rural university were walking or driving alone after midnight (21 percent), and night clubs (20 percent).

Ninety-five percent of the foreign students attending the urban university reported avoiding places due to the threat of criminal victimization. The situation avoided by the largest percentage of these foreign students was ghettos.

A larger percentage of foreign students at the urban university than at the rural university reported carrying weapons (53 percent versus 43 percent). Foreign students carrying weapons report carrying mace most often. Other means of protection utilized by foreign students are: knives, black jacks, stun guns, handguns, whistles, and "street sense."

Tables 2 and 3 list the worries of foreign students attending the rural and urban universities. The tables show foreign students' worries (in raw numbers), in order of magnitude.

Only three students verbalized from which racial group they were afraid of being attacked. Two Korean students attending the rural university mentioned being afraid of being assaulted by Japanese students. One Arab student attending the urban university mentioned being worried about being attacked by Jewish students and discriminated against by Jewish professors.

*Multi-variate analysis*

Multiple regression was used in the analysis of both groups to assess the influence of selected predictor variables on the dependent variable (worries about crime). The predictor variables were: age, sex, whether all of their time in the United States was spent at their present university, length of time spent in the United States, marital status, if children lived in the household, the average self-perceived ability in the English language score, past victimization experiences before and while living in the United States and those numbers of past victimization experiences, their self-perceived vulnerability score, if they avoid places, and if they carried a weapon. All of the predictor variables were entered at one time. Partial correlation coefficients were used to assess the contribution of the predictor variables by controlling the effects of other variables in the equation.

**TABLE 1**

**SELF-PROTECTIVE BEHAVIORS**
(in percentages)

| TYPE OF BEHAVIOR | Rural Midwestern University (N=67) | Urban Eastern University (N=82) |
|---|---|---|
| Avoid Places? | | |
| No | 27 | 5 |
| Yes | 73 | 95 |
| Carry a Weapon? | | |
| No | 57 | 47 |
| Yes | 43 | 53 |
| Means of Self-Protection | | |
| Knife | 14 | 17 |
| Mace | 76 | 33 |
| Black jack | 6 | 10 |
| Stun gun | 4 | 6 |
| Hand gun | - | 10 |
| Street sense | - | 14 |
| Whistle | - | 10 |

**TABLE 2**
**RANK-ORDERING OF WORRIES AMONG STUDENTS AT A LARGE RURAL MID-WESTERN UNIVERSITY[a]**

| Worry | Most serious |
|---|---|
| Failing in school | 22 |
| Racial attacks | 10 |
| Poor health | 7 |
| Family here in the United States | 6 |
| Getting mugged | 5 |
| Lack of money | 3 |
| Family back home | 4 |
| Job satisfaction upon returning home | 2 |
| Being morally good | 1 |
| Contracting AIDS | 2 |
| Becoming addicted to drugs | 1 |
| Choosing the right friends | - |
| Breaking up with boyfriend or girlfriend | - |

**TABLE 3**
**RANK-ORDERING OF WORRIES AMONG STUDENTS AT A LARGE URBAN EASTERN UNIVERSITY[b]**

| Worry | Most serious |
|---|---|
| Failing in school | 13 |
| Racial attacks | 2 |
| Poor health | 3 |
| Family here in the United States | - |
| Getting mugged | 32 |
| Lack of money | 5 |
| Family back home | 8 |
| Job satisfaction upon returning home | 4 |
| Being morally good | 2 |
| Contracting AIDS | 6 |
| Becoming addicted to drugs | 2 |
| Choosing the right friends | 2 |
| Breaking up with boyfriend or girlfriend | - |

a N=63; four students indicated "no worries"
b N=79; three students listed "no worries"

*Rural university results*

Regression results for the foreign students at the rural university reveal four significant variables which together explain six percent of the variance in these foreign students' worries about crime. The significant variables that were negatively correlated with worries about crime were: age, sex, whether they had been the victim of a crime in their native country, and whether they had children living with them in the United States.

Females and younger foreign students were more worried about criminal victimization (Beta= -.42 and -.50). If a foreign student had not been the victim of a crime in his or her native country that individual was more worried about crime (Beta=-.45). The more often a foreign student had been the victim of a crime in his or her native country, the more worried that individual was about becoming the victim of a crime in the United States (Beta=.40). The above-mentioned variables were all significant at the .05 level.

If a foreign student had children living in the house, he or she was not worried about victimization (Beta=-.40). This variable was significant at .10. Because this was an exploratory study, the more liberal significance level was included. The null hypotheses were rejected in the t and F-tests.

The conclusion is that the independent variables as well as the overall regression equation, are helping to predict rural foreign students worries about crime (F=2.70 at .05). Given the low percentage associated with the variables that explain this group's worries, more study is needed.

*Urban university results*

Regression analysis results from subjects at the urban university show that the percentage of variance explained by the four statistically significant independent variables is .31. Those subjects having heard about the victimization experiences of other foreign students tended to be more worried about becoming the victim of a crime, and this relationship was positive (Beta=.12).

A subject's perceptions about his or her ability in the English language was correlated with subject's worries about victimization (Beta=.14). The less comfortable the subject was with his or her ability to master the English language, the greater he or she worries about a victimization experience.

Foreign students having been the victim of a crime outside of the United States were more worried about becoming the victim of a crime while in the United States (Beta=.21). Those foreign students who believe that future victimization experiences were likely were also more worried about a victimization experience occurring (Beta=.12). The null hypotheses in both the F (F=9.5 at .05) and t tests were rejected. The overall equation is significant and the independent variables have explanatory value for predicting these foreign students' worries about crime.

## DISCUSSION, IMPLICATION AND SUGGESTIONS FOR FUTURE RESEARCH

Overall, foreign students from the urban university felt more vulnerable to and worried more about becoming the victim of a crime than foreign students at the rural university. Urban foreign students ranked getting mugged as their biggest worry while rural students ranked getting mugged as their fifth biggest worry. Regression results show different predictor variables influencing foreign students' worries about crime depending upon the type of university: urban or rural. Results among the foreign students at the rural university reveal that younger subjects were more worried than older subjects. A review of the past literature stresses that older people are more worried about becoming the victim of a crime. Given the higher victimization rates among younger foreign students, perhaps they feel less emotionally prepared to study abroad. Consistent with past studies was the finding that females are more worried about becoming a victim of crime than males. The female students tended to use more behaviors to insulate themselves from a possible victimization experience, i.e., carrying mace and avoiding more places.

Those foreign students at the rural university having been the victim of a crime in their native countries might have desensitized themselves about the likelihood of the occurrence of crime and, thus, worried about its occurrence less. But, the greater the number of times that they had been victimized in their native country, the greater the worries about becoming the victim of a crime in the United States. Prior victimization studies reveal that the occurrence and frequency of past victimization experiences result in greater worries about becoming the victim of a crime. The occurrence and frequency of past victimization experiences while in the United States were not significant predictors in rural foreign students' worries about becoming the victim of a crime.

Those foreign students at the rural university who had children living in their households were not as worried about becoming the victim of a crime as those students who did not have children living with them. One possible explanation for this finding might be that having children in the home kept them from going to those places where they might get victimized. Foreign students at the rural university ranked worrying about getting mugged as their fifth biggest worry. Perhaps, those with children worried more about other more immediate concerns that may or may not be related to their children.

Foreign students who considered their mastery of the English language to be poor tended to worry more about becoming the victim of a crime. Particularly, since they may be surrounded by strangers unfamiliar with their language.

Urban foreign students, believing it was likely they could be the victim of a crime (calculating the odds of a victimization experience), also tended to worry more about becoming the victim of a crime. Those foreign students having heard about the victimization experiences of other foreign students were correspondingly more worried about becoming the victim of a crime. Foreign students attending the urban university who had been the victim of a crime in their native country were more worried about becoming the victim of a crime in the United States.

The findings in this study of urban foreign students are consistent with previous studies with the exception of self-perceptions of ability in the English language. This variable was absent from previous research.

There are several implications that can be drawn from this study. The ramifications are incorporated here into practical suggestions that can be used by United States embassy personnel in foreign countries, counselors of international students in the United States, the police, and the general population. These data show that a large number of foreign students are crime victims. The elderly and females may have irrational fears about crime because their victimization rates are lower. But, foreign students' fears are rational because their victimization rates are high. Something must be done to help this vulnerable group.

Among the steps that should be taken to reduce foreign students' fear and victimization are tests of foreign students' language skills. Embassies could test foreign students' ability in English and counsel them so that the lack of being able to articulate English will not result in higher worry levels. Embassy personnel can prepare foreign students for study in the United States by informing them of possible worries that they might have which could interfere with their studying. In addition, these personnel might offer strategies for handling such worries if they occur. In so doing, embassy personnel can offer an obligatory orientation program to assist foreign students' preparedness to travel and study abroad.

These data also could be used by counselors in international services and by college deans to develop policy for addressing the potential worries of foreign students once they arrive and begin studying in the United States.

Finally, these study results should assist United States citizens coming into regular contact with foreign students, as well as the general population, in being sensitized to the nature of the potential problems of non-United States citizens studying at American universities. Everyone, particularly the police, should be aware of foreign students' worries. They should help in their transition to the United States, striving to make foreign students feel at home and welcome in a culture that may be frightening to them.

## CONCLUSION

There are many opportunities for future research in the fear of crime area. This study could be replicated on samples of foreign students stratified by native country so that further exploration of worries by country of origin can occur. Results focusing on worries among college students native to the United States could be compared to results of worries among non-native students studying in the United States to determine if there are any differences between these two groups. Results comparing the worries of United States college students studying abroad with those worries of United States college students studying in the United States could be compared. As a result, the host country where United States students are studying could provide orientation programs which address potential worries these students might have.

Researchers should attempt to develop a uniform set of variables representing the different dimensions of concern about criminal victimization, such as fear, worry, and anxiety. Currently, researchers studying in this area use a wide variety of uni-dimensional variables that tap only the singular dimension of the concept. Thus, we lack a comprehensive understanding of this phenomenon. Employing a multi-dimensional variable would greatly enhance our understanding of this complex phenomenon, as would research into the fears of differing populations.

## REFERENCES

Brown, D. 1980. *Principles of Language Learning and Teaching*. Englewood Cliffs, NJ: Prentice-Hall, Inc.

Conklin, J. 1975. *The Impact of Crime*. New York: MacMillan.

Coston, C. 1992. *Worries About Crime: Rank-Ordering Survival Concerns Among Urban Transient Females*. Paper presentation made at the Annual Meeting of the American Society of Criminology.

______. 1988. *Fear of Crime Among New York City's Shopping-Bag Ladies.* Doctoral Dissertation, Rutgers University, Ann Arbor, MI: Dissertation Abstracts.

DuBow, F.; M. Edward; and G. Kaplan. 1979. *Reactions to Crime: A Critical Review of the Literature.* Washington, D.C.: U.S. Department of Justice.

Erskine, H. 1974. "The Polls: Fear of Violence and Crime." *Public Opinion Quarterly* 38:131-145.

Federal Bureau of Investigation. 1991. *Uniform Crime Reports.* U.S. Department of Justice, Washington, D.C.: U.S. Government Printing Office.

Garofalo, J. 1987. "Reassessing the Lifestyle Model of Criminal Victimization." In *Positive Criminology,* edited by M.R. Gottfredson and T. Hirschi. Newbury Park, CA: Sage.

Gibbs, J. 1986. *Fear of Crime: A Concept in Need of Clarification.* Paper presentation at the Annual Meeting at the American Society of Criminology.

Gordon, M. and S. Riger. 1989. *Female Fear.* New York: Free Press.

Hanrahan, K. 1990. *Exploring Fear Of Crime Among Elderly Urban Females.* Doctoral Dissertation, Rutgers University, Ann Arbor, MI: Dissertation Abstracts.

Hindelang, M. 1974. "Public Opinion Regarding Crime, Criminal Justice, and Related Topics." *Journal of Research in Crime and Delinquency* 11: 101-106.

Hindelang, M.; M. Gottfredson, and J. Garofalo. 1978. *Victims of Personal Crime: An Empirical Foundation for a Theory of Personal Victimization.* Cambridge, MA: Ballinger Publishing Co.

Hossain, M. 1983. "Social Determinants of Foreign Students Length of Stay In U.S." *International Journal of Contemporary Sociology* Vol. 20 Nos. 3 and 4.

Lewis, O. 1982. "Urbanization Without Breakdown: A Case Study." *Scientific Monthly* 75: 31-41.

Lodhi, A. and C. Tilly. 1983. "Urbanization, Crime and Collective Violence in Nineteenth Century France." *American Journal of Sociology* 79: 296-318.

Lynch, K. 1990. *The Image of the City.* Cambridge, MA: Technology Press.

Merry, S. 1981. *Urban Danger: Life in a Neighborhood of Strangers.* Philadelphia: Temple University Press.

Moumen, F. 1985. *Attitudes, Motivation and Orientation in Learning English as a Second Language.* Master's Thesis, Indiana University, Bloomington, IN.

National Crime Commission: U.S. President's Commission on Law Enforcement and the Administration of Justice. 1967. *Task Force Report: Crime and Its Impact - An Assessment.* Washington, D.C.: U.S. Government Printing Office.

Roberts, B. 1989. *Organizing Strangers.* London: University of Texas Press.

Simmel, G. 1950. *The Sociology of George Simmel.* Glencoe, IL: Free Press.

Sparks, R. 1982. *Research on Victims of Crime: Accomplishments, Issues.* New York: National Institute of Mental Health.

Spaulding, S. and M. Flack. 1976. *The World's Students in the United States: A Review and Evaluation of Research on Foreign Students.* New York: Praeger, Inc.

U.S. Department of Justice. 1990. *Sourcebook of Criminal Justice Statistics.* Washington, D.C.: U.S. Government Printing Office.

Von Hentig, H. 1948. *The Criminal and His Victim: Studies in the Socio-Biology of Crime.* Hamden, CT: Archon Books.

Wirth, L. 1991. "Urbanism as a Way of Life." *American Journal of Sociology* 44:1-29.

# DRUGS AND VIOLENCE IN GANGS

*David Fattah is the co-founder of the House of Umoja in Philadelphia. Twenty five years ago, the House of Umoja began providing residential and non-residential services to juvenile gang members. It is widely regarded as the nation's most effective gang violence prevention program. Fattah received a bachelor's degree in business administration from Temple University.*

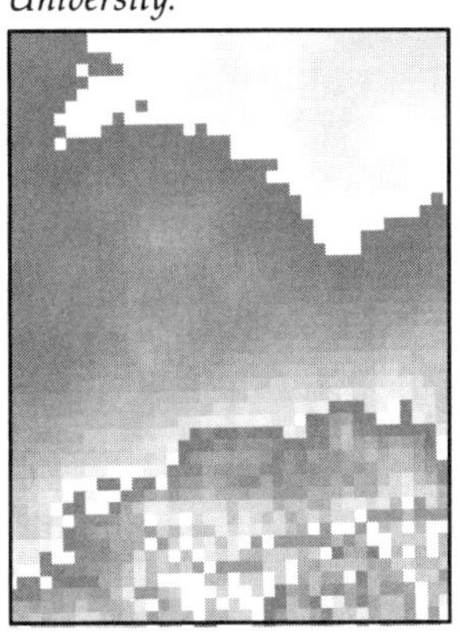

## VIOLENCE AND FEAR

The modern gang is a sophisticated organization with an unwritten charter, philosophy, claimed turf, communications system, purpose and agenda. Hundreds of thousands of children and adults belong to gangs. Thousands more are recruited each year.

Some gangs, as well as some individual gang members, are involved in drug dealing and violence. The violence includes armed and unarmed murders, aggravated assaults, batteries, and robberies. Each year, the violence associated with gang-related drug dealing claims thousands of lives. Many of the victims are not gang members. Small children frequently are accidentally hit in the wild shoot outs among rival drug dealing gang members. Sometimes the hits are intentional. As Woodson (1993) notes: "When a drug deal goes bad, a retalitory drive-by shooting may target any resident of a neighbohrood and is not necessarily limited to the offending gang members." And recent data from the Philadelphia Police Department indicate that drug dealing and homicide are related, with homicide rates over 125 percent higher in areas plagued by intense drug dealing activity than in other areas of the city.

The violence associated with gang-related drug dealing has created a climate of fear. This climate is so oppressive that it inhibits the level of community involvement necessary to address it. Single women, senior citizens, and non-participating youth are among the most fearful. Victims of these crimes, as well as witnesses to these crimes, often are afraid to cooperate with police investigations and prosecutions of offenders. And, the fear is so great, it is difficult to determine who the "good guys" are.

The drug dealing, the violence, and the fear all combine to create a situation making it more difficult to reduce gang drug dealing and the violence associated with it. These problems create barriers to reducing risk factors and enhancing neighborhood resilency.

## VIOLENCE AND GANGS

To fully understand the problems and to identify realistic options, several myths or misconceptions must be dispelled. Among these are: 1) the belief that gang-related drug dealing and violence are new problems; 2) the perception that gang members can be readily identified on the basis of their ethnic heritage, place of residence or dress; and 3) the belief that police suppression alone will remedy the problems.

When thinking about gang drug dealing and violence problems, many assume these are new problems - ones presenting novel challenges to urban communities. However, gangs are not a recent phenomenon in American history. According to Stark (1981), gangs were active in New York and Philadelphia throughout the 1800s. These early gangs "began as secret patriotic societies, political clubs, and volunteer fire companies." During the early 1900s, youth gangs emerged. Stark (1981) explains:

> At the turn of the century, however, youth gangs typically started as neighborhood play groups, evolved into teams and clubs with numerous followers, and generated a hierarchy of leadership based on loyalty and physical and mental skills.

The emergence of youth gangs did not signal the end of adult participation in gangs. Following passage of the Volstead Act, prohibiting the manufacture and importation of liquor, the established adult gangs quickly filled the demand for the then-illegal beverages. The illegal liquor trade was filled with violence. Chicago was not the only city that experienced mass murders among rival gang members fighting turf wars to control the market. And lucrative liquor markets were not the only vices customers demanded and over which rival gangs fought. Prostitution and gambling brought huge profits for gangs, as did drugs such as marijuana and heroin. Youth gangs did not then, nor do they now, control the profitable vice-related illegal businesses.

When thinking about youth gang members, most picture them as unemployed, poverty-stricken, functionally-illiterate, African-American or Mexican-American teenagers wearing some identifying clothing or colors. This perception is influenced by police department gang lists, that frequently are compiled on the basis of some "gang member profile." Contrary to popular belief, gang members are not necessarily uninformed. According to Woodson (1993), Watkins maintains that the "Crips" employ white youth "to sell and transport cocaine because they are not as likely to be stopped by police."

Perceptions of gang members also are influenced by scholarly studies on gangs. Since the turn of this century, numerous scholars have studied youth gangs (Thrasher 1927; Cohen 1955; Cloward and Ohlin 1960; Short 1974; Horowitz and Swartz 1974; Stark 1981; Woodson 1993). Thrasher (1927), in his study of 1,313 gangs, may have set the stage for a long and consistent series of simplistic analyses of gangs. Most of the studies view gangs as collections of wayward youth engaged in "senseless" violence (Haskell and Yablonsky 1982). However, they fail to recognize that even these so-called "youth" gangs include adults. These adults plan and direct gang recruitment efforts and gang activities, including drug dealing and violence.

These studies also fail to note that gang members are not just unemployed, poverty-stricken, functionally-illiterate, African-American and Mexican-American youngsters residing in inner cities. Gang members often are gainfully employed in legal businesses. Although most gang members reside in poor inner-city neighborhoods, many are white and can be found living in affluent suburban neighborhoods in Kansas or riding motorcycles through the mountains in Idaho. And many gang members are not functionally illiterate. They regularly read newspapers to obtain updates on gang members' exploits. And, given the skills required to deal drugs, functional literacy is required.

Perhaps most important, and most frequently ignored, is the fact that gangs are not inherently evil or totally devoid of any positive attributes. Gangs offer their members love, companionship, friendship, loyalty, and trust. They also help members and their families with living expenses, such as rent and utility payments, clothing and medicine purchases, and transportation.

There also is a belief that police suppression alone will stop gang drug dealing and the violence associated with it. The causes of drug dealing and violence are beyond the control of police. Police are able to respond after crimes occur. However, they are not equipped with the necessary resources to address the underlying causes of these crimes prior to their commission.

## VIOLENCE AND DRUG DEALING

Some gangs, having many juvenile members, are involved in drug dealing and the violence associated with the drug trade. Obviously, the drug trade provides a source of revenue for gangs. According to Woodson (1993), Kramer of the Los Angeles Police Department reports that four local gangs receive over $1 million a week from drug sales.

Gang involvement in drug dealing is not new. In 1978, Moore studied Chicano gangs. She found they were involved in marketing heroin. Moore (1978) also found these gang members used heroin and were involved in violence.

In 1981, McBride found that drug dealing and violence are related. He explains:

> The illegal situation generates an environment in which violence or murder is used to eliminate local competitors and informers, and to maximize profits for the seller or minimize expenses for the buyer. ... However, because of the extremely large amounts of money involved, violence often emerges within the context of the control of markets. ... Conflict over distribution and markets also appears to create a good deal of violence among large importers and dealers.

And in 1993, Woodson found that turf wars are claims "to a portion of a lucrative drug market" rather than just to specific street corners. According to Woodson (1993), gang members, including the Los Angeles-based "Crips" and "Bloods," commonly sell crack and cocaine and use the profits to purchase weapons. He laments: "Clearly, the street gangs of the nineties are more violent, more heavily armed - and, tragically, younger - than those of previous years."

I have found in Philadelphia that much of the distribution of crack and cocaine is under the control of an organization known as the "Junior Black Mafia." It is commonly called the JBM. The JBM was organized by the remnants of the original "Black Mafia," which was comprised of gang members. The "Black Mafia" began in 1974. It recruited young men into the heroin trade.

Young African-American males, ranging in age from 14 to 17 years, are employed by the JBM as its street corner lookouts and for protection. These youngsters are not easily distinguishable from youth simply lounging out of boredom on the same street corners. The lookouts and protectors are loosely structured and refer to themselves as a "posse." Posse is a Jamaican term synonymous with the American term gang. The posse concept was borrowed from Jamaican drug dealers using young men to terrorize drug dealing competitors as well as the general community. Law enforcement authorities in Philadelphia recently reported arrests of a substantial number of reputed JBM members.

Woodson (1993) suggests that gangs, drugs and violence problems are likely to increase. He notes the emergence of Asian gangs having connections with heroin organizations and having "the potential for extreme violence." Woodson (1993) also notes the national expansion of gang drug dealing networks, with 75 of 78 large cities reporting problems with a gang, crew, or posse.

## CREATING VIABLE OPTIONS

Despite the sobering nature of the task before us, there are many things that can be done to reverse the frightening trends. Gang-related drug dealing and the violence associated with it can be reduced. It will require many years of hard work on the part of agencies and organizations in the public and private sectors. No quick-fix solutions are available. But we can positively impact the problem if the following steps are taken:

1. During the spring and summer of 1993, various meetings were held around the country. The first of these was held in Kansas City and entitled "The National Urban Peace and Justice Summit." At the various meetings, former and current gang members called for the immediate creation of 500,000 jobs. In their view, to counteract the attractiveness of gangs and drugs, those in or likely to join gangs need to attach themselves to positive aspects of their communities. Jobs are an important part of this positive attachment process.

2. Given the national nature of gang networks, a national taskforce on gangs should be established. This taskforce should be funded by government agencies and private organizations. However, it should be designed and managed by neighborhood-based organizations working to reduce gang drug dealing and violence.

3. Drug dealing gangs based on both coasts and in Chicago are extending their drug marketing efforts to large and small cities throughout the entire nation. Law enforcement personnel, neighborhood-based organizations, and other concerned parties should be trained in how to recognize and respond to the presence of these gangs. A national training and research institute on gangs should be established. This institute should be funded by government agencies and private organizations. However, it should be designed and managed by neighborhood-based organizations working to reduce gang drug dealing and violence. Its research staff should include African-American and other non-white researchers having lived in inner-city neighborhoods

plagued by gangs, drugs and violence. In this way, the research will be relevant and have practical application to the problems experienced by those living at risk and in fear of gang drug dealing-related violence.

4. Immediate efforts should be taken to contain the spread of gang drug dealing and violence. This can be accomplished in several ways. Two of the most important are: a) prevent drug use and abuse by targeting pre-teens; and b) prevent gang recruitment by targeting pre-teens.

5. Implementation of the House of Umoja "Adella System." This system is an Afrocentric grievance procedure directed toward violence avoidance through counseling, mediation, and conflict resolution training. It was developed over the 25 years of the House's existence and has proven effective with thousands of warring gang members.

## CONCLUSION

Gangs, drugs and violence are a volatile mixture, causing the deaths of thousands of urban residents each year. Although the problem of gang drug dealing-related violence currently is increasing, a wholistic long-term plan can reverse these frightening trends. Our perceptions of the problem, youngsters residing in urban areas, and the capacity of law enforcement agencies to respond must change. And adequate resources must be given to neighborhood-based organizations to enable them to fully participate in efforts designed to humanely address one of the most difficult challenges facing this nation.

## REFERENCES


Cloward, R. and L. Ohlin. 1960. *Delinquency and Opportunity: A Theory of Delinquent Gangs.* New York: Free Press.

Cohen, A. 1955. *Delinquent Boys: The Culture of the Gang.* New York: Macmillan.

Haskell, M. and L. Yablonsky. 1982. *Juvenile Delinquency* (3rd ed.). Boston: Houghton Mifflin Company.

Horowitz, R. and G. Swartz. 1974. "Honor, Normative Ambiguity and Gang Violence." *American Sociological Review* 39: 238-251.

McBride, D. 1981. "Drugs and Violence." In *The Drugs-Crime Connection,* edited by J. Inciardi. Beverly Hills, CA: Sage.

Moore, J. 1978. *Homeboys: Gangs, Drugs, and Prison in the Barrios of Los Angeles.* Philadelphia: Temple University Press.

Short, J. Jr. 1974. "Youth Gangs and Society: Micro and Macrosociological Processes." *Sociological Quarterly* 36:3-19.

Stark, E. 1981. "Gangs and Progress: The Contribution of Delinquency to Progressive Reform." In *Crime and Capitalism: Readings in Marist Criminology,* edited by D. Greenberg. Palo Alto, CA: Mayfield Publishing Company.

Thrasher, F. 1926. *The Gang*. Chicago: University of Chicago Press.

Woodson, R. Jr. 1993. "Gang Violence: A National Epidemic." *Agenda: The Alternative Magazine of Critical Issues* 3:2-15

# BLACK FEMALE DELINQUENCY

*Helen Taylor Greene is an assistant professor. She teaches criminology and criminal justice courses at Old Dominion University. Greene received her doctorate degree in criminology and criminal justice from the University of Maryland in College Park.*

Throughout the 20th century the development of youth has been an important issue in the black community. Currently, black adolescents are described as an endangered species because of negative trends in their education, employment, delinquency and crime, substance abuse, pregnancy and other social indicators (Taylor amd Gibbs 1989). Yet, these youth are still only a minor component of literature on adolescence (McKenry et al. 1989). And, most studies of young black females focus primarily upon school experiences, pregnancy, mothering, and sexual behavior.

Decades ago, the eminent black sociologist, E. Franklin Frazier (1949), stated that criminality among "Negroes" had its roots in juvenile delinquency. While there has been extensive research on delinquency in the black community, studies of black female delinquents are rare. This is surprising because in 1990 black women represented almost half of all female prisoners under state or federal jurisdiction (Bureau of Justice Statistics 1992). If Frazier was correct, it is necessary to increase our understanding of black female delinquency to prevent criminality.

## MEASURING BLACK FEMALE DELINQUENCY

Several sources of data are used to describe the extent of juvenile delinquency. Traditional sources include: (1) the Federal Bureau of Investigation's *Crime in the United States,* an annual publication commonly referred to as the Uniform Crime Reports; (2) *Juvenile Court Statistics, Children in*

*Custody,* and *Update on Statistics* published by the Office of Juvenile Justice and Delinquency Prevention (OJJDP). The data sets document the nature of delinquency which consists primarily of property crimes and minor offenses. However, data sources are of limited import for determining the extent of delinquency generally, and black female delinquency in particular.

Most juvenile crime statistics include narrative summaries and tables with race and gender information. But, they do not lend themselves to simultaneous race and gender analyses. For example, the 1991 *Update on Statistics* includes a table entitled "Race and Gender Distributions of Arrests Involving Persons Under Age 18, 1990." In it, the percent of arrests are presented in the following categories: white, black, other, male, and female. Thus, the table provides only aggregated data.

In 1988, Congress mandated the disaggregation of juvenile custody data by offense, race, sex and age (OJJDP 1991). Unfortunately, these revisions have only been partially implemented. Disaggregated tables, which include both race and gender, are still not available. Until these revisions are made, the number of black females under 18 who were arrested, referred to juvenile court for either delinquency or status offenses, or institutionalized remains unknown.

Even when the data are disaggregated, the wide array of institutions that confine delinquents further exacerbate the measurement problem. Juveniles may be held in public or private juvenile facilities, state and federal prisons, local jails, treatment facilities and mental hospitals (Hawkins and Jones 1989). While the exact number of black female delinquents in confinement remains unknown, there is evidence they are overrepresented (Hawkins and Jones 1989; Pope and Feyerherm 1990a, 1990b).

Alternative sources of data, including victimization and self report studies, do permit limited analyses of disaggregated race and gender factors. The *National Crime Victimization Survey* provides annual data on victims of crimes of violence (excluding murder), crimes of theft, and household crimes. Crimes of violence include attempted and completed rape, robbery, and aggravated and simple assault. Crimes of theft include completed and attempted personal larceny, with or without contact. Household crimes include attempted and completed burglary, household larceny and motor vehicle theft.

The *National Crime Victimization Survey* data is one of the better sources of information on black juvenile females. According to this data, in 1991, black females ages 12-15, reported lower rates of victimizations (28.4) than white females in the same age group (35.2) for crimes of violence (See Table 1).

**TABLE 1**
**VICTIMIZATION RATES FOR FEMALES 12-19 BY RACE AND AGE**

| | | Rate Per 1,000 Persons in Each Age Group | |
|---|---|---|---|
| Race, Age | Total Population | Crimes of Violence | Crimes of Theft |
| Black | | | |
| 12-15 | 1,081,950 | 28.4 | 63.5 |
| 16-19 | 1,054,050 | 65.1 | 54.6 |
| White | | | |
| 12-15 | 5,392,650 | 35.2 | 95.1 |
| 16-19 | 5,292,160 | 60.1 | 105.6 |

Source: *National Crime Victimization Survey*, Criminal Victimization in the U.S., 1991. Table 11.

Black females 16-19 had higher victimization rates (65.1) than white females 16-19 (60.1) for crimes of violence. For crimes of theft, black females in both age groups (12-15 and 16-19) had lower rates of victimizations than white females (Bureau of Justice Statistics 1992). Although useful, it is difficult to determine who victimized these females. Furthermore, this data excluded: (1) race, age and gender comparisons for specific types of crimes (robbery, rape); (2) juveniles under age 12; and (3) murder and minor and status offenses, which frequently are committed by juveniles. Thus, this data, while disaggregated by gender and race, has very little information on juveniles.

The Institute for Social Research's *Monitoring the Future* series is an unusually comprehensive data set funded by the National Institute of Drug Abuse. It is an annual survey of high school seniors and includes both delinquency and victimization data. These data have limitations. However, they do provide some useful information on black females.

The Institute for Social Research Studies contain both delinquency and victimization data. In a secondary analysis of the 1985-1988 data, respondents reported fewer delinquent acts than victimizations (Taylor Greene 1992). Of the 13,227 respondents, only three percent had been involved in a serious fight, seven percent in a gang fight, three percent had hurt someone badly, 18 percent had stolen something under $50, and 12 percent had been involved in a store theft two or more times. Forty-six percent had been victims of a theft under $50, 35 percent had been victims of a theft over $50, and 68 percent had been victims of deliberate property damage two or more times. The mean number of delinquent acts by females appear in Table 2.

**TABLE 2**

**MEAN NUMBER OF FEMALE SELF-REPORTED DELINQUENT ACTS BY RACE**

| Race, Sex | (N) | S. Fight | (N) | G. Fight | (N) | Hurts |
|---|---|---|---|---|---|---|
| Black Female | (36) | 1.5 | (66) | 1.6 | (22) | 1.8 |
| White Female | (181) | 1.5 | (511) | 1.6 | (116) | 1.4 |

| | (N) | Theft Less than $50 | (N) | Store Theft | (N) | Trespass | (N) | Trouble w/Police |
|---|---|---|---|---|---|---|---|---|
| Black Female | (317) | 1.6 | (194) | 1.7 | (447) | 3.0 | (371) | 2.7 |
| White Female | (1838) | 1.6 | (1264) | 1.5 | (3560) | 3.2 | (2911) | 2.0 |

Source: Helen Taylor Greene, "Self-Reported Delinquency Among the Nation's High School Seniors," 1992.

Like the *National Crime Victimization Survey* data, the Institute for Social Research data have limitations. Many minor and status offenses are excluded, only high school seniors are included and blacks are underrepresented. Nevertheless, because its findings are consistent from year to year, the Institute for Social Research data are considered reliable.

Methodological problems of both official and unofficial delinquency data sources always will exist. However, disaggregating the data will improve our estimation of the extent and nature of black female delinquency.

## THE STATUS OF RESEARCH ON BLACK FEMALE DELINQUENTS

As a multidisciplinary topic, delinquency research appears in criminology and criminal justice, sociology, psychology, adolescence, psychiatry, drug issues, law, social work, and family violence journals. Because black scholars, regardless of discipline, often publish their research in black journals, delinquency research can be found in those journals as well.

Prior to the 1970s, many studies of delinquency in the black community appeared in black journals and periodicals. Several topics were examined, including delinquency in general (Beckham 1931; Diggs 1940; Frazier 1932, 1949; Douglas 1959; Willie 1965), the relationship between delinquency and class (Blue 1948; Epps 1967), personality (David 1932; Watts 1941), and community factors (Moses 1936).

Between 1930-1960 many studies appeared in the *Journal of Negro Education,* which published a special issue on Negro Delinquency in its 1959 Summer Yearbook. Contributing authors included (black and white scholars) Kenneth B. Clark, Ruth Shonle Cavan, Negley K. Teeters, David Matza, Carroll L. Miller, Joseph D. Lohman, Benjamin Mays, and Albert J. Reiss, Jr. Articles addressed the problem of delinquency, factors associated with delinquency, and the effectiveness of prevention programs.

Not surprisingly, much of the early research focused on males. Only two studies, by Chivers (1942) and Clarke (1959), included brief statements on girls. Chivers (1942) described black girls as being ignored by the police unless they were "hardened" or involved in interracial acts. Clarke (1959) provided a table on race and sex of juvenile delinquents and noted that the proportion of female offenders is higher among blacks than whites.

During the past two decades, extensive research on delinquency in the black community has continued to examine general delinquency and males (Alexander 1976; Gay 1981; Gray-Ray et al. 1990; Hawkins and Jones 1989; Mendez 1987; Okwumabua et al. 1989; Singleton 1989; Swan 1977; Staples 1976; Taylor 1988; Wright 1975). Very few studies analyze black female criminality or delinquency (Laub and McDermott 1985).

When black female delinquents are included, comparisons are often made between black females and either black males or white females. When race or gender are discussed, the simultaneous effects of both factors usually are not discussed (Bishop and Frazier 1988; Horowitz and Pottieger 1991). Studies, which include black female delinquents, frequently focus on one or more of the following topics: family structure (Austin 1978; Datesman and Scarpitti 1975; Farnworth 1984); self and opportunity theory (Datesman et al. 1975); status offenders (Datesman and Aickin 1984); alcohol consumption (Brinson 1991; Gay 1981; Higgins et al. 1977); gangs (Bowker and Klein 1983); seriously crime involved youth (Laub and McDermott 1985; Horowitz and Pottieger 1991); juvenile justice processing (Ageton 1983; Cernkovich and Giordano 1979; Datesman and Scarpitti 1975); and racial differences in female delinquency (Austin 1978; Cernkovich and Giordano 1979; Datesman and Aickin 1984; Datesman and Scarpitti 1980; Laub and McDermott 1985; Ward and McFall 1986; Young 1980).

Although there is no consensus, it is generally believed that black girls are more delinquent than white girls (Laub and McDermott 1985). After reviewing available studies of racial differences in female delinquency, Chesney-Lind (1992) concluded that there is less support for this commonly held belief. While noting differences, Chesney-Lind emphasized that white girls are slightly more delinquent than their nonwhite counterparts.

Of the studies that include black females, only eight discuss them in detail (Arnold 1990; Austin 1978; Bowker and Klein 1983; Datesman and Aiken 1984; Datesman and Scarpitti 1975; Datesman et al. 1975; Farnworth 1984; Laub and McDermott 1985) (See Table 3). Two include discussions of both young and adult black females (Arnold 1990; Laub and McDermott 1985); three compared young black and white females (Austin 1978; Datesman and Aiken 1984; Datesman et al. 1975); and two compared minority males and females (Datesman and Scarpitti 1975; Farnworth 1984). Only one focused entirely upon black female delinquents (Bowker and Klein 1983).

In two studies (Bowker and Klein 1983; Arnold 1990), explanations of black female delinquent behavior were presented. Bowker and Klein attributed black girls' involvement in delinquency and gang behavior to social structural explanations, including racism, sexism, poverty and limited opportunity structures. Psychological factors such as personality, relations with parents, and problems associated with heterosexual behavior were less important. Arnold argued that young black girls, of lower socioeconomic status, engage in "precriminal" behaviors (including running away from home, stealing and truancy), to resist victimization. As a result of their resistance and structural dislocation (from family or school), they pay a tremendous price including addiction, crime, and incarceration.

The limited number of "within-group" studies of black female delinquents may be due to several factors including insufficient data, emphasis on quantitative research, and limited scholarly interest in black females. Or, it may result from what McKenry et al. (1989) describe as the failure of many scholars to recognize the uniqueness of the black adolescent experience.

The study of black female delinquents is best described as underdeveloped. While often included, they are rarely the major focus of research. Thus, not only is more research important, but different research methods and strategies may be necessary.

**TABLE 3**
**RESEARCH ON BLACK FEMALE DELINQUENTS**

| Author(s) | Date | Focus | Data/Source | BF | BM | WF |
|---|---|---|---|---|---|---|
| Arnold | 1990 | Process of victimization/ criminalization | Prison and jail inmates | ✓ | | |
| Austin | 1978 | Race, father absence and delinquency | 5,545 Jr./Sr. high school students (CA) | ✓ | | ✓ |
| Bowker and Klein | 1983 | Explanations of gang membership | 229 black female juveniles in Los Angeles | ✓ | | |
| Cernkovich and Giordano | 1979 | Male/female delinquency | | | | |
| Brinson | 1991 | Alcohol users | 71 youth (age 12-20) | ✓ | ✓ | |
| Datesman and Aickin | 1984 | Status offenders (escalation) | 689 youth | ✓ | ✓ | ✓ |
| Datesman and Scarpitti | 1980 | Status offenders | | ✓ | ✓ | |
| Datesman, Scarpitti, and Stephenson | 1975 | Female delinquency | | ✓ | | ✓ |
| Farnworth | 1984 | Male/female delinquency | | | | |
| Laub and McDermott | 1985 | Black female juvenile offenders 12-17 | NCS 1973-1981 | ✓ | ✓ | ✓ |
| Silverman et al. | 1990 | Black adolescent crack users | | | | |
| Taylor-Gibbs | 1981 | Depression/suicide among female delinquents | 48 females 13-18 | ✓ | ✓ | |

## FUTURE RESEARCH ISSUES

Future studies of black female delinquency should examine contemporary issues, including involvement in gangs and violent crimes, and prevention strategies. Emphasis should be placed on collaborative research as well as comparative studies.

Recognizing the limitations of available data and previous studies, researchers should improve methods for studying black female delinquency. It is essential that researchers include more black females in their samples and conduct "within-group" studies. Researchers must also: (1) develop and utilize alternative sources of data; (2) include both delinquent and nondelinquent adolescent females; and (3) identify existing national and international Africana scholarship.

Understanding black female delinquency will be greatly enhanced when more reliable data is available. Until then, secondary analyses of existing data sets that can be disaggregated should be undertaken. Data collected at the local, state and federal levels may contain race and gender information, although it is not always published. Utilizing these sources, secondary analyses can be conducted to examine black female juveniles' involvement in criminal and status offenses.

More "within-group" studies of black females also are needed. Quantitative and qualitative within group research can facilitate useful comparisons within different groups of black female delinquents and with nondelinquents. Then, more salient issues can be addressed. To date, research has focused on the lower class in urban areas, virtually ignoring middle class black females and those residing in suburban or rural areas. Within group studies will facilitate analyses of both class and regional differences.

Although we do not know the extent of delinquency, the majority of youth, including young black females, are not delinquent. Those that are usually commit property crimes and minor offenses. Nevertheless, there is increasing concern that more females are involved in violent personal crimes and joining gangs. Although they probably represent a very small portion of delinquents, researchers should study young black female involvement in violent crime and gangs.

Researchers also must identify strategies for preventing delinquency. Family and community factors that contribute to delinquency resistance should be examined. The negative effects of family dysfunction and structure (single parent families) have received considerable attention in delinquency research. While they are areas of concern, we must begin to identify successful socialization strategies utilized in single, two-parent, and extended families (grandparents, aunts and uncles).

Families often depend upon community resources which are instrumental in preventing delinquency. The effect, if any, of mentoring programs, Big Brothers, Big Sisters, Boys and Girls Clubs, sororities, churches and other organizations in preventing black female delinquency also should be examined.

Because there are so few criminologists interested in black female delinquents, collaboration across disciplines is necessary. Collaboration should include individuals working directly with black female juveniles in the juvenile justice system, social service agencies and community programs. In this area, recent initiatives targeting "at-risk" youth should be examined to determine the extent of programming designed specifically for black females.

Black female criminologists have been in the vanguard of research on black women in the criminal justice system (Arnold 1990; Mann 1984, 1988, 1989; Taylor Greene 1981; Young 1980, 1986). As their numbers increase, they, along with sister scholars in other disciplines, will make significant contributions in this area. However, this will require recognition of the importance of funding black female delinquency research.

In light of the contribution by black and white scholars in the area of female delinquency, intradisciplinary collaboration is important. For example, Chesney-Lind (1989) recommends field observations and listening to girls to better understand their situations, choices and behaviors. She identifies family and school settings, racism and poverty as relevant factors to be considered. Collaborative efforts will build upon and advance prior female delinquency research. Specifically, in the study of black females, issues such as female and male peer influences, drug use and sales, and patterns of abuse could be addressed.

Lastly, future research must include international studies of black female delinquency. Africana scholarship on this topic should be identified. Specific attention should be paid to black girls in the Caribbean, South America, Latin America, Africa, and European countries with large black populations. Faculty exchange programs, study abroad and educational travel can be used as vehicles to conduct comparative research in other countries. Academicians in the United States and abroad must form partnerships to facilitate the exchange of faculty and students, to hold conferences, and to develop resource centers on black female delinquents here and abroad.

## SUMMARY

Hopefully, during the next decade the study of black female delinquents will flourish, nationally and internationally. As we build the body of knowledge, not only will we increase our understanding of these juveniles, but ultimately, we may reduce their numbers in the juvenile justice process.

**REFERENCES**


Ageton, S. S. 1983. "The Dynamics of Female Delinquency." *Criminology* 21:55-564.

Alexander, G. G. 1976. "The Role of Police and the Courts in the Survival of Black Youth." *Journal of Afro-American Issues* 4:235-40.

Arnold, R. A. 1990. "Processes of Victimization and Criminalization of Black Women." *Social Justice* 17:153-66.

Austin, R. L. 1978. "Race, Father-Absence, and Female Delinquency." *Criminology* 15:487-504.

Beckham, A. S. 1931. "Juvenile Delinquency and the Negro." *Opportunity* 9:300-302.

Bishop, D. M. and C. S. Frazier. 1988. "The Influence of Race in Juvenile Justice Processing." *Journal of Research in Crime and Delinquency* 22:309-28.

Blue, J. T. Jr. 1948. "The Relationship of Juvenile Delinquency, Race, and Economic Status." *Journal of Negro Education* 17:469-77.

Bowker, L. H. and M. W. Klein. 1983. "The Etiology of Female Juvenile Delinquency and Gang Membership: A Test of Psychological and Social Structural Explanations." *Adolescence* 18:739-51.

Brinson, J. A. 1991. "A Comparison of the Family Environments of Black Male and Female Adolescent Alcohol Users." *Adolescence* 26:877-84.

Bureau of Justice Statistics. 1992a. *Correctional Populations in the United States, 1990.* Washington, D.C.: U.S. Department of Justice.

_______. 1992b. *Criminal Victimization in the United States, 1991.* Washington, D.C.: U.S. Department of Justice.

Cernkovich, S. A. and P. C. Giordano. 1979. "A Comparative Analysis of Male and Female Delinquency." *Sociological Quarterly* 20:131-45.

Chesney-Lind, M. 1989. "Girls' Crime and Women's Place: Towards a Feminist Model of Female Delinquency," *Crime and Delinquency* 35:5-29.

Chesney-Lind, M. and R. G. Shelden. 1992. *Girls, Delinquency, and Juvenile Justice.* Pacific Grove: Brooks/Cole.

Chivers, W. R. 1942. "Negro Delinquent." *National Probation Association Yearbook* (1942):46-59.

Christianson, S. 1981. *Index to Minorities and Criminal Justice.* Albany, NY: The Center on Minorities and Criminal Justice, State University of New York.

Daniel, R. P. 1932. "Personality Differences Between Delinquent and Non-Delinquent Negro Boys." *Journal of Negro Education* 1:381-87.

Datesman, S. K. and M. Aickin. 1984. "Offense Specialization and Escalation among Status Offenders." *Journal of Criminal Law and Criminology* 75:1246-75.

Datesman, S. K. and F. R. Scarpitti. 1980. "Female Delinquency and Broken Homes." *Criminology* 8:51-69.

Datesman, S. K., F. R. Scarpitti, and R. M. Stephenson. 1975. "Female Delinquency: An Application of Self and Opportunity Theories." *Journal of Research in Crime and Delinquency* 12:107-23.

Diggs, M. H. 1940. "Problems and Needs of Negro Youth as Revealed by Delinquency and Crime Statistics." *Journal of Negro Education* 9:311-20.

Douglass, J. H. 1959. "The Extent and Characteristics of Juvenile Delinquency Among Negroes in the United States." *Journal of Negro Education* 28:214-229.

Epps, E. G. 1967. "Socioeconomic Status, Race, Level of Aspiration and Juvenile Delinquency: A Limited Empirical Test of Merton's Conception of Deviation." *Phylon* 28:16-27.

Farnworth, M. 1984. "Male-Female Differences in Delinquency in a Minority Group Sample." *Journal of Research in Crime and Delinquency* 21:191-212

Federal Bureau of Investigation. 1992. *Crime in the United States.* Washington, D.C.: U.S. Government Printing Office.

Frazier, E. F. 1932. "Juvenile Delinquency." In *The Negro Family in Chicago.* Chicago: University of Chicago Press.

_______. 1949. "Crime and Delinquency." In *The Negro in the United States.* New York: McMillan Co.

Gay, J. E. 1981. "Alcohol and Metropolitan Black Teenagers." *Journal of Drug Education* 11:19-26.

Gray-Ray, P. and M. C. Ray. 1990. "Juvenile Delinquency in the Black Community." *Youth and Society* 22:67-84.

Hawkins, D. F. and N. E. Jones. 1989. "Black Adolescents and the Criminal Justice System." In *Black Adolescents,* edited by R. Jones. Berkeley: Cobb and Henry Publishers.

Higgins, P. C., G. L. Albrecht, and M. H. Albrecht. 1977. "Black-White Adolescent Drinking: The Myth and the Reality." *Social Problems* 25:215-24.

Horowitz, R. and A. E. Pottieger. 1991. "Gender Bias in Juvenile Justice Handling of Seriously Crime Involved Youths." *Journal of Research in Crime and Delinquency* 28:75-100.

Journal of Negro Education. 1959. *Summer Yearbook.*

Laub, J. H. and M. J. McDermott. 1985. "An Analysis of Serious Crime By Young Black Women." *Criminology* 23:81-98.

Mann, C. 1984. *Female Crime and Delinquency.* University, AL: The University of Alabama Press.

_______. 1988. "Getting Even? Women Who Kill in Domestic Encounters." *Justice Quarterly* 5:33-51.

_______. 1989. "Minority and Female: A Criminal Justice Double Bind." *Social Justice* 16:95-112.

McKenry, P. C., J. E. Everett, H. P. Ramseur, and C. J. Carter. 1989. "Research on Black Adolescents: A Legacy of Cultural Bias." *Journal of Adolescent Research* 4:254-64.

Mendez, G. A. Jr. 1987. "Crime and Policy in the African-American Community." *Annals of the American Academy of Political and Social Science* 494:105-10.

Office of Juvenile Justice and Delinquency Prevention. 1991. *Children Taken Into Custody, 1989.* Washington, D.C.: U.S. Department of Justice.

_______. 1990. *Juvenile Court Statistics, 1987.* Washington, D.C.: U.S. Department of Justice.

_______. 1991. *Juveniles Taken Into Custody: Fiscal Year 1990 Report.* Washington, D.C.: U.S. Department of Justice.

Okwumabua, J. O., T. M. Okwumabua, B. L. Winston, and H. Walker Jr. 1989. "Onset of Drug Use Among Rural Black Youth." *Journal of Adolescent Research* 4:239-46.

Pope, C. E. and W. H. Feyerherm. 1990a. "Minority Status and Juvenile Justice Processing: An Assessment of the Research Literature (Part I)." *Criminal Justice Abstracts* 22:327-35.

_______. 1990b. "Minority Status and Juvenile Justice Processing: An Assessment of the Research Literature (Part II)." *Criminal Justice Abstracts* 22:527-42.

Singleton, E. G. 1989. "Substance Use and Black Youth: Implications of Cultural and Ethnic Differences in Adolescent Alcohol, Cigarette, and Illicit Drug Use." In *Black Adolescents,* edited by R.L. Jones. Berkeley: Cobb and Henry.

Staples, R. 1976. "Black Crime and Delinquency." In *Introduction to Black Society.* New York: McGraw-Hill.

Swan, L. A. 1977. "Juvenile Delinquency, Juvenile Justice and Black Youth." In *Black Perspectives on Crime and the Criminal Justice System,* edited by R.L. Woodson. Boston: G.K. Hall and Co.

Taylor, R. L. 1989. "African-American Inner City Youth and the Subculture of Disengagement." *Urban League Review* 12:15-24.

Taylor-Gibbs, J. 1981. "Depression and Suicide Behavior Among Delinquent Females," *Journal of Youth and Adolescence* 10:159-67.

_______. 1989. "Black Adolescents and Youth: An Update on an Endangered Species." In *Black Adolescents,* edited by R. Jones. Berkeley: Cobb and Henry Publishers.

Taylor Greene, H. 1979. *A Comprehensive Bibliography of Criminology and Criminal Justice Literature by Black Authors From 1895-1978.* Hyattsville, MD: Ummah Publications.

_______. 1981. "Black Women in the Criminal Justice System." *Urban League Review* 6:55-61.

_______. 1992. *Self Reported Delinquency among the Nation's High School Seniors.* Paper presented at the Academy of Criminal Justice Sciences, Pittsburgh, PA.

Ward, C. I. and R. M. McFall. 1986. "Further Validation of the Problem Inventory for Adolescent Girls: Comparing Caucasian and Black Delinquents and Nondelinquents." *Journal of Consulting and Clinical Psychology* 54:732-33.

Watts, F. P. 1941. "A Comparative Clinical Study of Delinquent and Nondelinquent Negro Boys." *Journal of Negro Education* 10:190-207.

Willie, C. V. 1965. "Race and Delinquency." *Phylon* 26:240-46.

Wright, B. M. 1975. "Bangs and Whimpers: Black Youth and the Courts." *Freedomways* 15:178-87.

Young, V. 1986. "Gender Expectations and Their Impact on Black Female Offenders and Victims." *Justice Quarterly* 3:305-27.

_______. 1980. "Women, Race, and Crime." *Criminology* 18:26-34.

Young, V. and A. Sulton. 1991. "Excluded: The Current Status of African-American Scholars in the Field of Criminology and Criminal Justice." *Journal of Research in Crime and Delinquency* 28:101-116.

# FAMILY AND DELINQUENCY: AFRICAN-AMERICAN FEMALE-HEADED HOUSEHOLDS AND CHRONIC MALADAPTIVE BEHAVIOR BY JUVENILES

*Dorothy Taylor currently is an assistant professor at the University of Miami where she teaches sociology courses. She also is a clinical social worker. Taylor received her doctorate degree in criminology from Florida State University. She also holds a master's of social work degree from Wayne State University.*

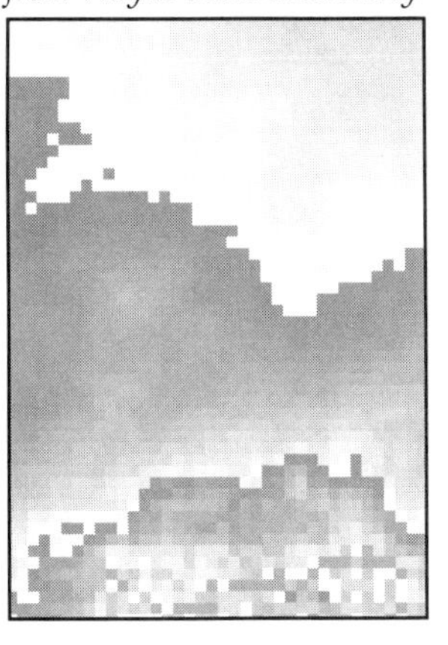

## INTRODUCTION

The recent dramatic growth of the single-parent, female-headed household has been well documented. The United States Department of Labor (1985) reports that between 1975 and 1985 the number of African-American female-headed households in the United States increased by more than 50 percent from two million to three million. This comprises nearly 30 percent of all female-headed families (*Black News Digest* 1985).

The Department of Labor (1985) also reports that female-headed families experience poverty rates three times greater than all families and five times greater than those of married-couple families. Furthermore, the rates of poverty are dramatically highest for African-Americans, with approximately half of the African-American female-headed families living in poverty.

Many theories of crime and delinquency argue that strong relationships exist between poverty and crime, including Merton's (1964) anomie, Cohen's (1955) middle-class measuring rod, and Cloward and Ohlin's (1960) differential opportunity. Thus, the data on female-headed families and poverty is relevant to discussions about crime and delinquency.

A report by the National Center for Juvenile Justice (1985) reveals that African-American children are overrepresented in institutions for delinquents. The U.S.

Department of Justice's Office of Juvenile Justice and Delinquency Prevention reports that African-American and other minority youths constitute more than 50 percent of the juveniles in public-custody institutions. The 1987 Children in Custody Census shows that more than 80,000 juveniles were in public and private facilities. Between 1985 and 1987, the minority population in these facilities increased from 25,809 to 30,128. African-American juveniles showed the greatest increase over the two year period, from 18,174 to 20,898 (*Juvenile Justice Bulletin* 1988).

In Lerman's (1991) study, wherein he attempts to update the United States on the number of juvenile delinquents in various institutions, he concludes that along with being referred to the juvenile justice system, delinquent youths also are referred to mental health, child welfare, and alcohol and drug abuse organizations. Lerman (1991) states that "America's system for counting youth are 3 to 5 years behind current usage and yield deficient resident and admissions data" (p. 465).

Lerman (1991) further reports that data regarding juvenile detention centers, for the public sector, for the year 1987, was not available until 1990. And, in 1990, placement information regarding private institutions was only available for 1985. This study leaves the research community with the question of whether "incomplete mid-1980 data are sufficient bases for determining youth policies for the 1990's" (p. 479).

A substantial body of empirical literature addresses the effects of family factors on juvenile delinquency. However, much of the data was not gathered in a theoretical context. Some of the studies used widely varying designs and methods of analysis. Others relied upon social, social psychological, or economic variables to explain the high rates of delinquent behavior in female-headed households. Very little research has focused on the interpersonal dynamics of female heads of households, their children, and maladaptive behaviors.

Existing family and delinquency literature shows a general relationship between bonding and delinquency: the greater the juvenile's bonding to the parental figure, the more strongly he or she is bonded to the parent's expectations, and consequently to conformity to the legitimate standards of the larger society (Hirschi 1969; Rutter and Giller 1984; Shoemaker 1984). The existing literature on African-American female-headed families devotes little attention to the interaction between the parent and the child, and on whether this interaction contributes to or deters the development of the child's maladaptive behavior.

This paper addresses this issue. The present research was designed to determine the relationships between female-headed households and juvenile maladaptive behavior by exploring interpersonal bonding factors related to parent-child relationships. This research was designed not only to increase our knowledge of African-American female-headed households and their effect on juvenile delinquency, but also to suggest new directions for future study.

## THEORETICAL BACKGROUND

The research on the relationship between family structure and juvenile delinquency has been dominated by a variety of alternative and sometimes conflicting theoretical models. In reviews of family and delinquency literature, it has been suggested that the relationship between family and delinquency has not received the same attention as other areas of research and theory development because criminological proponents minimize the relevance of family variables. During the past three decades, however, there has been a revival of concern about factors involved in this relationship. Since the late 1950's when a renewed interest in the effects of family structure was introduced into the literature on family and delinquency, researchers have focused on several major issues and have developed various sociological theories.

Among these theories, there is a consensus that parent/child relationships influence behavior. Some theorists propose that bonding between parent and child inhibits maladaptive behavior (Liska and Reed 1985). Many investigators report that when the parent provides affection households headed by single parents experience no more delinquency than two-parent families (McCord 1982). When researchers traced child abuse, neglect, and rejection, however, they reported that parental rejection had a greater impact on delinquency than did child abuse or neglect (Loeber and Stouthamer-Loeber 1986; McCord 1983a).

Social control theorists have contributed significantly to the renewed interest in the effects of family factors on juvenile delinquency (Empey and Lubeck 1971; Hirschi 1969; Nye 1958; Reckless 1961; Nettler 1978). Empey and Lubeck (1971) report that familial interaction, as measured by "boy-parent harmony," predicted juvenile maladaptive behavior more accurately than did whether the child resided in a father-only or two-parent home. Hirschi (1969) found that delinquency was related more to parental attachment (the psychological and emotional connection the child feels toward the parent and the extent to which the child cares about the parents' opinions and feelings) than to whether the juvenile lived in a two-parent home. Nettler (1978) contends that attachment to parents is strongly associated with lawful conduct among youth, and this relationship holds regardless of social class.

The Gluecks (1961) identified family interaction variables such as attachment and discipline as the most important in relation to chronic delinquency. Laub and Sampson (1988) also found that family functioning is an important factor when considering juvenile maladaptive behavior. However, these and similar studies are inconclusive (Herzog and Sudia 1973; Loeber and Stouthamer-Loeber 1986; Rankin 1983; Rosen and Neilson 1982; Rutter and Giller 1984; Wilson and Herrnstein 1985). The findings of various studies suggest that the relationship between single-parent homes and delinquency is unreliable when official data are used in measuring delinquency and weak when self-report data are used (Rankin 1983; Wilson and Herrnstein 1985). A principal concern regarding this work is the possibility of ineptness in examining situations that may be connected to family structure and to delinquency (Empey 1982; Rosen 1985; Rutter and Giller 1984).

Although the literature on family and delinquency is not limited to the issues discussed above, it provides a useful framework for a discussion of the African-American female-headed household and delinquency, with which this investigation is concerned.

The conjecture that female-headed families, particularly those receiving welfare, produce more juvenile delinquency than other families is associated most commonly with African-Americans (Chilton and Markle 1972; Clark and Koch 1975). However, Wilson and Herrnstein (1985) report their research indicates little is known about the effects of child rearing in either a two-parent or single-parent African-American family.

Rosen's (1985) study provides some insight. Rosen's (1985) study characterized the structural and functional correlates of African-American and Caucasian families. He includes such structural factors as single-parent homes, father's presence, social class, and the size of the family. The two functional measures he examined are the quality of father-and-son interaction and parental involvement. Interaction with father proved to be the most pertinent factor for African-Americans. Among African-Americans, factors relating to family size, social class, and father's presence were associated with delinquency. The relationships were less clear-cut for Caucasians. The single-parent home factor was of no consequence for either group.

Most research focusing on the relationship between African-American female-headed families and delinquency tends to be inconclusive. Some research findings suggest that being reared in a single-parent family is associated with a greater prevalence of juvenile delinquency among African-Americans (Anderson 1968; Chilton and Markle 1972; Clark and Koch 1975; Monahan 1957); others reveal no correlation (Robins and Hill 1966; Rosen 1970). Several of these investigations were cross-sectional, comparing juveniles in broken and in intact homes. Because the findings vary, one cannot reach firm conclusions on causality.

The study by Kellem et al. (1982) appears to be the type of investigation needed in determining the effect of African-American female-headed households on juvenile chronic maladaptive behavior. The Kellem study, which demonstrates possible theoretical links between family structure and juvenile delinquency, includes approximately 1,000 African-American children living in Chicago. About one-third of these children reside in female-headed households, another one-third live in two-parent homes, and the remainder live with mothers and their mothers' live-together-partner. They were identified shortly before birth and are being followed throughout their lives.

For several years, the Kellem study will measure the connection between family structure, personality characteristics, and socioeconomic status. The children were classified by their teachers as "adapting" or "maladapting." The maladapting children were classified further as either aggressive or nonaggressive. Upon entering the third grade, the children from female-headed families were much more likely to be considered by their teachers as "maladapting" than those from other family types, especially two-parent families. When they entered high school, boys from female-headed families were more likely than others to admit having committed various acts of delinquency (Kellem et al. 1982). The data resulting from this inquiry have yet to be completely analyzed.

## RESEARCH DESIGN

The purpose of the current study is to provide an analysis which will increase our understanding of factors underlying juveniles' participation in maladaptive behavior. The study seeks to ascertain whether bonding variables related to the parent-child relationship, as well as the natural support system of the single parent, are related to the occurrence of juvenile chronic maladaptive behavior. The principal approach taken here is to determine which of these bonding factors (social control variables) has the greatest potential influence on juveniles' behavior.

For the purpose of this study, a maladaptive child is any child who engages in a pattern of behavior that is sufficiently troublesome to warrant acceptance by the Early Attention Program of the agency which provided the secondary data for this study. This behavior may be serious or nonserious. Some behaviors considered serious in this study are pregnancy, shoplifting, carrying a concealed weapon, assault on a classmate, armed robbery, and selling and using drugs. The nonserious behaviors would include such behaviors as running away from home, disruptive behavior, destructive behavior, loitering, truancy, and nonviolent school problems. To be deemed chronically maladaptive, the juvenile must exhibit more than one type of occurrence of maladaptive behavior. Serious maladaptive behavior in a juvenile is any behavior whose consequences would be criminal sanctions for an adult, or which might have a devastating effect on the juvenile's future, such as adolescent pregnancy.

## *Data*

This study uses a cross-sectional descriptive methodology employing secondary data from the records of an agency responsible for counseling juveniles in Detroit. The cross-sectional design is used for making observations at a single point in time (Levin 1977; Hagen 1982). Specifically, the data are taken from an analysis of the agency's extensive intake forms, psychosocial history reports, progress notes, communication questionnaires for juveniles and parents, and case disposition reports.

Levin (1977), Hagen (1982), and other researchers have given several reasons to support the use of secondary data analysis in this inquiry. First, the short time involved in the information-collecting procedure is cost-effective. Second, secondary data are useful when confidentiality is an issue. In addition, such data assure considerable anonymity regarding the private lives of the juveniles and their parents (Babbie 1983; Sellitz et al. 1976).

The study population included 140 first time African-American juvenile offenders and children referred from other sources, such as school and family, to the Early Attention Program of the Children's Aid Society between 1984 and 1987.

The parents ranged in age from 20 to 60, but only one was over 40 and was a grandparent rather than a parent. The median age of the parents was 38 years, with most being between 31 and 40 years old.

The gender of the juveniles was distributed relatively evenly: approximately 49 percent were male and 51 percent were female. The juveniles ranged in age from five to 19 years, with a mean age of 13.7 years. (The Early Attention Program was expanded to assist youths under age eight or over age 17 in cases where the circumstances so warranted and the Juvenile Court so ordered.) Most of the youths (57.9%) were between ages 11 and 15.

A 71-item instrument was developed for data collection. Along with the demographic variables of the parents and juveniles and the parental socioeconomic variables, data were collected on interpersonal (bonding) variables which were identified by a panel (comprised of a psychiatrist, a psychologist, and a social worker) and a review of prior studies in the literature. These variables include: 1) Did the parent contact the agency willingly? 2) Does the juvenile have a curfew? 3) Does the parent attend school activities? 4) Does the parent assist the juvenile with homework? 5) Does the parent give the juvenile one-on-one time? 6) Does the parent prepare and share meals with the juvenile? 7) Do the parent and the juvenile attend religious services? 8) Is the parent consistent in disciplining the juvenile? 9) Does the parent encourage participation in family decision making? 10) Is the parent willing to trust the child? 11) Does the parent listen to/communicate with the juvenile? 12) Is the juvenile involved in cultural/ethnic activities? 13) Is the parent involved in leisure activities with the juvenile? 14) Are the juvenile's television/movies monitored by the parent? 15) Is the parent involved in the juvenile's medical/dental care? 16) Does the parent have a "natural" (in-home) support system?

*Statistical analysis procedure*

The means of analyzing the data included univariate, bivariate and multivariate analyses. The univariate statistics were examined to ascertain the frequency, valid percentage, and number of missing cases associated with each of the 71 items included in the analysis.

From the bivariate and multivariate procedures, tables were constructed and examined for significant relationships. Tests of significance used chi-square (Babbie 1983; Sellitz et al. 1976). The appropriate measure of association for this data analysis is Kendal's tau.

The interpersonal bonding factor (IBF) scales were computed. The interpersonal bonding factor was the mathematically scored scale of the 16 interpersonal bonding factors (See Table 1).

Of the 71 items of data collected, 14 were associated with the interaction between the parent and the juvenile. Of the 14, the most important bonding factor was the parents' consistency in disciplining the juvenile. Although the first two bonding factors indicated on Table 1 are not interaction variables, they are deemed very important to the bonding process because human service literature is now emphasizing the importance of the individual's natural support systems for healthy functioning as well as for crisis intervention (Baker 1977). The importance of the natural support system also is emphasized in correctional institutions (Roberts 1983).

The importance of the parent contacting the agency willingly was suggested by the Early Attention Program counselors. They indicated the propensity for delinquency status was decreased when the parent brought the child to the agency prior to any interaction with juvenile authorities, such as law enforcement officials.

**TABLE 1**

**Percentage Distribution of Support and Bonding Factors**

| | Yes % | No % | Total N |
|---|---|---|---|
| Does parent have any natural support? | 24.5 | 75.5 | 140 |
| +Did parent contact agency willingly? | 54.3 | 45.7 | 138 |
| Does juvenile have a curfew? | 52.2 | 47.8 | 138 |
| Does parent attend school activities (PTO, etc.)? | 30.7 | 69.3 | 137 |
| Does parent assist juvenile with homework? | 13.9 | 86.1 | 137 |
| Does parent give the juvenile one-on-one time? | 30.0 | 70.0 | 140 |
| +Does parent prepare and share meals with juvenile? | 30.0 | 70.0 | 140 |
| Do parent and juvenile attend some form of religious service? | 23.7 | 76.3 | 139 |
| +Is parent consistent in disciplining the juvenile? | 15.1 | 84.9 | 139 |
| *Does parent encourage juvenile's participation in family decision making? | 28.6 | 71.4 | 140 |
| *Is parent willing to trust the child? | 46.4 | 53.6 | 140 |
| *Does parent listen to and communicate with the juvenile? | 44.3 | 55.7 | 140 |
| *Does parent encourage juvenile's involvement in cultural/ethnic activities? | 10.7 | 89.3 | 140 |
| *Is parent involved in leisure activities with juvenile? | 15.1 | 84.9 | 139 |
| *Does parent monitor juvenile's television and/or movie selection? | 21.6 | 78.4 | 139 |
| *Is parent involved in juvenile's medical and/or dental care? | 97.1 | 02.9 | 139 |

*The category "yes" includes various responses. The category "No" relates only to "No".

+These factors are most important in preventing delinquency.

## FINDINGS

The findings produced by this inquiry show a relationship between bonding factors and juvenile behavior. The most outstanding interpersonal bonding factors were parents willingly contacting the agency, being consistent in disciplining their children, and preparing and sharing meals with their children. The children of these parents tended to display less chronic maladaptive behavior than other juveniles in the study.

The absence of a spouse in the home does not imply absence of in-home "natural" support. For the purpose of this study, natural support systems include the parents, siblings, or significant others living in the same household, who may have a positive influence on the individual's behavior. A large majority of the sample (76 percent) did not have any natural support, but the remainder who had such support was worth noting. These natural supporters were divided almost evenly between relatives and nonrelatives.

My experiences, as a foster care worker, a probation officer, a family counselor, and an independent presentence investigator, indicate that juveniles from female-headed households have a greater opportunity for uninvolvement in maladaptive behavior if their single parents have access to the inherent strengths of their natural support systems, especially in crisis situations. Bonding can occur in the absence of in-home support. However, the degree of bonding is affected by in-home support. In other words, if a single parent is assisted by a significant other in child rearing, the single parent can better provide the child with the support the child needs to alleviate stress and anxiety. Figure 1 shows the distribution of types of natural support.

In regards to the interpersonal bonding factors (Table 1), 54 percent (N=138) of the parents willingly contacted the agency. Over half, 69 percent (N=137), did not attend school activities, and 86 percent reported that they did not assist their children with homework. Only 30 percent of the parents reported giving the juvenile one-on-one time. Interestingly, the same percentage reported that they prepared and shared meals with the juvenile. It was reported that 24 percent of families (parents and juveniles) attend some form of religious activity. Discipline for 85 percent of the juveniles was reported as not consistent. In addition, the juveniles, as a whole, were not encouraged to participate in family discussions and decision-making processes. Slightly more than half (54 percent) of the parents were reluctant to trust the juvenile; fewer than half (44 percent) listened to or communicated with the juvenile.

It was reported that 85 percent of the parents did not participate in any leisure activity with the juvenile. An even greater proportion of the

FIGURE 1
Natural Support Factors, Specific and Reduced

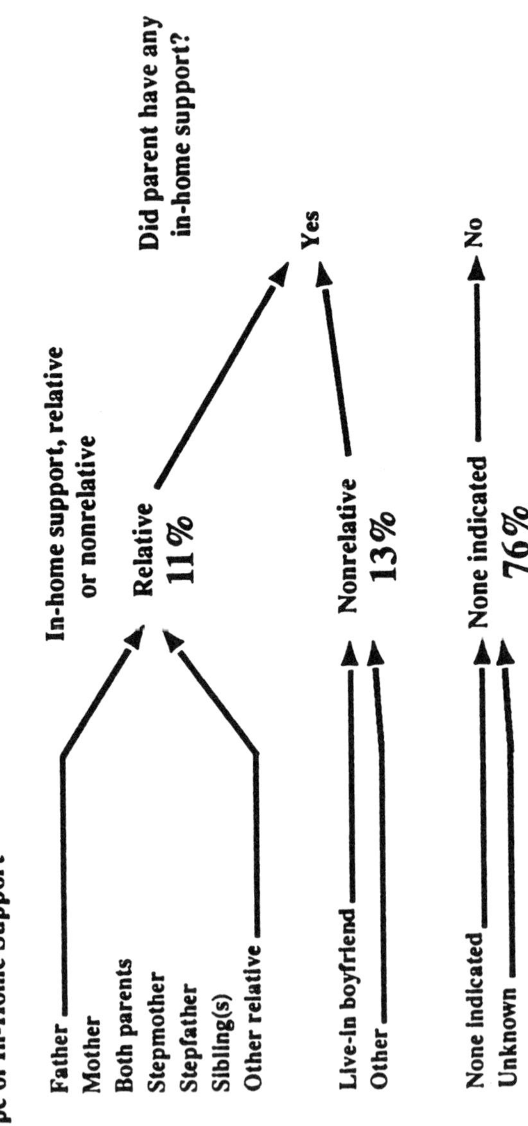

**TABLE 2**

**Relationship Between Bonding Factors and Range of Bonding**

| First Occurrence of Maladaptive Behavior | | |
|---|---|---|
| | N of IBFS | Range of Bonding |
| Shoplifting | 2-06 | *Mid |
| Running away | 0-03 | Low |
| Truancy | 4-15 | **High |
| Disruptive behavior | 2-06 | Mid |
| Destructive behavior | 4-15 | High |
| Sexually acting out | 0-15 | ***Even |
| Insubordination | 4-15 | High |
| Fighting mother | 7-15 | High |
| Carrying a concealed weapon | 7-15 | High |
| Loitering | 4-06 | Mid |
| Assault on classmate | 4-06 | Mid |
| Disregard of family property | 0-01 | Low |
| Abandonment of 2-year-old | 7-15 | High |
| Sexual molestation | 4-06 | Mid |
| Provocative behavior toward parents and teachers | 7-15 | High |
| Extensive criminal behavior | 7-15 | High |
| Leaving home without permission | 7-15 | High |
| School problems | 7-15 | High |
| Armed robbery | 2-03 | Mid |
| **Second Occurrence of Maladaptive Behavior** | | |
| Shoplifting | 4-06 | Mid |
| Running away | 4-06 | Mid |
| Truancy | 0-03 | Low |
| Disruptive behavior | 7-15 | High |
| Destructive behavior | 4-06 | Mid |
| Sexually acting out | 0-03 | Low |
| Pregnancy | 2-06 | Mid |
| Insubordination | 4-15 | High |
| Fighting mother | 2-06 | Mid |
| Drug involvement | 0-01 | Low |
| Selling drugs | 0-03 | Low |
| Using drugs | 0-03 | Low |
| Assault on classmate | 4-15 | High |
| Extensive criminal behavior | 0-01 | Low |
| Leaving home without permission | 4-15 | High |
| School problems | 7-15 | High |
| Lying to parent alot | 2-06 | Mid |

* Marginal
** Marginally high
*** Evenly distributed

juveniles, 89 percent, reportedly did not participate in any type of cultural/ethnic activity. Television and movie selections were monitored, at least occasionally, in only 22 percent of the cases. Nearly all parents, 97 percent, reportedly were involved in the juvenile's health care. Except for this factor, only about half of the juveniles had interpersonal bonding factors present in their homes.

The maladaptive incidents reported by the Early Attention Program counselors included 29 different types of behavior ranging in severity from trouble at school to armed robbery (See Table 2). The most frequent first type of maladaptive behavior was truancy, exhibited by 50 percent of the juveniles. A sizable proportion (44.3 percent) had no second incident.

In regard to the relationships between bonding and maladaptive behavior, the juveniles involved in shoplifting had two to six bonding factors for the first incident of maladaptive behavior. Runaways had fewer (0-3) factors, indicating less bonding. Juveniles involved in truancy had four to 15 factors, suggesting a marginally high degree of bonding. Sexually acting out appeared to be distributed more evenly between zero and 15 factors. Oddly, however, juveniles experiencing school problems scored very high (7-15) on the scale, a sign of greater bonding.

When the second incidents of maladaptive behavior were considered, juveniles participating in truancy had zero to three factors, suggesting less bonding. Sexually acting-out juveniles also had zero to three factors. Surprisingly, the juveniles exhibiting insubordination had four to 15 factors, a sign of more bonding. The majority of juveniles exhibiting nonviolent problems also had a high number of bonding factors (seven to 15). Sixty juveniles had no second incidents of maladaptivity.

## CONCLUSION

A great deal of research on family and juvenile conduct addresses the concept of attachment or lack of attachment in single-parent or two-parent families. The main approach of this research is to examine more closely the bonding factors considered by mental health professionals to have the greatest potential influence on juveniles' conduct within female-headed African-American households.

While this investigation lends support to social control theory, particularly as it relates to the identification of important family interactions that function as controls against juvenile chronic maladaptive behavior, it also provides a valuable blueprint for a new theoretical model to approach a major social problem. The broad perspective of social control theory, from which the bonding variables were obtained, proves to be instructive. Significant relationships among several of the interpersonal bonding factors and juvenile chronic maladaptive behavior suggest that internal family dynamics are important in influencing such behavior. More chronic maladaptive conduct was exhibited by juveniles between 11 and 19 years of age when the parents did not willingly contact the agency. Less such conduct occurred among male youths whose parents willingly contacted the agency. The most influential interpersonal bonding factors among parents were willingly contacting the agency, being consistent in disciplining their children, and preparing and sharing meals with their children. The children of these parents tended to display less chronic maladaptive conduct than other youths in the study.

In reference to serious and nonserious maladaptive conduct and levels of bonding, youths displaying first occurrences of maladaptive behavior had two to six bonding factors, indicating a smaller degree of marginal-level bonding. Two youths, however, exhibited 13 or 14 factors; this finding calls into question the validity of self-report data. Bonding factors ranged from zero to 15 among youth displaying nonserious behavior.

In regard to natural support systems, the absence of a natural (in-home) support system was found to be significant in two of the bonding factors. When parents failed to give their children one-on-one time and when they lacked any natural support, the incidence of maladapative conduct was higher. The percentage of children displaying maladaptive conduct was very high in households where parents with nonrelatives (live-in significant others) as natural support did not prepare or share meals with the juveniles. The same situation occurred when parents were not consistent in disciplining their children.

These findings also support recent research showing that socialization variables concerning direct parent-child relationships are the strongest predictors for juvenile conduct. This study reveals that bonding influences some antisocial behaviors but not others. Due to the nature of the available data, individual differences due to genetic background or differences due to learning and experiences were not taken into consideration. For example, problems with learning disabilities, dyslexia and hyperactivity could be responsible for individuals exhibiting poor school performance but scoring high in bonding. Many questions remain unanswered.

Future research on sibling relationships in the female-headed household could offer additional insight into juvenile maladaptive conduct in African-American families. Researchers have noted that a child's position in the family (eldest, middle, or youngest) influences his or her ability to bond with the parent(s) and siblings in the family. Baker (1977) also suggests that sibling rivalry could play a very direct role in influencing the occurrence of juvenile maladaptive conduct. Another major area of concern is a more developed theoretical integration between the bonding process and the natural support system. Early intervention to control delinquency, school problems, and other maladaptive behaviors can be based on both the bonding and the natural support systems of families like those studied here.

These findings might not be generalizable beyond this sample. However, they can be useful to researchers in assessing the relationship between family functioning and various types of maladaptive behavior across diverse populations and cultures.

From a policy standpoint, this research may prove helpful for professionals in their intervention with African-American juveniles and their parents. This study is important because it challenges the myth that children from female-headed African-American families are destructive and dysfunctional. There is strong bonding in these families. This study further demonstrates that solid bonding factors, such as consistent discipline, and sharing meals, which at one time were nationwide ordinary family events, deter maladaptive conduct in children of these families. This research offers a guide for providing bonding strategies, which can be introduced, through various workshops, to African-American females heading households as a method of contributing to juvenile crime prevention.

## REFERENCES

Anderson, R.E. 1968. "Where's Dad? Parental Deprivation and Delinquency." *Archives of General Psychiatry* 18:641-649.

Babbie, E. 1983. *The Practice of Social Research.* Belmont, CA: Wadsworth.

Chilton, R.J. and G. E. Markle. 1972. "Family Disruption, Delinquent Conduct and the Effect of Subclassification." *American Sociological Review* 37.

Clark, S.H. and G.G. Kock. 1975. "A Study of Self-Reported Delinquency in Charlotte/Mecklenberg." *Popular Government.*

Cloward, R. A. and L. Ohlin. 1960. *Delinquency and Opportunity.* New York: Free Press.

Cohen, A. K. 1955. *Delinquent Boys.* New York: Free Press.

Empey, L.T. and S.G. Lubeck. 1971. *Explaining Delinquency.* Lexington, MA: Lexington Books.

Empey, L. 1982. *American Delinquency: Its Meaning and Construction.* Homewood, IL: Dorsey.

Hagen, F. 1982. *Research Methods In Criminal Justice and Criminology*. New York: Macmillan.

Herzog, E. and E.E. Sudia. 1973. "Children in Fatherless Families." *Review of Child Development Research* 3:141-232.

Hirschi, T. 1969. *Causes of Delinquency*. Berkeley, CA: University of California Press.

Kellem, S.G., R.G. Adams, H.C. Brown, and M.E. Ensminger. 1982. "The Long Term Evolution of the Family Structure of Teenage and Older Mothers." *The Journal of Marriage and the Family* 44:539-544.

Laub, J.H. and R.J. Sampson. 1988. "Unraveling Families and Delinquency: A Reanalysis of the Gluecks' Data." *Criminology* 26:355-380.

Lerman, P. 1991. "Counting Youth in Trouble in Institutions: Bringing the United States Up to Date." *Crime & Delinquency* 37: 465-480.

Levin, J. 1977. *Elementary Statistics in Social Research*. New York: Harper and Row.

Liska, A.E. and M.D. Reed. 1985. "Ties to Conventional Institutions and Delinquency: Estimating Reciprocal Effects." *American Sociological Review* 50:547-560.

Loeber, R. and M. Stouthamer-Loeber. 1986. "Family Factors as Correlates and Predictors of Juvenile Conduct, Problems and Delinquency." In *Crime and Justice an Annual Review of Research*. Chicago: University of Chicago Press.

McCord, J. 1982. "A Longitudinal View of the Relationship Between Paternal Absence and Crime." In *Abnormal Offenders, Delinquency, and the Criminal Justice System*, edited by J. Gunn and D.P. Farrington. New York: John Wiley & Sons.

_______. 1983. "A Forty Year Perspective on Effects of Child Abuse and Neglect." *Child Abuse and Neglect* 7:265-270.

Merton, R.K. 1964. "Anomie, Anomia, and Social Interaction: Contexts of Deviant Behavior." In *Anomie and Deviant Behavior*, edited by M. B. Clinard. New York: Free Press.

Monahan, T. 1957. "Family Status and the Delinquent Child: A Reappraisal and Some New Findings." *Social Forces* 35:250-258.

National Center for Juvenile Justice. 1985. *Delinquency in the United States*. Pittsburgh, PA.

Nettler, G. 1978. *Explaining Crime*. New York: McGraw-Hill.

Nye, F. I. 1958. *Family Relationships and Delinquent Behavior*. New York: John Wiley & Sons.

Rankin, J.H. 1983. "The Family Context of Delinquency." *Social Problems* 30:466-479.

Reckless, W. C. 1961. "A New Theory of Delinquency and Crime." *Federal Probation* 25:42-46.

Robins, L. and Hill. 1966. "Assessing the Contributions of Family Structure, Class and Peer Groups to Juvenile Delinquency." *Journal of Criminal Law, Criminology, and Police Science* 57:325-334.

Rosen, L. 1985. "Family and Delinquency: Structure of Function." *Criminology* 23:553-573.

______. 1970. "Matriarchy and Lower Class Negro Male Delinquency." *Social Problems* 17:175-189.

______, and K. Neilson. 1982. "Broken Homes." In *Contemporary Criminology.* New York: John Wiley & Sons.

Rutter, M. and H. Giller. 1984. *Juvenile Delinquency.* New York: The Guilford Press.

Sellitz, C., L.S. Wrightman, and S.W. Cook. 1976. *Research Methods in Social Relations.* New York: Holt, Reinhardt, and Winston.

United States Department of Justice. 1988. *Juvenile Justice Bulletin.* Washington, D.C.: U.S. Government Printing Office.

United States Department of Labor. 1984. *The United Nations Decade for Women, 1976-1985: Employment in the United States.* Washington, D.C.: U.S. Government Printing Office.

______. 1985. *Women Who Maintain Families. Fact Sheets.* Washington, D.C.: U.S. Government Printing Office.

Wilson, J. Q. and R. J. Herrnstein. 1985. *Crime and Human Nature.* New York: Simon and Schuster.

# BLACK PERSPECTIVES ON POLICE BRUTALITY

*Helen Taylor Greene is an assistant professor. She teaches criminology and criminal justice courses at Old Dominion University. Greene received her doctorate degree in criminology and criminal justice from the University of Maryland in College Park.*

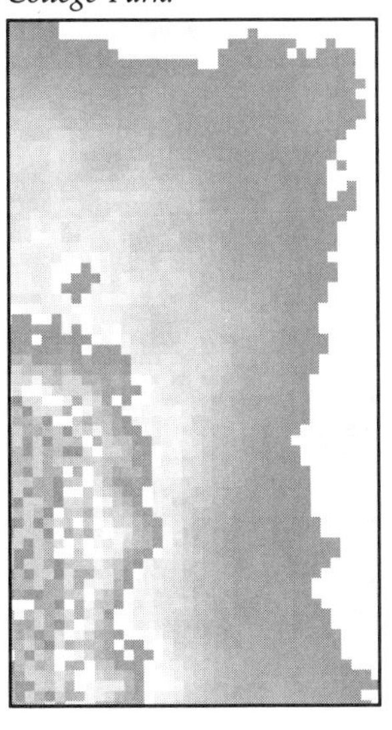

## INTRODUCTION

Police brutality always has been a critical issue in criminal justice. It most recently resurfaced as a result of the 1991 Rodney King incident in Los Angeles. King was brutally beaten by police. Upon their acquittal of criminal charges in 1992, deadly civil disturbances occurred.

While blacks are disproportionately the victims of excessive use of force, their perspectives on the issue receive little attention. Black perspectives on police brutality refers to recurring themes appearing in the writings of black authors on crime and justice related issues. These themes include the effects of social, economic, and political conditions, as well as racism and oppression, on crime and justice.

Black perspectives historically have been published in black periodicals such as *Black Scholar* and the *Howard Law Journal*. Young and Sulton (1991) correctly note that these perspectives, and those of other black criminologists, have been virtually ignored by white criminologists.

This paper was developed in an effort to identify black perspectives on police brutality. Emphasis was placed on identifying research, change agents and victims of police brutality. The identification process included reviewing literature in several special collections and libraries, including Howard University's Moorland Spingarn Research Center, the Library of Congress, Hampton University's Peabody Collection, and the libraries at Norfolk State University and Old Dominion University. A content analysis was completed of available research, significant historical and contemporary incidents of police brutality involving black victims, and black police officers' accounts. Information also was obtained from civil rights organizations and governmental agencies.

Four interrelated contextual frameworks are used to discuss black perspectives on police brutality: historical, sociological, political and criminal justice. Each provide different though related contexts and themes for understanding police brutality. The historical context traces the problem of police brutality from slavery to the present. It is helpful in understanding the police role throughout American history. It includes issues that are frequently over-looked. Police involvement in slave patrols, lynchings, race riots, the civil rights movement, and more recent civil unrest are useful historical themes.

**BLACK PERSPECTIVES ON POLICE BRUTALITY: ANALYTICAL FRAMEWORK**

| Historical Context | Sociological Context | Political Context | Criminal Justice Context |
|---|---|---|---|
| Slave Patrols | Racism | Political Repression | Administration of Justice |
| Jim Crow Laws | Discrimination | Powerlessness | Police Violence |
| Lynchings | Social and Economic Conditions | Political Movements | Unequal Treatment of Black Victims |
| Race Riots | American Cultural Values and Norms | Political Prisoners | Black Police Ascendancy |
| Civil Rights Movement | Subculture of Policing | Political Ascendancy | Black Police Organizations |
| Civil Unrest 1960s-1990s | | Judicial Decisions | Red Squads |
| | | Legislation Initiatives | Situational Characteristics |
| | | | Prevention and Control |
| | | | Comparative Criminal Justice |

The sociological context takes into consideration racism, discrimination, other social and economic conditions, American cultural values and norms, and the subculture of policing. Within a sociological context, the impact of social movements and social change on policing are better understood. For example, during the civil rights movement, questionable police practices and treatment of demonstrators not only became more visible, but were also challenged.

Within a political context, brutality can be examined by taking into consideration political repression, powerlessness, political movements, political prisoners, political ascendancy, judicial decisions, and legislative initiatives. Black political ascendancy and political repression of both civil rights activists and militants are among the themes most frequently mentioned by black authors when discussing police brutality.

The criminal justice context recognizes the police as part of the administration of justice process. Though closely related to the political context, the criminal justice context focuses on specific situational characteristics of brutality incidents. It also is within this context that the ascent of black police, and their role as change agents for preventing and controlling police brutality, can be examined in a meaningful way.

These contexts are interrelated. Myrdal (1944), although not black, provides a useful example of the historical, sociological and criminal justice contexts of police brutality. He noted that southern policemen, regardless of rank, had a low opinion of black people. Myrdal (1944) explained:

> In many, but not all, Southern communities, Negroes complain indignantly about police brutality. It is part of the policeman's philosophy that Negro criminals or suspects, or any Negro who shows signs of insubordination, should be punished bodily, and that this is a device for preventing crime and for keeping the "Negro in his place" generally. It is apparent, however, that the beating of arrested Negroes—frequently in the wagon on the way to jail or later when they are already safely locked up—often serves as vengeance for the fears and perils the policemen are subjected to while pursuing their duties in the Negro community. (p. 541)

## DEFINING POLICE BRUTALITY

Police brutality is usually defined as the unlawful use of physical force by officers in the performance of their duties. Excessive use of force is prohibited by state and federal statutes. Police brutality incidents occur in a variety of situations including routine traffic stops where no arrest is made, arrests, in-custody handling during investigations preceding arrest, during custodial interrogations, and during civil disturbances. The brutality might take the form of a severe beating, a deadly choke hold, or a shooting.

Black perspectives on police brutality include several definitions and references to different types of behavior. Staples (1974) refers to acts of violence used in the interest of political and economic elites as "legitimate" violence. Smith (1981) uses the term "police crime" to describe a range of violent acts by police, including unwarranted use of deadly force, unnecessary use of violence, any form of physical and mental torture, harassment or intimidation, frame-ups, illegal wiretaps, illegal searches and seizures, verbal abuse, and coverups. Reaves (1991) notes that police brutality is more than injury which requires medical treatment. He also includes wanton destruction of one's property.

## EXTENT OF BRUTALITY

It is difficult to determine the extent of the excessive use of force by police. Documenting all instances of brutality is difficult, in part, because there is no central source of information on brutality incidents. However, actions taken against black activists and their organizations have been documented in several books and articles authored by blacks (See Haynes 1970; *Black Scholar* 1981; Lumumba 1981; Jones 1988; Hilliard 1993).

Several black scholars trace police violence and repression back to slavery. According to Smith (1981), slave codes enabled slave patrols to whip, intimidate, and murder slaves. During the post-Reconstruction period, policemen were used to enforce Jim Crow laws. Police officers also were involved in lynchings that occurred in this century.

## POLICE BRUTALITY INCIDENTS

Numerous historical and contemporary examples of police brutality are described in detail in the literature. Describing each incident is beyond the scope of this paper. But several police brutality incidents are discussed below because they provide insight into the nature of brutality and blacks' responses to it.

Throughout the Civil Rights Movement of the 1960s, police used clubs, dogs, and water hoses and savagely beat and arrested blacks for demonstrating, often peacefully, against segregation. Similar incidents were reported during efforts to register black voters. The Council of Federated Organizations collected testimonies from victims of police violence for the purpose of offering them in evidence in a suit brought against the sheriff and other elected officials in Mississippi. Fifty-seven testimonies were chosen to show the cruelty and harassment suffered by civil rights activists. The brutalities described in these testimonies were committed by public servants. They included arrests on false charges and brutality by the police. The brutality incidents frequently approached sadistic cruelty and on occasion resulted in death.

By 1968, the Civil Rights Movement had taken a more militant approach. When black nationalists, often referred to as militants, began advocating the use of physical violence, white liberals and middle class blacks looked upon them with disdain. According to Haynes (1970), militants became easy targets of political repression. Several authors have described the political repression of black militants (Haynes 1970; Smith 1981; Smith 1988; Lumumba 1981; Marable 1984; Jones 1988). Of these, most identified federal, state and local police as the primary agents of political repression.

Although many black individuals and organizations were targeted, the destruction of the Black Panther Party provides the most poignant example of the police role in political repression of black militants. Black academicians and former Panthers have written extensively on political and police repression of this group (Haynes 1970; Karenga 1976; Pinkney 1978; Marable 1984; Jones 1988; Brown 1992; Hilliard 1993). Many Black Panther party members were killed, imprisoned, or forced into exile during what Haynes (1970) referred to as the "Police-Black Panther Conflict."

In October 1966, the Black Panther Party was founded by Huey P. Newton and Bobby Seale in Oakland, California. They, and many other young blacks, were frustrated and disillusioned with black organizations perceived as being dominated by middle class blacks (Jones 1988). The Panthers were revolutionary in their philosophy, dress, and tactics. For example, while many organizations criticized police actions against blacks, the Panthers believed they could end police brutality by organizing armed, self-defense groups (Boyd 1993).

In 1967, the Black Panther Party gained national attention. In May of that year, they disrupted the California State Legislature with an armed delegation. In October, an officer was killed during a Panther-police shoot-out in Oakland (Jones 1988). The Panther's philosophy and tactics were viewed as threatening by police and many citizens.

In addition to the resistance from the black middle class, militants often were involved in violent confrontations against one another. Haynes (1970) suggests militants may have killed other militants.

Jones (1988) provides an in-depth analysis of political repression of the Panthers in the Oakland Bay area. He notes how harassment and public order laws frequently were used to legally repress Party members. Covert activities, sometimes involving the United States Department of Justice's Federal Bureau of Investigation, also were used to neutralize the Black Panther Party. These acts included discouraging involvement by grocery stores and churches in the Panther's Free Breakfast Program, disrupting circulation of the *Black Panther* newspaper, disrupting speaking engagements, and causing dissension both within and outside the organization (Jones 1988).

More recently, former Panthers have discussed some of their personal experiences while members and leaders of the Panthers (Newton and Brown 1993; Hilliard 1993). Although many Panthers survived the destruction of their political organization, many others died, were incarcerated or chose to live in exile.

Throughout the 1970s, 1980s and continuing into the 1990s, police brutality incidents have occurred. Pierce (1986) suggests that there is a systemic and cyclical sequence to the emergence of police brutality. This sequence includes periods of relative quiescence, catalytic police incident, community/political outcry, police sensitivity training, return to relative quiescence.

Examples of Pierce's sequence can be found by examining incidents occurring in Florida. Two recent controversial brutality incidents, leading to community outcry and civil unrest, are the LaFleur and McDuffie cases. In 1979, the home of Nathaniel LaFleur, a school teacher, mistakenly was raided by Dade County police officers. In December, Arthur McDuffie was killed following a police chase. However, the catalytic incident which resulted in a community outcry in 1980 was the acquittal of officers involved in McDuffie's death.

Community outcry also occurred after the April 1992 acquittal of those police beating Rodney King in Los Angeles. This outcry proved to be the most devastating and deadly riot to occur in decades. A year earlier, Rodney King was brutally beaten by police officers after a high speed chase. A resident of an apartment complex near the scene of the beating captured the incident on videotape. Citizens in Los Angeles and across the country were outraged by the incident. In April 1992, when the officers involved were acquitted, there was an immediate, violent outbreak, which further devastated already strained police community relations. Dozens of people were killed, nearly a thousand injured, and thousands jailed. Arson, looting, and other destruction reportedly resulted in over $200 million worth of damage.

Unlike earlier civil unrest, property damage extended beyond the black community in Los Angeles. While south central Los Angeles was the hardest hit, Beverly Hills also was affected. Schools were closed, mail service was discontinued, final examinations at area colleges and universities were canceled, and federal troops were requested by city officials. Disturbances also occurred in other cities, including Madison, Wisconsin, Las Vegas, Atlanta, San Francisco, Minneapolis, Seattle, and Eugene, Oregon. Peaceful demonstrations were held in Baton Rouge, Louisiana, Kansas City, Missouri, Newark, New Jersey and other cities.

Cornell West (1992) describes what happened in Los Angeles as neither a race riot nor a class rebellion. He views it as a multiracial, transclass and largely male display of justified social rage. More importantly, though frequently overlooked, the failure of the police to prevent or control the revolt demonstrated police discontent as well.

The implications of the Los Angeles civil unrest forced many federal, state and local officials to more closely scrutinize police brutality. Then-Attorney General Richard Thornburgh, at the behest of Michigan Congressman John Conyers, directed the Civil Rights Division of the United States Department of Justice to investigate 15,000 police brutality complaints received since 1987.

The National Association for the Advancement of Colored People (NAACP) conducted hearings on police brutality in various cities around the country. Elected officials, police administrators, academicians, and citizens participated. The NAACP held hearings in an attempt to document the extent of police brutality, and how police and elected officials were responding to complaints against the police. The NAACP recently issued a report on police brutality. This report has stimulated interest on the part of law enforcement agencies to review their use of force policies.

These NAACP efforts were not their first to curb police brutality. A decade earlier, the NAACP responded to police violence by implementing the federally funded Police-Citizen Violence Project (Fleetwood 1982). Unlike previous efforts to address citizen concern for police brutality at the local level, this project was national in focus. It specifically targeted police departmental firearms policies. A strategy for developing firearms policies was presented in a manual made available to community groups.

Since the late 1960s, black police officers also have been change agents for reducing the number of brutality incidents. Working within police departments, many have been instrumental in revising use of force policies. Although their contributions in this area are not well documented, several black police officers have written about their experiences in law enforcement (Palmer 1973; Harris 1989; Reaves 1991).

During the 1970s, as increasing numbers of black police officers were hired and promoted, black police became change agents within their departments and organizations. Palmer (1981) contends that black police initially were used against black people. However, when properly organized, black officers are one of the strongest and most effective agents for change, providing protection for the black community's law enforcement interests (Palmer 1981).

In August 1972, black police representing 29 organizations in 25 cities and 14 states held a conference in St. Louis, Missouri. They formed the National Black Police Association. One of its stated purposes is to work towards reform in existing departments and to eliminate police corruption, brutality and racial discrimination. Four years later, the National Organization of Black Law Enforcement Executives (NOBLE) was formed. It has several goals including the establishment of effective means and strategies for dealing with racism in the field of criminal justice (Reaves 1991).

## CONCLUSION

Brutality incidents, and the civil unrest which often accompanies them, continue. The perspectives of blacks should be considered as this nation searches for solutions. A national commission, comprised of black civic leaders, black scholars, and police officials, should be formed to coordinate efforts to prevent and control police brutality. A part of their mission should be to accurately document the extent of brutality incidents, to review use of excessive force policies, set standards for federal, state and local law enforcement agencies, and identify future research needs.

The reports of this commission and the perspectives of blacks should be incorporated into college courses. Criminologists, sociologists, political scientists and historians should diversify their courses by incorporating black perspectives on police brutality. Both undergraduate and graduate courses on law enforcement, violence, criminal justice, as well as topical courses on blacks, crime, political repression, and numerous other issues will benefit from including these perspectives which have traditionally been ignored.

## REFERENCES

*Black Scholar*. 1981. *Special Issue on Police Violence*. 12(1).

Blackstock, N. 1975. *Cointelpro: The FBI's Secret War on Political Freedom*. New York: Vintage Books.

Boyd, H. 1993. "All Power to the People." *Emerge* 4:40-44.

Conyers, Jr., J. 1981. "Police Violence and Riots." *Black Scholar* 12:2-5.

Brown, E. 1992. *A Taste of Power: A Black Woman's Story*. New York: Pantheon Books.

Churchill, W. 1988. *Agents of Repression: The FBI's Secret War Against the Black Panther Party and the American Indian Movement*. Boston, MA: South End Press.

Copeland, V. 1970. *The Crime of Martin Sostre*. New York: McGraw-Hill.

Caldwell, L. and H. Greene. 1980. "Implementing a Black Perspective in Criminal Justice." In *Improving Management in Criminal Justice*, edited by A. W. Cohn and B. Ward. Beverly Hills, CA: Sage.

Dean, J. 1976. *Cointelpro: The FBI's Secret War on Political Freedom*. New York: Vintage.

"Detroit Police Officers Beat Man to Death with Flashlight." 1992. *The Virginian Pilot and Ledger Star*. November 7, p. A3.

Fleetwood, M. 1982. "The NAACP Response to Police Violence." *The Crisis* 89:27-29.

Georges-Abeyie, D. 1992. "Law Enforcement and Racial and Ethnic Bias." *Florida State University Law Review* 19:717-26.

Goldstein, R. J. 1977. *Political Repression in Modern America: 1870 to the Present*. New York: Schenkman.

Harris, S. 1989. *A Reason for Being: The Syl Harris Story*. New York: Carlton Press.

Haynes, Jr., A. B. 1970. "Police Black Panther Conflict." In *In Black America*. Los Angeles: Presidential Publishers.

Hilliard, D. and L. Cole. 1993. *This Side of Glory*. New York: Little Brown.

Hersey, J. 1968. *The Algiers Motel Incident*. New York: Alfred A. Knopf.

Jones, C. 1988. "The Political Repression of the Black Panther Party 1966-1971, The Case of the Oakland Bay Area." *Journal of Black Studies* 18:415-34.

Karenga, R. 1976. *The Roots of the U.S.-Panther Conflict: The Perverse and Deadly Games Police Play*. San Diego, CA: Kawaida.

Lacayo, R. 1991. "Law and Disorder." *Time* 137:18-21.

Lumumba, C. 1981. "Short History of the U.S. War on the R.N.A." *Black Scholar* 12:72-81.

Marable, M. 1984. *Race, Reform, Rebellion: The Second Reconstruction in Black America*. Jackson: University Press of Mississippi.

Moss, K. 1983. "Racial Injustice in Miami." *The Crisis* 90:48-49.

Moss, L. 1977. *Black Political Ascendancy in Urban Centers and Black Control of the Local Police Function: An Exploratory Analysis*. San Francisco: R&E Research Associates.

Myrdal, G. 1944. *An American Dilemma: The Negro Problem and American Democracy*. New York: Harper & Brothers.

Palmer, E. 1973. "Black Police in America." *Black Scholar* 5:19-27.

Pierce, H. B. 1986. "Blacks and Law Enforcement: Towards Police Brutality Reduction." *Black Scholar* 17:49-54.

Pinkney, A. 1978. *Red, Black and Green: Black Nationalism in the United States*. New York: Cambridge University Press.

Porter, B. and M. Dunn. 1984. *Miami 1980: A Different Kind of Riot*. Lexington, MA: D.C. Heath and Company.

Raine, W. 1977. *Perception of Police Brutality in South Central Los Angeles*. San Francisco: R&E Associates.

Reaves, J. N. 1991. *Black Cops*. Philadelphia: Quantum Leap.

Smith, D. 1981. "The Upsurge of Police Repression: An Analysis." *Black Scholar* 12:35-56.

Smith, Jr., J. C. 1988. "The MOVE Bombing: An Annotated Bibliographic Index." *Howard Law Journal* 31:95-142.

Southern Regional Council. 1952. *Race and Law Enforcement: A Guide to Modern Police Practices*. Atlanta, GA.

Staples, R. 1974. "Violence in Black America: The Political Implications." *Black World* 23:16-34.

Taylor Greene, H. 1979. *A Comprehensive Bibliography of Criminology and Criminal Justice Literature by Black Authors from 1895 to 1978*. Hyattsville, MD: Ummah.

Young, V. and A. Sulton. 1991. "Excluded: The Current Status of African-American Scholars in the Field of Criminology and Criminal Justice." *Journal of Research in Crime and Delinquency* 28:101-16.

West, C. 1992. "Bridging the Gap." *The Virginian Pilot and Ledger Star*. August 2, pp. C1, C3.

**NOTE:** Funding for this study was provided by Old Dominion University.

# AFRICAN-AMERICAN AND LATINO PRISONERS' RESPONSES TO A DIAGNOSIS OF HIV/AIDS

*Laura Fishman is an associate professor. She teaches criminology and criminal justice courses at the University of Vermont. Fishman received her doctorate degree in sociology from McGill University.*

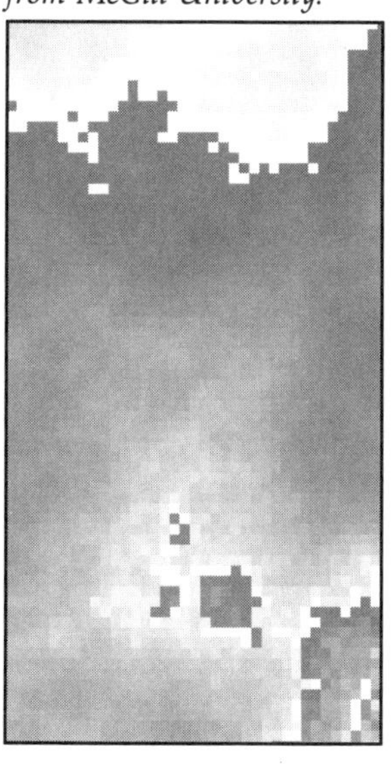

## INTRODUCTION

The typical response to a diagnosis of HIV infection of the African-American and Latino prisoners, incarcerated in upper New York State prison systems, is the outcry, "My God! I've got the 'monster'!" HIV infection is a catastrophic event, especially for prisoners. Many prisoners believe that a "diagnosis of HIV / AIDS" is tantamount to a sentence of death. Those infected must not only confront a deadly disease but the stigma associated with it.

Imprisonment, especially when coupled with AIDS, produces so many stressors that the coping abilities of prisoners are challenged in the extreme. Sometimes the demands exceed an individual's ability to survive. When AIDS is involved, the normal crises associated with imprisonment, such as separation and loss, are compounded. AIDS, a mysterious disease, carries with it a tremendous stigma. Thus, the stresses associated with the disease are both more acute and more complex than those associated with other life-threatening illnesses. It is likely that the social stigma of the disease, in addition to that associated with imprisonment, has a tremendous impact on prisoners' ability to cope on a daily basis.

This paper examines the reactions of African-American and Latino prisoners to a diagnosis of AIDS and the accommodative strategies these prisoners adopt in order to cope with this life threatening disease. I focus on this population because African-

American and Latino prisoners are predicted to be disproportionately affected by the AIDS virus in the future (See Des Jarlais et al. 1984; Des Jarlais and Friedman 1987, 1988; Friedman et al. 1986; Rogers and Williams 1987; Potler 1988). The numbers currently affected are high. Hammett (1987) reported that 28 percent of a sample of New York State prison admissions from New York City jails in December 1987 to January 1988 had histories of IV drug use and 44 percent of them were HIV seropositive in anonymous testing.

There is consensus within the literature that following a diagnosis of AIDS, persons with AIDS report the uncertainty of their situation is compounded by fears of social abandonment. They become anxious that they will be subjected to workplace hostilities, familial rejection, police harassment, anti-gay violence and rejection by health care providers (Christ and Wiener 1985; Foster 1988; Kowalewski 1988; Sandstrom 1990; Weitz 1993).

HIV antibody testing is available to concerned persons "on the streets" as well as in correctional and drug treatment facilities. A positive test result means an individual could actually have the virus in his or her system. To be diagnosed as AIDS infected means the individual is at the final and symptomatic stage of HIV infection. Given this, AIDS is a continuum extending from initial infection with the HIV, through a long asymptomatic period, and then to the development of AIDS, the final and symptomatic stage of HIV infection. An HIV diagnosis, therefore, is not an immediate death sentence (See Hopp and Rogers 1989).

To date there has been no systematic investigation of prisoners' reactions to a diagnosis of HIV infection. The literature on the reactions of gay men may be useful. This literature notes that upon a diagnosis of HIV positive gay men experience a shift in identity from that of a "typical" normal person to one with difficult, special and potentially stigmatizing problems (Christ and Wiener 1985; Kowalewski 1988; Sandstrom 1990.) The person with AIDS is left with the new identity of a damaged person who must accept the illness label.

Morin and Batchelor (1984) report that in the general population the emotional reactions of those with AIDS, following a diagnosis of HIV positive, include the usual psychological reactions that accompany the diagnosis of a life-threatening illness. These reactions, consistent over a diverse population of persons with AIDS, include fear of death and dying, anger, guilt, fear of exposure of lifestyle, fear of contagion, loss of self-esteem, fears of decreased social support and increased dependency, isolation, stigmatization, concerns and confusion over options for medical treatment, and an overriding sense of gloom and helplessness associated with a degenerative illness (Batki et al. 1988; Christ and Wiener 1985; Holland and Tross 1985; Joseph et al. 1987; Kelly and St. Lawrence 1988;

Namir et al. 1987; Rubinow and Joffee 1984, 1987; Sandstrom 1990; Shaw 1992; Weitz 1989, 1991).

The existing literature on gay men with HIV/AIDS provides a basis for predicting the responses of African-American and Latino prisoners with HIV/AIDS. Research on gays with HIV/AIDS suggests prisoners with HIV/AIDS might initially accommodate to this life threatening disease and its concomitant stigma in four ways.

The first is *denial*. Denial has been viewed as both functional and dysfunctional when used as a coping mechanism (Foster 1988; Joseph et al. 1987; Kelly and St. Lawrence 1988). Denial can help persons with HIV/AIDS deal with the constant threat of death and may let them live sanely on a day-to-day basis. But the danger of denial is that it precludes taking precautions to protect oneself from the onslaught of the disease.

The second is *passing*. Goffman (1963) notes that passing can be used by the less severely stigmatized. They carry on their lives just as they had before receiving the diagnosis in order to appear "normal."

The third is *avoidance*. Patterns of avoidance, which can prove to be stigma-provoking, most commonly take the form of withdrawing into the home; shying away from interactions with others, especially in public places; and limited sociable involvement. This strategy can assist persons with HIV/AIDS in coping with hostile public reactions because it conveys an appearance of normalcy. But avoidance can exacerbate the person's distress rather than mobilize social and health-related support.

The fourth is *affirmation*. Affirmation assumes such forms as acknowledging the HIV diagnosis (Christ and Wiener 1985; Coates et al. 1984; Kelly and St. Lawrence 1988). "Going public" can provide such benefits as limiting the impact of the illness on their social lives. It also allows persons with HIV/AIDS to obtain social support as well as support from health-related agencies. In addition, those who avow the illness are usually able to better tolerate stress.

Little attention, however, has been directed toward documenting the strategies employed by prisoners or intravenous drug abusers to deal with a diagnosis of HIV/AIDS. The present paper attempts to fill this gap in the literature.

The traditional conception of prison is of a "closed system," or what Goffman (1961) terms a "total institution." A "total institution" is one which completely absorbs and structures the identities of the actors within it. Given this, prisons traditionally have been characterized as extremely control-limiting environments. For example, Clemmer's (1940) "universal factors of prisonization," Sykes' (1966) "deprivations of imprisonment" and Goffman's (1961) prison as a "total institution" emphasize the restrictions on a prisoner's sense of autonomy and self-esteem and the limited opportunity for inmates to make choices (Goffman

1961; Goodstein et al. 1984; Irwin 1970; Sykes 1966; Sykes and Messinger 1960; Thomas 1977; Toch 1977; Wheeler 1961). One goal of this study is to determine whether African-American and Latino prisoners with HIV/AIDS focus on the opportunities for action and personal control, or whether they choose inaction.

This paper examines the conditions under which a diagnosis of HIV infection occurs and the consequences it may have for African-American and Latino prisoners. This paper also examines ways in which prisoners cope with the HIV/AIDS life-threatening disease, as well as with the effects of uncertainty and the expectation of social rejection.

## METHOD

The preliminary findings reported here are based on research-in-progress that focuses on 60 African-American and Latino male prisoners with HIV/AIDS and currently incarcerated in five upstate New York maximum and medium security correctional facilities. This population was identified by obtaining access to upstate New York correctional facilities. Within each facility, arrangements were made by health care providers knowing the identity of prisoners with HIV/AIDS. These prisoners were informed of the research project and their cooperation was requested. The study population was confined to only those prisoners who were known to health care providers as having HIV/AIDS and having served at least six months.

All the men who participated in this study did so voluntarily. The participants were assured of confidentiality and all interviews were conducted in a manner which respected their dignity and made them feel comfortable with the data collection process. In-depth interviews were conducted with each prisoner. These interviews ranged in length from two to five hours. The length of the interview session depended upon the health and willingness of the inmate. Each prisoner was informed about the project and his informed consent was obtained. The interviews were structured to obtain information regarding the man's family background, prior arrests and convictions, how he learned he had contracted HIV/AIDS and how he copes with HIV/AIDS. While the interviews followed no rigid structure, an interview guide was used to ensure that the same basic topics were raised with each prisoner.

All 60 African-American and Latino prisoners lived in New York City. Thirty-two of the men were African-American and the remaining twenty-eight were Latino. (The term Latino in this context refers to a number of different ethnicities — Cubans, Puerto Ricans and Dominicans.) The majority were members of the lower class. Only seven men had been steadily employed prior to imprisonment. The remainder were unemployed at the time they were arrested. Most men were getting money by robbing, stealing, doing con jobs or drug dealing.

Fifty-eight were heterosexual intravenous drug users and two were homosexual. The preponderance of IV drug users indicates the effects of both geographical location and the tendency for drug users to be arrested for crimes punishable by imprisonment. The prisoners also lived within an area of New York City which has a relatively high incidence of AIDS among intravenous drug users.

Most of the men had extensive criminal histories and reported they had spent time in prison prior to the current incarceration. The prisoners were serving sentences ranging from three years to life and primarily for drug-related crimes. Most had been convicted of serious crimes, such as assault, homicide, sexual offenses or sale of unregulated drugs. And most had been previously convicted on two or more charges.

The data collected are analyzed with the "grounded theory" and "constant comparative" procedures developed by Glaser and Strauss (1967) and Charmaz (1983). Since the "grounded theory" method emphasizes discovery and theory development, data collection and analysis proceeds simultaneously so that a theoretical understanding of the phenomenon is constantly revised as more data are collected. And on the basis of the "constant comparative" method, information from data sources will be subjected to rigorous comparisons, cross-checking and validation with respect to the experiential frame and life space of the prisoners with HIV/AIDS.

## LIFESTYLES ON THE STREETS

Prior to their incarceration, most of the African-American and Latino men participated in a lifestyle which placed them at risk to contract the HIV virus. The men's accounts of their lives strongly resemble the fast-living lifestyle portrayed by Fishman (1990).

According to the men, they actively pursued at least three elements of fast living: (1) heavy drinking or drug consumption; (2) frequent absences from home with peers, hanging out on the streets, in local bars, or in shooting galleries where intravenous drug users gather to purchase or use drugs; (3) unsteady relationships with wives or sexual partners; (4) toughness in which the men act in a violent manner; and (5) involvement in criminal and quasi-criminal activity. For instance, one prisoner recalled how he pursued a fast lifestyle:

> In the 70's, I started using heroin and I had a habit. ... I sold heroin to other blacks. We were going wild. I stayed away from home two weeks at a time. We had a lot of crews at the

time. We made a lot of money. We had a nice apartment and some fine clothes. We had everything we needed and more. I stayed at the apartment for weeks on end and then I'd come home and crashed. I stole the rent money from my mother and did not come home for weeks after that.

Within the context of fast living, most of the men's activities were precursors to contracting the HIV virus.

Almost all the men reported drinking excessively or heavy drug consumption; most were primarily abusers of heroin, cocaine and crack. More than half of the men went on periodic binges or consumed large quantities of alcohol or drugs on a daily basis. A small number of men used both alcohol and drugs.

The sharing of works for injecting drugs is part of the fast lifestyle pursued by the men in the study population. By custom, tradition or necessity, intravenous drug abusers share their needles, syringes, drug paraphernalia, cookers and supply of drugs. Most of the men who were intravenous drug users reported they shared drugs or drug paraphernalia with one or more persons prior to their diagnosis. A few reported they were most likely to share needles and drug paraphernalia when they frequented shooting galleries. (In shooting galleries, injection equipment can be rented and needles/syringes are often shared with strangers.) African-American prisoners were significantly more likely to report they had injected drugs in a shooting gallery than were Latinos.

Prior to 1983, most HIV/AIDS prisoners were ignorant or misled; they did not know HIV infections came through shared needles and sex. A few who reported sharing drug paraphernalia stated they had changed their behaviors in some way once they learned how AIDS was transmitted.

Most of the men reported they had not established stable, legitimate employment which regularly produced enough income to support their drug consumption patterns. Consequently their lives consisted of intermittent involvement in crime, jobs and hustles. They stole, robbed or sold drugs whenever opportunities arose to do so. They did a variety of odd jobs such as painting apartments, delivering messages, or moving furniture. None of these activities provide a stable income or an income sufficient to maintain a decent standard of living, one which would place them above the poverty line.

The fast lifestyle can frequently lead to multiple sexual partners. Some African-American men admitted that they had achieved the status of a "player of women," one using women solely as sexual objects. Oliver (1989) notes that African-American men will act as "players of women" as an acceptable alternative to the traditional definitions of manhood.

The men opt to redefine manhood in terms of toughness, sexual conquest and thrill seeking. One prisoner illustrates the point:

> When I was working I started to use heroin. I met a lot of girls on the job and I wanted to keep my ejaculation going. I wanted to prolong the ejaculation. I met this girl who had a raw sexual appetite and I had a long night with her. I first got high on dope and then we kept going at it. I found that using dope helped me to keep going. Then one day I was going with this girl. I wanted to make a night she won't forget. I got some money together and did a bag of dope. It worked. From there I started doing dope two or three times a week. I wanted to be the super stud. I kept meeting girls and fooling around.

Hence, the men's accounts reveal that their role as "player of women" places them at risk for HIV infection.

Drug-using behavior is linked with sexual behavior. Some drugs increase the desire for sex or the circumstances surrounding drug use create opportunities for sexual activity. The men in the study population reported an association between needle sharing and sexual activity. For these men, high-risk sexual behavior (multiple sexual partners and no condoms) was the norm.

Of these, a little over half reported between two and 10 sexual partners during the year prior to their incarcerations, the remainder indicated more than six. Two men reported over 20 homosexual contacts. This sexual behavior was linked with drug-using behavior in that these men had sex to obtain drugs or money. Some men reported that they were infected because they had multiple sexual partners. Others mentioned that they were uncertain as to how they contracted AIDS because they had been heavy drug users and had numerous sexual partners, both high risk forms of behavior.

The picture that emerges is that with the advent of AIDS, fast living has become synonymous with risky behavior, particularly when fast living encompasses drug-use-related risk. Drug consumption precipitates some additional risks as a result of the failure to think clearly and as a result of the chaos and instability from the constant pressure to hustle. According to the men, drug using behavior clouds one's mind and thus causes HIV risky behavior. Many men said that they were unable to control their behaviors when using drugs. Some seldom exercised self-restraint to avoid used needles or to use condoms. Even among the few men who were aware of the risks of infection, some were unable to implement risk-reduction strategies. These men were so consumed by the quest for money and drugs that they ignored or assumed the risk.

As one prisoner related:

> When I was on the streets, I knew that I was high risk. I was too busy doing other things. I had no time to think about AIDS. I was only thinking about getting a package of drugs and shooting up as much as I could. I was shooting up as much as I sold drugs. I was not making money but I was getting high. I'd get enough money to do it over and over again. It's called backward hustling.

Knowledgeable prisoners commonly found it difficult to translate their knowledge about HIV transmission into a change of behavior. Contracting AIDS became just another risk among the many risks they encountered on a daily basis (e.g., risks of arrest, overdosing, or becoming the victim of theft, violence or other illnesses related to drug use). Risk-taking is intrinsic to maintaining a drug habit. These men said these risks were of more pressing concern than the risk of AIDS. Their risk choices were made at the expense of prioritizing for their physical and psychological well-being.

The risk of death was a part of the intravenous drug user's subculture long before AIDS (See Des Jarlais and Friedman 1987). Drug users already face the threat of death with each injection. According to Friedman et al. (1986), even though AIDS usually causes a slower and more painful death than overdosing, intravenous drug users' fatalistic acceptance of the risk of death as part of their lifestyle reduces the deterrent effect of AIDS. Another impediment to the perception of AIDS as a health risk is the prisoners' difficulty in distinguishing AIDS as a singularly important cause of death compared with the many causes of death in their communities.

AIDS risk-related behaviors, therefore, are not divorced from a myriad of other risk-taking behaviors. The prisoners' accounts reveal that although they were aware, prior to their diagnosis of HIV infection, their behavior might result in the transmission of AIDS, the risk was one of many risks imbedded in the fast lifestyle.

## DIAGNOSIS AND ITS AFTERMATH

Since 1985, people have been able to ascertain if they have been infected with HIV by taking a test. However, from the study population, the men usually were incarcerated when they were tested for HIV infection. Since HIV/AIDS testing is not required upon incarceration, testing for HIV/AIDS infection is done on a voluntary basis.

Many of these men were aware of their risky behavior while on the streets but postponed getting an HIV antibody test until they were incarcerated. Some were more willing to be tested once the symptoms of HIV infection started to appear (e.g., rashes, fevers, night sweats and swollen lymph nodes). A few were tested upon being hospitalized for some opportunistic infection which suggested AIDS. A few of the men, on the streets, sought testing at an earlier stage of the HIV disease. Two, however, were hospitalized and subsequently tested for AIDS.

Those men receiving a diagnosis of HIV infection, either at HIV testing facilities or from doctors in community hospitals, reported they generally were treated sympathetically and received detailed and accurate information about their condition and prognosis. Often they reported they were immediately counseled by nurses and social workers who filled the role of sympathetic listener as well as providing some support. Men who were tested at either Rikker's Island or the medium security prison were likely to report similar experiences. Most of the men tested in maximum security prisons reported they were not as fortunate. They were more likely to report they were given the news briskly and insensitively. Most said they were not provided with psychological supportive follow-up from health care personnel. Frequently they were informed they should expect to live only a few months to two years even though they had yet to develop any life-threatening infections.

## REACTIONS TO A DIAGNOSIS OF HIV/AIDS INFECTION

The reactions of prisoners with HIV / AIDS to their diagnosis widely vary. Most prisoners report intense emotional reactions to the crisis of a diagnosis of HIV / AIDS infection. The men in the study population report a range of immediate emotional reactions such as disbelief, shock, numbness, guilt, fear, anger and depression.

A common response made by the prisoners is to consider their diagnosis "a death sentence" whether they are asymptomatic but infected or whether they have AIDS. A similar response has been reported by intravenous drug abusers (Des Jarlais et al. 1984; McCoy and Khoury 1990). For example, a prisoner related his reaction to a diagnosis of HIV positive:

> I thought that I had AIDS. I thought that HIV was AIDS. I thought that I had only months to live. I prayed to God to kill me now. I flipped and went crazy. All I had heard on the news was that AIDS was a killer disease and it will kill me in months. I just thought that I had months to live.

In the street culture, distinctions among being HIV-infected, having AIDS and being in imminent danger of death are seldom made. Those men who reported severe death anxiety also reported that at the time of diagnosis they did not receive sufficient information about the meaning of the test.

A diagnosis of HIV/AIDS created new uncertainties for the men. They expressed uncertainty about how they will die, how they will live from day to day, and how much longer they can expect to live. In turn, these reactions undermine the prisoners' ability to understand the immediate effects of their condition, to cope with the demands of the illness, and to deal with the demands of their everyday lives.

Many prisoners coped with the uncertainties of their new status by becoming fatalistic. Fatalism provides a way to cope with the anxieties and uncertainties about imminent death. Some men maintained "It's God's will!" or "We're all going to die anyway" to assuage their death anxieties. Death is seen as a part of the life cycle, an inevitable outcome that brings closure to a life story. Such a perspective assists them to face death.

Some expressed fears of disability and of suffering and pain. To them, fear of death was minimal in comparison to the fear of what their lives might become. All the men have seen members of their communities stricken with AIDS. Being ill with AIDS therefore terrifies them as they become anxious about the manifestations of the disease for which there is currently no remedy. As one prisoner said:

> I've seen guys in the last stages of the disease and it hurts. It's like looking at myself in the mirror. It scares the shit out of you. I've seen guys whose bodies are raw meat, lesions, teeth came out, nails fall out. I've seen a lot of them. I used this as an excuse to keep drugging. It was inevitable. I'd be like that. I'd look in the mirror and I'd say, "God, when I get like that, let me die or let me get busted and die in jail so my kids do not see me like that."

Less frequently, prisoners revealed they felt feelings of loss after learning about their diagnosis. Feelings of loss are reportedly a common response to a diagnosis of HIV infection (See Weitz 1989, 1991). A few felt anguish about the loss of their future, the loss of educational and occupational opportunities or the loss of intimate contacts with their children, wives and families. More, however, expressed grief about their loss of health and a normal life span.

Feelings of guilt can be induced by an HIV diagnosis. Some men felt guilty about infecting their sexual partners or their young children.

They also expressed some guilt about the amount of pain and suffering their diagnosis may cause their sexual partners or family members.

Finally, the uncertainty about their status with their families, friends and fellow prisoners is most worrisome. A common theme among prisoners is their expectation of rejection by the significant people in their lives. Weitz (1991) and Sandstrom (1990) make a similar observation about persons with AIDS reactions to a diagnosis of HIV infection. Because of the massive stigma attached to AIDS, prisoners frequently worry about the possibility of rejection by society, the loss of casual acquaintances and the abandonment of close friends, associates, lovers and families.

African-American and Latino prisoners with HIV/AIDS are not unfamiliar with being labeled "them" or "other." They have experienced such labeling repeatedly as economically oppressed minorities and as members of cultures whose values hold them inferior. As people of color, they have already been stigmatized by poverty, race and intravenous drug use and they have been repeatedly the targets of social control measures. Understandably, they wish to avoid new forms of stigmatization that are likely to accompany disclosure of their health status.

African-American prisoners are more likely to be fearful about disclosing their status than Latino prisoners. All reported they did not immediately disclose their status because they feared physical harm, stigma, abandonment and rejection. One prisoner explained:

> A lot of people don't want to be looked at as gay or that they have indulged in homosexual activity. They would rather be considered an intravenous drug user. They fear that other people will look at you like trash. I have to take care of myself and am not concerned how they [i.e., prisoners and prison personnel] see me. But around here there is a lot of worry about how people see you.

Following diagnosis, most men were not likely to turn to their friends or acquaintances for support. However, Latino prisoners were more likely to disclose to their close friends than African-American prisoners. These Latinos noted that the Latino community has more solidarity than the African-American community and therefore Latinos are less likely to make derogatory remarks about fellow Latinos prisoners with HIV/AIDS and less likely to ostracize their "amigos." According to the African-American men in the study population, the African-American community tends not to form tight knit peer groups. Consequently, ostracism is more likely to be keenly experienced by African-American prisoners because they do not have a solid support group to buffer the hostility that emanates from the larger prison community.

Some of the prisoners have not disclosed their condition to other inmates. All those prisoners who have not disclosed their condition believe that disclosure is fraught with danger. Knowing that so many prisoners and correctional personnel fear or despise those who have the illness, many worry about how their fellow prisoners will react. A typical observation made by a prisoner with HIV infection is:

> Some inmates with HIV disease assume that their [the other prisoners] response will be unsympathetic. Some, for example, consider that inmates are going to reject them. They will talk about them behind their backs. Others fear that the inmates will retaliate, as by burning them out of their cells. So they decide not to tell their fellow inmates.

The aftermath of a diagnosis for prisoners with HIV/AIDS is a time of distress, confusion and disruption. The anticipation of social rejection, the anxieties about how the illness will affect their lives, as well as the anxieties about death and dying, are deeply felt, aggravating their situation. Despite all the difficulties they face because of the uncertainty, they are not helpless. They find ways to reduce or, if necessary, to live with the uncertainty. The accounts of prisoners reveal that they employ a variety of coping strategies to make their lives bearable as well as to present what they consider to be "normal" faces. The most commonly used strategies are: (1) passing, (2) self-isolation, (3) insulation, (4) acting up and (5) affirmation. The particular strategies employed vary according to the progression of their illness at the time of diagnosis, the personal meanings they attach to their illness, and whether or not they were incarcerated at the time of diagnosis.

## PASSING

As Goffman (1963) notes, those with a "spoiled" identity may seek to pass as normal by carefully suppressing the information. Passing is generally employed in the early stages of the illness when the more telltale physical signs have not yet become visible.

Whether they are on the streets or incarcerated, many prisoners with HIV/AIDS reported they are fearful about the "dangers" which could emerge from full medical disclosure. They respond to their fears by "passing" in order to maintain others' perceptions of them as "normal." Within the prison system, they attempt to hide any visible signs that they are infected, try to appear "conventional" by participating in their normal round of activities, attempt to conceal any identifying medications, avoid eating any high protein meals available at the cafeteria, and dissociate themselves from prisoners known to be infected with the disease. To dissociate themselves, they hesitate to sit with them in the cafeteria, to share their food with them, to converse with them or even to sit next to them in the medical infirmary waiting room.

When on the streets, prisoners attempted to hide their illness from families, friends, associates and sexual partners. Fatalistically, they simply go about "business as usual." They continue their involvement in a fast-living lifestyle in which the "hustle" remains any legitimate or illegitimate activity that can generate income to purchase drugs. Given this, several men continued in their roles as "players of women." One felt no ethical obligation to reveal his diagnosis to his sexual partners. Two others argued that these women were probably infected anyway and therefore were not at risk from having sex with them. One prisoner explains:

> I was still smoking crack and drinking. I'd get high whenever I could. When I had the money, I'd get some crack. I was not too much for women at this point in my life. Women did not really interest me. I did have some sex with women. I had sex with those I knew before I went to the hospital. I felt that I didn't need to tell them. They'd get upset. So why bother. I did not use condoms because I had had sex a few times with them before I was HIV positive. If I infected them before I went into the hospital, then it did not matter now if I had sex with them again. I did not change my lifestyle.

Several men said that they hid their illness from their families. For example, they snuck their medications into their homes or lied to their families about their medications or trips to the clinics. One man routinely transferred pills to another medicine bottle because he feared that family members would recognize the drug as one used to treat HIV. Another made his bed whenever he experienced night sweats so that his mother would not suspect he might be ill.

## SELF-ISOLATION

Some men chose to avoid any interaction with either prisoners or guards. After a diagnosis of HIV infection, 13 men, incarcerated in maximum security prisons, reported doing this. Initially these men felt that their status had been dramatically and shamefully shifted from "ordinary prisoners" to "prisoners with HIV/AIDS." Their diagnosis made them ashamed and embarrassed. Two of these men, whose diagnosis came as a consequence of severe illness, isolated themselves because they believed their physical conditions provided major clues that they were AIDS infected. Under these circumstances, they perceived negotiations with both prisoners and guards to "normalize" their situation could be problematic. As a result they avoided all situations where their HIV/AIDS status might become known, e.g., they did not go to the hospital to pick up their nutrient supplement because it would immediately identify them as HIV-positive. They avoided any social contacts where it might become an issue, e.g., hanging out with the men in the prison yard, participating in recreational activities or participating in work activities. And they avoided developing friendships or acquaintanceships.

Their self-enforced isolation was effective insofar as they reported they seldom encountered any stigmatizing situations. But as a result of this self-isolation, their social lives deteriorated significantly and visits to the medical services were fairly non-existent.

## INSULATION

Some prisoners reported they chose a more selective withdrawal strategy whether they were on the streets or within the prison system. They made an effort to disengage from many but not all social involvements. These men said they selectively informed family members and a handful of trusted associates (e.g., running partners, friends and sexual partners) about their diagnosis. It is within these circles of family or friends that the men previously received socio-emotional support. Contacts with those outside this circle was minimized as they believed these contacts were likely to be hostile and rejecting.

Latinos are more likely than African-Americans to disclose to a small network of trusted friends and family members. They want to ensure for themselves some insulation from potentially threatening interactions as well as to receive the support they need. They therefore experienced some relief from the stigma and in turn some relief from their fears about the illness.

## IMPLICATIONS OF PASSING, SELF-ISOLATION AND INSULATION

Although hiding their illness protects prisoners from rejection and danger, it creates other problems. The infected prisoners can never be entirely certain how well their deception is working. "Keeping the secret" requires uninterrupted vigilance. The men therefore try not to respond to or encourage even friendly inquiries about their health. They carefully watch every word and gesture when they are around other men or prison guards. As long as they can conceal information or avoid situations in which they might have to conceal information, they assume that others will regard them as "normal."

Another basic problem is that those who "pass" or seek self-isolation deprive themselves of the emotional or practical support they might otherwise receive. As noted in the literature, having social support has been identified by persons with all stages of HIV infection as the single most helpful resource (Batchelor 1984; Corless and Pittman-Lindeman 1988; Joseph et al. 1984; Kelly and St. Lawrence 1988; Morin and Batchelor 1984; Zich and Temoshok 1987). Within the prison community, social support provides infected prisoners with some assistance in obtaining scarce resources (e.g., alternative meal preparation), protection from other prisoners and assistance when ill. Social support also provides infected prisoners with a network of fellow sufferers which can mitigate their sense of "uniqueness" and "aloneness."

"Keeping the secret" prevents prisoners with HIV/AIDS from making full use of the medical facilities, educational materials and counseling services which are available. The need to avoid stigmatization places these men at high risk of dying sooner than those who avail themselves of social support and medical treatment. As one prisoner with HIV/AIDS observed:

> Then there is what I call the willful type of dying. He is a guy who is infected but he does not want anyone to know about it. He even avoids going to sick call. Sometimes these guys have a nervous breakdown and then we know. Sometimes, there are no obvious signs that they have AIDS. Some of these guys die alone in their cells.

Finally, this imposed secrecy places a heavy burden on those who are "living a lie." Having to field questions and remarks from family or friends who have a mistaken notion about what is happening in their lives or who have become suspicious about their health can create considerable strain. Thus, secretiveness itself can result in severe emotional stress for prisoners with HIV/AIDS.

## ACTING UP

A diagnosis of HIV infection can escalate the pace of fast living and therefore the criminality of some men on the street. For those who are imprisoned, such a diagnosis can actually precipitate verbal and physical behavior and self-destructive behavior. Six men who were incarcerated at the time of their diagnosis and six men who were diagnosed on the streets reported doing this. All the men who acted up reported they were responding to the popular belief that AIDS results in certain death as well as to fears and anxieties about loss of health and sexuality, isolation and social abandonment.

According to the men's accounts, the momentum of a fast lifestyle quickens its pace. Following their diagnosis the men increased their drug consumption. Most went on binges that lasted for as long as they had drugs or the means to purchase them. Criminal activities were repeated more frequently to produce income to cover these extended binges. A few men reported that all their tangible assets were sold or traded for drugs and two men lost their permanent residences. Their existence focused more intensely on getting money, buying drugs and consuming them. As one prisoner reported:

> My drug addiction took its toll. I did crack, coke and I got fired, lost my car. I sold all my property. My VCR, stereo, jewelry. I found myself in a room by myself with a habit. I went to Puerto Rico. My nephew took me to Puerto Rico. I was going downhill. The crack was bugging me out. I was hearing things. I stayed there a month and then I came back and got a job. I worked for the month of January. And then I got PCP and wound up in the hospital.

Only two admitted they continued to engage in unprotected sex with numerous sexual partners. During their runs of cocaine or cocaine crack, most reported they were awake for days at a time. All reported they neglected to eat, sleep regularly and tend to basic hygiene.

Given the constraints of prisons, drug use, criminal behavior and interpersonal conflict are tightly controlled. The range of opportunities to act up are fairly narrow. Even so, security measures do not prevent highly volatile prisoners from stabbing, fist fighting, engaging in gang warfare and attempting suicide. Believing they were going to die anyway, "acting up" is a response to felt social isolation, the perceived hopelessness of the disease and fears of the debilitating illness. A prisoner, incarcerated in a detention facility, recalled how he acted up:

> When I found out I was HIV positive, it was through a gorgeous black woman. She was a nurse and she sat down and told me. My world just dropped. I never cried about it. The first time I cried was 10 days later. I got back into the jail and I went on a mission. I did crazy stupid things. I stabbed four

> guys, hit one guy on the head with a phone. I prepared to commit suicide. I took a bed sheet and tried to hang myself. And I was trying to kill everybody. I hurt six people in 10 days. I took the sheet into the shower to hang myself. A guy went to get Pete and between them and 20 other guys, they held me down. I had this disease. I did not know what to do. I could not handle a simple disease. All I knew was that it was a killer disease. I just wanted to get it over with.

Given this overwhelming sense of helplessness and fear, the men in the study population said that they became intransigent prisoners.

These men waged open warfare with prison personnel, flouting authority and brazenly defying regulations. Some swore or argued with officers and two went as far as attacking some officers. This aggressive behavior extended to fellow prisoners. Some were quick to lash out with a stream of profanity or to throw a punch or to knife inmates whenever they felt infringed upon. These direct confrontations with staff or fellow prisoners were perceived as futile and ceased after a few months duration and endless days in the "hole;" most began to tone down their behavior.

An alternative to acting up is to turn the aggression inward. In confinement, several men turned to suicide as a mechanism to deal with their despondency over having a life-threatening illness and the stigma associated with it. As one prisoner related:

> When I first found out, I was in Auburn. I thought that I took the wrong diagnosis. I heard the news from the doctor that I will die in three months from this disease. I got a rope and I was going to hang it up to the corner of my cell and hang myself. I told a CO [i.e., correctional officer] that I was going to hang myself. I told him that I had this problem. He saw me trying to throw the rope up to a part of the ceiling that I could then hang myself from. He got the other CO and they stopped me. They asked me why did I do it? I wanted to die before I got really sick from this problem.

Suicide attempts assumed the form of wrist slashing with a crude, handmade knife or inept jobs of hanging. Two men attempted suicide more than once but provided no other management problems to the staff. The suicide attempts, however, stopped within two months following diagnosis.

Another form of directing the aggression towards oneself is self-mutilation or what the prisoners term "cutting." Two inmates with histories of "cutting" themselves, escalated this practice following their diagnosis. Both men reported feelings of demoralization, anger and social abandonment. Their behavior persisted throughout their incarceration.

## IMPLICATIONS OF ACTING UP

There are some benefits to "acting up" following the diagnosis of HIV infection. Escalation of fast living, drug use and criminal activities leave little time for focusing on the constant threat of imminent death and the regular use of drugs medicates their anxieties. On the other hand, attempting suicide or self-mutilation can compel others to take notice and do something to help. One prisoner ended up in the psychiatric unit and received treatment; others were placed in the protective custody unit which provided a less threatening environment in which to spend time. None, however, received counseling about the disease.

Acting verbally and physically in an aggressive manner reinforces the prisoners' perceptions that they are still "tough" and strong "macho" men. By acting in this manner, they can deny the stigma of the illness and anxieties about their loss of manliness. By exaggerating their "toughness" and "machoism," they can hide the illness from themselves.

This strategy is not as effective as the prisoners anticipate. As long as they employ this strategy, they risk the progression of the disease. Initially, they are willing to risk death for they believe they are already dead. In some respects, this strategy brings them closer to the death they previously flirted with during their involvement in drugs and crime. At best, the prisoners are able to achieve a momentary attenuation of the fears and anxieties they found most difficult to handle. Linked to this, however, is a sense of inevitability about their getting into trouble with the "law" and this undermines the effectiveness of the "acting up" strategy they adopted.

## GOING PUBLIC: AFFIRMATION

Whenever others are aware that a prisoner is infected, an open-awareness context is established (Glaser and Strauss 1965). Following a diagnosis of HIV/AIDS, 16 African-American and Latino prisoners at the medium security prison and seven African-American and Latino prisoners at the maximum security prisons reported that they have opted for full disclosure. Only two Latino prisoners opted to disclose when they were on the streets.

Affirmation is the technique used by these prisoners. Most choose to directly attack the roots of the stigma. The decision to "go public" about their illness is not an easy one. Nevertheless, most do choose to reveal their condition. When the men made their disclosures, they usually provided cues as to how others could continue to relate to them as "normal" prisoners. As one prisoner with HIV reported:

> Once I was afflicted, I was afraid that they'd change towards me. Me being a barber. I had to touch them. I thought, "There goes my career." We did a seminar — that is John, José, and Manuel and I. We put it out there. This is what we have. I sorta hoped that some of them would back away. I'm overly generous. I give them anything they want if I have it. If someone is hungry, I give food. If someone wants cigarettes, I give. I'm always giving. I'm too nice. At the end of my speech, I told them that I have a problem. I even told them that I hoped that it would push some of them away because I gave them too much. No one moved away. No minute change in their behavior. They still ask me for things. They still come to get their hair cut. A guy named Tito, he called me over and said, "I heard you have HIV. Shit, I don't give a damn what you have." We're friends and there's no change in anything. People here end up defending us. They know that this thing is not caught casually.

Affirmation can bring relief to those who participate in disclosure. Full disclosure means moving out of secrecy and discarding the mask which burdens them. In most cases the prisoners reported few instances in which they experienced rejection, abandonment or hostile responses from those with whom they had developed friendships or acquaintanceships or from most family members. In many cases, family members and their friends already suspected and subsequently were relieved to discover their suspicions were well-founded. "Going public" also can relieve others of the burden of maintaining "the secret."

A few prisoners broke the secret at public meetings of the prison population during educational sessions about HIV/AIDS. Most prisoners, however, simply stated privately to their friends that they had HIV/AIDS. Others presented the information through bravado. They put on what amounts to a show to convince others that they were, in fact, still functioning and worthwhile human beings. A few prisoners had no choice but to go "public," such as those in the AIDS ward of city hospitals and of maximum and medium security prisons.

## IMPLICATIONS OF AFFIRMATION

According to the men, going public often brings with it rewards which outweigh the costs. Self-disclosure may win emotional support from others and promote adaptive coping.

Affirmation also appears to be associated with a more positive adjustment. Prisoners who affirm their diagnosis are more likely to report less emotional and physical distress than prisoners who have withheld this information from others. As a consequence of affirmation, they are more likely to associate with other persons with the disease and in some cases, to act in an altruistic manner toward the infected. This form of interaction reduces the prisoners' feelings of degradation and shame. Another benefit which is derived from affirmation is the freedom to take advantage of the treatment and medication offered in prison infirmaries and to arrange for AIDS counseling, if available. In this sense, affirmation can directly influence a prisoner's health, longevity and sense of well-being.

Also beneficial is contact with others who are coping with a similar life crisis. A final advantage is that many prisoners benefit by reaching the stage of acceptance (Sandstrom 1990). By accepting, prisoners experience an identity shift; they identify with their HIV/AIDS status. Prisoners learn to accept the limitations HIV/AIDS imposes on them and the life-threatening aspects of the disease. They come to realize they can still manage their lives by reacting to the disease with more reason than emotion.

## GETTING ARRESTED

Arrest came as no surprise to the prisoners coping with a diagnosis of HIV infection by "passing" or "acting up" on the streets. Although they anticipated their arrest, they faced it with mixed emotions. Incarceration can precipitate feelings of anger, resentment, remorse, depression and despair. At the same time, some of these prisoners welcomed incarceration with a sense of relief.

The prisoners' accounts explained the reasons for feelings of relief. In most cases the relief was based on the expectation that prison would be able to control their behavior which they believed had become uncontrollable and threatening to their well-being. Most anticipated that prison would break the cycle of fast living, alcohol and drug abuse and criminality.

As noted earlier, when on the streets, the lives of these prisoners could be characterized as uncertain, chaotic and dangerous. Many of these men could no longer deal with their illness, their lives or their habits. All were painfully aware that they are courting death by their risky behavior. Consequently, prison was a relief from the burdens of street life.

For some men, especially those in medium security prisons, daily life in prison is easier, less frustrating and more secure than life on the streets. Prison provides housing which is often far better than the homeless shelters where some prisoners had been living. It furnishes three meals a day, accessible medical care for prisoners with HIV/AIDS and clean clothes. Prison can be a more stable place to live because the factors which contribute to drug use and criminal behavior are tightly controlled (Fleisher 1989). Incarceration, especially in the medium security prison, not only grants many prisoners time to handle their drug habits but also to get a grip on dealing with their HIV infection. As one man said:

> They say that I have the virus... I cannot tell how long I had it. I could have had it for 15 years. But coming to jail has saved me. I'm living a normal lifestyle here. Before I detoured away from this lifestyle. I was not going to work, I was partying, doing drugs and having sex. Like I'd pick up a girl and I would not know anything about her. Jail might save you. Like from killing someone. It saves you because it gives you rest, proper sleep, proper exercise. I'm up in the mountains and I get the proper air. You get into the norms of society. Outside you fall off the system.

Another prisoner reported:

> If I had stayed in the street, I'd be dead. I picked up a gun that day. I then got my check and four weeks later I went through $467 dollars. I did not pay rent or food. I used this money for crack, coke and alcohol. I got the gun and I stuck up dealers for drugs in Washington Heights. I did it before. I got into a fight on the train and I got arrested. It's more than a coincidence God prevented me from hurting anyone or myself. I was just out of control. I could have gotten my head blown off.

## CONCLUSIONS

Previous studies have shown, after a diagnosis of HIV infection, persons with HIV/AIDS experience uncertainty based on fears of death and dying, fears of debilitation and death without dignity, and fears of social abandonment. This study-in-progress suggests these fears may have an even greater impact on prisoners with HIV/AIDS than on other infected populations. African-American and Latino prisoners must cope not only with the stigma of being an HIV/AIDS sufferer but with additional stigmas — the stigma of being an intravenous drug user, a prisoner and a person of color. The ways in which these prisoners cope, however, differs based on where they learned they contracted the virus. Some heard the "news" while on the street; others were told they were HIV positive while incarcerated within the New York State prison system.

Following a diagnosis of HIV infection, the prisoners employed some form of accommodative mechanism which would ameliorate the uncertainties of their situation. It is important to note that the prisoners' most common form of accommodation was to insulate themselves from anticipated rejection by others and at the same time to deny the presence of a life-threatening disease. Both strategies, "passing" and self-insulation, allowed them to continue participating in the normal round of life. Other prisoners resisted the illness by "acting up." By escalating their drug consumption, criminal and fast-living activities and their intransigent and suicidal behavior, they "cover up" their stigmatized status. By making their appearance and lifestyles even more exaggeratedly deviant, they hope to effectively conceal their diagnosis from family members, associates and even themselves. The prisoners actively stave off labeling themselves as "prisoners with HIV/AIDS." They have a stake in maintaining their identities as "normal" in order to sustain their relations with others and to reinforce their own notions that they are "ordinary" prisoners.

Prisoners who affirm their status derive a sense of normalcy as well as the means to gain the emotional and medical support they need. Prisoners with HIV/AIDS who "pass," isolate themselves or "act out," experience greater distress and depression than those who affirm their illness.

It should be noted that in a qualitative study of this kind, where random sampling methods are not used, the question of the generalizability of the findings arises. This study-in-progress is exploring coping in only 60 African-American and Latino men with HIV/AIDS self-selecting themselves to participate in this study. Given that participation is voluntary, the study population underrepresents those prisoners having failed to utilize the prison medical facilities. Thus, these same prisoners perhaps are employing some coping strategies not mentioned here. However, as a preliminary exploration, the information presented here provides some important clues as to how prisoners cope with a diagnosis of HIV/AIDS.

The findings presented here further suggest that a diagnosis of HIV infection does not necessarily deter intravenous drug users from behavior that can exacerbate the progression of the illness. There is some tentative evidence among those infected with HIV that there is increased morbidity associated with needle use and drug consumption (Friedman et al. 1986).

A striking feature of the prisoners' accounts is the difference among forms "acting up" assumes on the streets and within the prison systems. The streets provide more choices of accommodative strategies than the prison system. As a "total institution," with its extreme regimentation and security measures, the prison severely curtails opportunities to choose a drug and criminal oriented fast-living lifestyle. Within these constraints, prisoners are more likely to cope with a diagnosis of HIV/AIDS by denying its existence and by keeping busy through participation in the normal rounds of life. These activities inadvertently promote a healthy style of living which is sadly lacking when the men are on the streets.

The current literature provides some clues as to possible forms of accommodation employed by intravenous drug users during times of crisis. A number of investigators observed a strong connection between intravenous drug use and criminal activity. The frequency of crime increases as the intensity of drug abuse increases. Heroin users commit two to six times as many crimes when they use drugs daily compared to when they use drugs less frequently (Ball et al. 1982; Johnson et al. 1985; Speckart and Anglin 1986). Crack users appear to commit amounts of crime at least equal to heroin users and tend to have higher rates of robbery, violent crimes and sexual offenses (Goldstein et al. 1989; Goldstein et al. 1990; Johnson et al. 1990). Others note that intravenous drug users are more likely to escalate their drug use and criminal activities when confronted with stress-provoking events (Khantzian et al. 1974; McCoy and Khoury 1990). A few observers suggest escalation of drug consumption and criminal deeds may occur after drug abusers receive a diagnosis of AIDS. It is suggested that drug abusers are resentful young men, already with little to lose, who may see their life chances as further diminished. Therefore, their motives for violence may increase (Berk 1990). AIDS and street crime may have a reciprocal relationship.

These findings elaborate upon the drug-crime nexus in the broader context of the drug abuser career. According to prisoners' accounts, following a diagnosis of HIV infection, the spiraling effects of some prisoners' drug use appear to cause an increase in criminal behavior. The relationship of drug use and criminal behavior appears to be more complex than previous research has indicated. It is significant that a diagnosis of HIV can precipitate a series of behaviors simultaneously, i.e.

fast living, drug consumption and criminal activities. These findings suggest that a simple cause-and-effect sequence does not fully capture the complexities of the drug-crime connection following diagnoses of HIV infections.

This paper has viewed African-American and Latino prisoners with HIV/AIDS through their accounts. These accounts confirm the literature's view of prisoners as passively and helplessly enduring their stigmatized and degraded status. But there is some evidence suggesting that prisoners actively manipulate their stigmatized status while attempting to establish "normalcy" for themselves. Often they are unable to reach this goal.

Further work is needed on the kinds of strategies employed by prisoners to cope with a diagnosis of HIV/AIDS infection. The present article suggests there is a variety of such strategies. This variety is a reminder that more research should be done to capture the full range of these coping strategies.

## REFERENCES

Ball, J.C., L. Rosen, J.A. Flueck and D.N. Nurco. 1982. "Lifetime Criminality of Heroin Addicts in the United States." *Journal of Drug Issues* 3:225-239.

Batchelor W.F. 1984. "AIDS: A Public Health and Psychological Emergency." *American Psychologist* 39:1279-1284.

Batki, S., J.L. Sorensen, B. Faltz, S. Madover. 1988. "Psychiatric Aspects of Treatment of IV Drug Abusers with AIDS." *Hospital and Community Psychiatry* 39:439-441.

Baxter, S. 1991. "AIDS Education in the Jail Setting." *Crime and Delinquency* 37:48-63.

Berk, R.A. 1990. "Drug Use, Prostitution and the Prevalence of AIDS." *The Journal of Sex Research* 27:607-621.

Christ, G.H. and L.S. Wiener. 1985. "Psychosocial Issues in AIDS." In *AIDS: Etiology, Diagnosis, Treatment and Prevention,* edited by V.T. DeVita, S. Hellman and S.A. Rosenberg. New York: J.B. Lippincott.

Charmaz, K. 1983. "The Grounded Theory Method: An Explication and Interpretation." In *Contemporary Field Research: A Collection of Readings,* edited by R. M. Emerson. Boston: Little, Brown and Company.

Clemmer, D. 1958. *The Prison Community.* New York: Holt, Rinehart, and Winston. (Originally published in 1940).

Coates, T.J., L. Temoshok and J. Mandel. 1984. "Psychosocial Research is Essential to Understanding and Treating AIDS." *American Psychologist* 39:1309-1314.

Corless, I.B. and M. Pittman-Lindeman. 1988. *AIDS: Principals, Practices, and Politics.* Washington: Hemisphere Publishing.

Des Jarlais, D.C., M.E. Chamberland, S.R. Yancovitz, P. Weinberg and S.R. Friedman. 1984. "Heterosexual Partners: A Large Risk Group for AIDS." *Lancet* 8415:1346-1347.

Des Jarlais, D.C. and S.R. Friedman. 1987. "HIV Infection Among Intravenous Drug Users: Epidemiology and Risk Reductions." *AIDS: International Bimonthly Journal* 1:67-76.

_____. 1988. "The Psychology of Preventing AIDS Among Intravenous Drug Users." *American Psychologist* 43:865-870.

Fishman, L.T. 1990. *Women at the Wall: A Study of Prisoners' Wives Doing Time on the Outside.* Albany, NY: State University of New York Press.

Fleisher, M. 1989. *Warehousing Violence.* Newbury Park, CA: Sage Publications, Inc.

Foster, Z. 1988. "The Treatment of People with AIDS: Psychosocial Consideration." In *AIDS,* edited by Corless and Pittman. Washington: Hemisphere Publishing.

Friedman, S.R., D.C. Des Jarlais and J.L. Sotheran. 1986. "AIDS Health Education for Intravenous Drug Users." *Health Education Quarterly* 13:383-393.

Glaser, B.G. and A.L. Strauss. 1965. *Awareness of Dying.* Chicago: Aldine.

_____. 1967. *The Discovery of Grounded Theory: Strategies for Qualitative Research.* Chicago: Aldine.

Goffman, E. 1961. *Asylums: Essays on the Social Situation of Mental Patients and Other Inmates.* Garden City, NY: Doubleday.

_____. 1963. *Stigma: Notes on the Management of Spoiled Identity.* Englewood Cliffs, NJ: Prentice-Hall.

Goldstein, P.J., H.H. Brownstein, P.J. Ryan and P.A. Bellucci. 1989. "Crack and Homicide in New York City, 1988: A Conceptually-Based Event Analysis." *Contemporary Drug Problems* 16:651-687.

Goodstein, L., D.L. MacKenzie and R.L. Shotland. 1984. "Personal Control and Inmate Adjustment to Prison." *Criminology* 22:343-369.

Hammett, T.M. 1987. *AIDS in Correctional Facilities: Issues and Options* (2nd ed.). Washington, DC: National Institute of Justice.

Holland, J.C. and S. Tross. 1985. "The Psychosocial and Neuropsychiatric Sequelae of the Acquired Immunodeficiency Syndrome and Related Disorders." *Annals of Internal Medicine* 103:760-764.

Hopp, J. and E. Rogers. 1989. *AIDS and the Allied Health Professions.* Philadelphia: F.A. Davis Company.

Irwin, J. 1970. *The Felon.* Englewood Cliffs, NJ: Prentice-Hall.

Johnson, B., P.J. Goldstein, E. Preble, J. Schmeidler, D.S. Lipton, B. Spunt and T. Miller. 1985. *Taking Care of Business: The Economics of Crime by Heroin Abusers,* Lexington, MA: Lexington Books.

Johnson, B.D., T. Williams, K.A. Dei and H. Sanabria. 1990. "Drug Abuse in the Inner City: Impact on Hard-Drug Users and the Community." In *Drugs and Crime,* edited by M. Tonry and J.Q. Wilson. Chicago: University of Chicago Press.

Joseph, J.G., C.A. Emmons, R.C. Kessler, C.B. Wortman, K. O'Brien, W.T. Hocker and C. Schaefer. 1984. "Coping with AIDS: An Approach to Psychosocial Assessment." *American Psychologist* 39:1297-1302.

Joseph, J.G., S.B. Montgomery, C.A. Emmons, J.P. Kirscht, R.C. Kessler, D.G. Ostrow, C.B. Wortman, K. O'Brien, M. Eller and S. Eshleman. 1987. "Perceived Risk of AIDS: Assessing the Behavioral and Psychosocial Consequences in a Cohort of Gay Men." *Journal of Applied Social Psychology* 17:231-250.

Kelly, J.A. and J.S. St. Lawrence. 1988. *The AIDS Health Crisis: Psychological and Social Interventions.* New York: Plenum Press.

Khantzian, E.J., J. Mack and A. Schatzberg. 1974. "Heroin Use as an Attempt to Cope: Clinical Observations." *American Journal of Psychiatry* 131:160-164.

Kowalewski, M.R. 1988. "Double Stigma and Boundary Maintenance: How Gay Men Deal With AIDS." *Journal of Contemporary Ethnography* 17:211-228.

Magura, S., A. Rosenblum and H. Joseph. 1991. "Aids Risk Among Intravenous Drug-Using Offenders." *Crime and Delinquency* 37:86-100.

McCoy, C.B. and E. Khoury. 1990. "Drug Use and the Risk of AIDS." *American Behavioral Scientist* 33:419-431.

Morin, S.F. and W.F. Batchelor. 1984. "Responding to the Psychological Crisis of AIDS." *Public Health Reports* 99:4-9.

Namir, S., D.L. Wolcott, F.I. Fawzy and M.J. Alumbaugh. 1987. "Coping with AIDS: Psychological and Health Implications." *Journal of Applied Social Psychology* 17:309-328.

Oliver, W. 1989. "Black Males and Social Problems: Prevention Through Afrocentric Socialization." *Journal of Black Studies* 20:15-39.

Potler, C. 1988. *AIDS in Prison: A Crisis in New York State Corrections.* New York: The Correctional Association of New York.

Rogers, M.F. and W.W. Williams. 1987. "AIDS in Blacks and Hispanics: Implications for Prevention." *Issues in Science and Technology* 89-94.

Rubinow, D.R. and R.T. Joffe. 1987. "Psychiatric and Psychosocial Aspects of AIDS." In *AIDS: Modern Concepts and Therapeutic Challenges*, edited by S. Broder. New York: Marcel Dekker, Inc.

Sandstrom, K.L. 1990. "Confronting Deadly Disease: The Drama of Identity Construction Among Gay Men with AIDS." *Journal of Contemporary Ethnography* 19:271-294.

Shaw, L.L. 1991. "Stigma and the Moral Careers of Ex-Mental Patients Living in Board and Care." *Journal of Contemporary Ethnography* 20:285-305.

Speckart, G. and M.D. Anglin. 1986. "Narcotics Use and Crime: A Causal Modeling Approach." *Journal of Quantitative Criminology* 2:3-28.

Sykes, G. 1966. *The Society of Captives.* New York: Atheneum.

Sykes, G.M. and S.L. Messinger. 1960. "The Inmate Social System." In *Theoretical Studies in the Social Organization of the Prison,* edited by R. Cloward. New York: Social Science Research Council.

Thomas, C.W. 1977. "Theoretical Perspectives on Prisonization: A Comparison of the Importation and Deprivation Models." *Journal of Criminal Law and Criminology* 68:135-145.

Toch, H. 1977. *Living in Prison: The Ecology of Survival.* New York: Free Press.

Weitz, R. 1989. "Uncertainty and the Lives of Persons with AIDS." *Journal of Health and Social Behavior* 30:270-281.

_____. 1991. *Life with AIDS.* New Brunswick, NJ: Rutgers University Press.

Wheeler, S. 1961. "Socialization in Correctional Communities." *American Sociological Review* 26:696-712.

Zich, J. and L. Temoshok. 1987. "Perceptions of Social Support in Men with AIDS and ARC: Relationships with Distress and Hardiness." *Journal of Applied Social Psychology* 17:193-215.

# A BROKEN CONTRACT: ARGUMENTS AGAINST THE DEATH PENALTY

*Charles R. See is associate director of the Lutheran Metropolitan Ministry Association and executive director of the Community Re-Entry Program in Cleveland. He was appointed by Ohio's Governor to serve on Ohio's Select Committee on Prisons. See also serves on Ohio's State Sentencing Committee.*

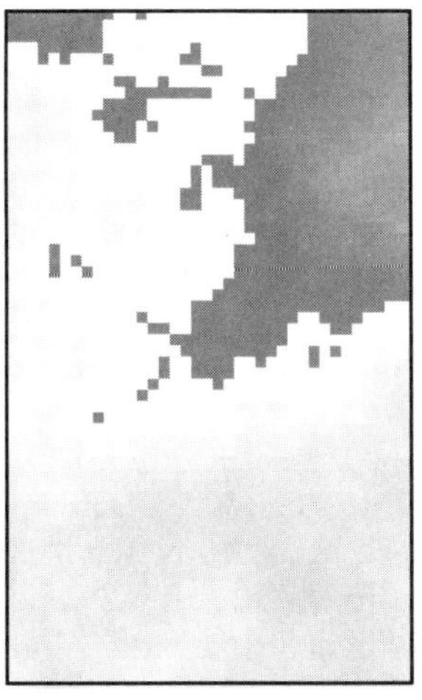

Thirty-six states authorize use of the death penalty. Thousands of offenders wait on death row for their turn to die by lethal injection, hanging, electrocution, firing squad or gas. Nearly half of these offenders are African-American (American Correctional Association 1993). Most suffer from the "poverty deprivation syndrome."

Calls for expansion of the use of the death penalty are heard across this nation. But first we must consider whether its use it just. Clearly, premediated murders and other capital crimes are among this nation's most devastating occurrences. The painful effects of these crimes are far reaching - touching the victim, his family, and their neighborhood. Americans have a right to expect their governments to take steps protecting them from such heinous acts. However, their governments must take only those steps that are just.

To reach a just decision, courts consider the offense and the offender. Mitigating and aggravating factors are reviewed. When considering the offender, courts frequently assume he is a self-willed, self-reliant, and self-directing individual consciously choosing among his many options the path leading him to commit a capital offense. And, when they decide in favor of the death penalty, they conclude the offender is an "evil" person having made a "bad" choice and deserving to die. The short-coming of this type of analysis is the failure to consider the context in which the offender acted. But the context must be considered before a just decision can be reached. And, when examining the context, imposition of the death penalty cannot be just.

## A MORAL CONTRACT

Beccaria (1963), writing in the late 1700s in Europe, was concerned with the administration of justice. He introduced the concept of open and fair trials, trials by juries, and punishment commensurate with the offense. Beccaria (1963) believed "Punishments that exceed what is necessary for the protection of the deposit of public security are by their very nature unjust" (p.13).

Beccaria opposed the death penalty for several reasons. He saw it as "the war of a nation against a citizen." He believed its ability to deter future crimes was questionable. He also thought the death penalty did not make sense. Beccaria (1963) states:

> [It is] absurd that the laws, which are an expression of the public will, which detest and punish public homicide, should themselves commit it, and that to deter citizens from murder, they order a public one. (p. 50)

And Beccaria (1963) opposed the death penalty because it is inconsistent with his social contract theory.

Essentially, Beccaria argues that there is a social contract wherein every member of the society transfers a piece of his freedom or a part of his rights to the government so that the government can govern and protect all members from the transgressions of others. But this social contract does not include the transfer to the government of the right to take one's life. Beccaria's social contract theory is intriguing. In my view, however, a moral contract is in place.

Each time a child is born, a moral contract commences between that child and the social institutions charged with the responsibility of providing him the necessary supports, resources, and instructions to become a healthy and productive member of those social institutions in particular and of society in general. The child is charged with the responsibility of learning the ways of these social institutions and abiding by their rules. The child also is expected to develop his own personal gifts and talents and use them to improve society.

There are four social institutions having responsibility to fulfill their part of this moral contract with each child. They are family, school, neighborhood, and church. These four institutions constitute the major source of supports, resources, and instructions for a child. It is from these sources that a child learns who he is, where he is from, what is expected of him, what he should aspire to accomplish in life, how he should treat others, his worth or value to himself and others, and what becomes of him after he dies.

At the beginning of his life, the child is totally dependent on these social institutions to discharge their part of the moral contract. To the degree these institutions fail, then to the extent the child will reflect that failure. These early patterns of failure, on the part of social institutions, will persist throughout the child's lifetime. However, intervening measures providing supports, resources and instructions for positive self-development may help reverse the negative impacts of these early patterns of failure.

In my view, these early patterns of failure are most noticiably seen in what I call the "poverty deprivation syndrome." This syndrome is a perpetual impoverished set of conditions grossly lacking in positive supports, adequate resources, and clear instructions. This syndrome is a living nightmare wherein small children are left to find their own way. Instead of finding social institutions readily providing supports, resources and clear instructions, small children find broken, bruised, deprived, hurting, hostile, and struggling collections of individuals consumed by the agony associated with their own existence.

It is within this context that most offenders committing capital crimes are socialized. But this context seldom is appreciated by courts considering the fate of the offender convicted of a capital offense.

**FAMILY**

The family of each child has an obligation to provide an environment wherein the child is loved, nurtured, guided, protected, and instructed. However, when that family suffers from the poverty deprivation syndrome, it is ill-equipped to provide the child the necessary experiences for positive self-development. It cannot properly socialize the child because it is dysfunctional. Parenting skills are lacking. Untreated substance abuse is present. Psychological, physical or sexual abuse are daily occurrences. Adequate food is absent - weeks may pass before a single meal containing the "minimum daily requirements" is eaten. Clothing and furnishings are sparse. Living spaces are crowded, cramped and unclean. And basic health care is a wish.

When the child discovers that his extended family members also suffer from the syndrome, his association with these family members serves to reinforce and encourage the internalization of negative concepts. The negative behavior of extended family members assures this child that their negative behavior, as well as his, are appropriate and acceptable.

A family suffering from the syndrome places its child at risk. During his most crucial formative years, the child constantly receives from his family images and sounds of brokeness, despair, failure, helplessness, hopelessness, and limitation. The child ages without the benefit of wise hands to guide and oversee his development. It is in this dysfunctional family that the child initially learns and practices the behavior he later exhibits in the classrooms of his school and on the streets of his neighborhood. In this family is where the child first learns indifference toward himself and others. And it is here that he initially learns violence.

## SCHOOL

The child, having learned the lessons taught by his dysfunctional family, encounters school at an age where it can make a significant difference in his life. School usually is this child's first interaction with a major social institution outside his family.

Schools are charged with the responsibility of educating the child and preparing him to participate in society as a law-abiding and productive adult. But the schools attended by the child living with families suffering from the poverty deprivation syndrome are less than adequate for these tasks because they too suffer from the syndrome. These schools simply are not able to prepare this child to compete in a highly complex society. According to Kozol (1991):

> Denial of "the means of competition" is perhaps the single most consistent outcome of the education offered to poor children in the schools of our large cities." (p. 83)

The schools attended by the syndrome-affected child are dysfunctional because they lack adequate supports, resources and instructions to do their jobs. They are under-funded, under-staffed, and under-supported by the general public. They are not equal to those schools attended by the affluent. According to Kozol (1991), the inequality stems from the currently popular conception of attaining equality in public education. He states:

> The notion of a "minimum" (rather than a "full") foundation represents a very special definition of the idea of equality. It guarantees that every child has "an equal minimum" but not that every child has the same. (p. 208)

These schools are packed with hundreds of children from families suffering from the syndrome. Thus, the schools must contend with numerous negative interactions among students, faculty, and staff. Classrooms, hallways, and lunchrooms are unsafe because of armed and unarmed confrontations. And even though these physically and emotionally bruised and battered children initially arrive at school with the same enthusiasm and intelligence as their affluent counterparts, by the fifth grade the school's inability to honor its part of the moral contract is reflected in the students' behavior. Students' best efforts at positive matriculation are thwarted by teachers having low expectations of them and by the violence surrounding them.

These schools more nearly resemble local reservations where babysitting takes place than public centers for learning and adult preparation. Rather than embracing the syndrome-affected children, these schools frequently treat them in a hostile fashion, labelling them delinquent rather than acknowledging that their behavior is learned. The syndrome-affected children receive no respect from the school. Thus, having received no respect at home or school, they have no respect for the people and property at school. School officials quickly reciprocate - no respect given equals no respect received. The circle of human degradation continues, with the syndrome-affected children receiving the message "You ain't worth much."

These children eventually learn that they are not part of the school's social fabric. Their grades, negative experiences with teachers, unrealized aspirations, unsuccessful attempts to be heard and understood, and failure to obtain needed supports, resources and clear instructions all combine to build their suspicions and rob them of hope. Other syndrome-affected children are in the same leaky boat. Together they find companionship and comfort. They form supportive alliances, which further reinforce negative images and behavior.

Although some of these double-syndrome-affected children muddle through to graduation from high school, more frequently than not they are unable to compete. The schools, like the family, have failed them.

## NEIGHBORHOOD

The neighborhood should provide a wholesome and nuturing environment for its resident children. But the neighborhood in which the poverty deprivation syndrome child resides also suffers from the syndrome. It is filled with brokeness, despair and violence. On the streets children see old dilapidated houses, run down cars, people lying in doorways, prostitutes, and drug dealers. On any given day, children witness a robbery of a starter jacket or fancy gym shoes, a violent argument between neighbors, a pimp beating a prostitute, or gang members shooting at each other. Adults even prey on these children, asking them for sexual favors or to serve as a drug courier. And when these children earn enough money, they buy small guns.

These children do not expect anyone to rescue them from the brokeness and despair. The family, schools, and friends all reinforce negative concepts. And they do not expect the police to protect them from the violence plaguing their neighborhood because the police too are violent.

There are traditional youth-oriented organizations available to provide services to the triple-syndrome-affected children. But these organizations, citing fear of crime or lack of funds to pay staff, close their doors before or shortly after dark.

Facing these and other closed doors, the triple-syndrome-affected children turn to and rely on other similarly situated children. Together, they interpret life and attempt to survive using the lessons learned from family and school and neighbors.

## CHURCH

Churches are an immensely important part of every neighborhood, including those suffering from the poverty deprivation syndrome. Their teachings and work positively touch the lives of many. But churches have not been successful in reaching the syndrome-affected children. Churches have failed to help these children understand and internalize the value of human life, as well as the abstract concepts of brotherly love, charity, faith, forgiveness, and hope. The syndrome-affected children then face a hostile and confusing world without a relationship with a God who is all powerful. Thus, these children are unable to draw on their spiritual resources because they have not been tutored regarding them.

Churches, once thought to be the keeper of the moral fabric of the neighborhood, have insulated themselves from many of the problems experienced by the poverty deprivation syndrome children. Churches frequently do not go seeking these children. And the children do not realize there is help in the church. Facing despair, hopelessness, and continual violence, these children lack even a spiritual base to undergird them or to help them establish a positive direction in their lives.

## EFFECTS OF FAILURES

By the time the poverty deprivation syndrome-affected child reaches age 10, he has learned well the lessons taught at home, in school, and on the streets of his neighborhood. He uses this information, gained from thousands of negative experiences with dysfunctional environments, to survive. His behavioral options and choices are determined by his experiences.

Thus, the child has fulfilled his part of the moral contract. He was charged with the responsibility of learning the ways of the socializing institutions in his environment. This he has done by becoming like those he sees in his environment. The fact that he commits a capital crime should surprise no one. As Susan Goodwillie (1993) explains:

> Everywhere, it seems, children are beset by violence - at home, at school, in their neighborhoods, among their peers, on TV, in the movies, wherever they go. Violence has become an everyday fact of life. ... No wonder our youth are filled with rage and anger and unfilled dreams, alienated from their parents, from one another, from us all. Their voices tell of horror beyond imagining. (p. xi)

Although the family, school, neighborhood, and church have failed to honor the moral contract for poverty deprivation syndrome children, society is quick to condemn these children. Their indictment should read:

> You did willfully and knowingly be born into poverty. You did conspire to have dysfunctional parents. With malice and forethought you did undermine the effectiveness of your schools. With cunning and gile you did under-fund the housing authority where you reside. You did with purpose and intent allow yourself to be hungry and cold and sexually abused and physically battered. And on one day in your struggle to survive, in the midst of the confusion you know life to be, you did commit a capital offense. We a jury of your "peers," although not having suffered any of these hardships, do hereby find you guilty without mitigation and do sentence you to die by the hands of the state. Next case please.

## CONCLUSION

America must do better by its poor than to reserve the death penalty for them when they fail. Their failure is due to a broken moral contract - one which was broken long before they were able to make choices. It is unjust that the contract has been broken. But it is more unjust that the poor be put to death.

**REFERENCES**

American Correctional Association. 1993. *Directory*. Laurel, MD: Author.

Beccaria, C. 1963. *On Crimes and Punishments*. New York: Bobbs-Merrill.

Kozol, J. 1991. *Savage Inequalities: Children in America's Schools*. New York: Crown Publishers.

Goodwillie, S. (editor). 1993. *Children's Express Voices from the Future: Our Children Tell Us About Violence in America*. New York: Crown Publishers.

# REDUCING THE INVOLVEMENT OF AFRICAN AMERICAN MALES IN THE CRIMINAL JUSTICE SYSTEM

*Elsie Scott is the deputy commissioner of training for the New York City Police Department. Scott received her doctorate degree in political science from Atlanta University.*

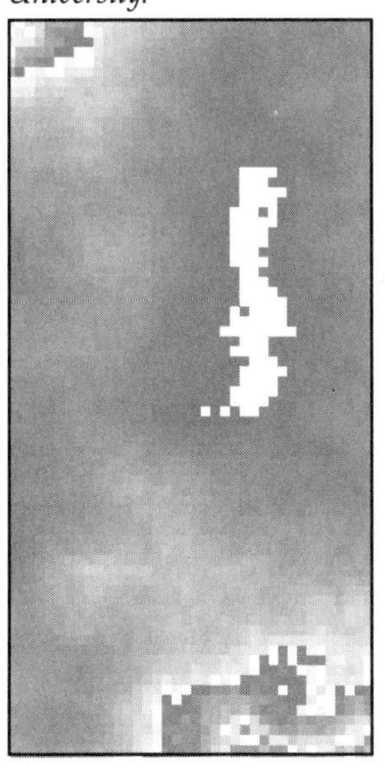

## INTRODUCTION

In recent years, policy-makers, practitioners and activists have devoted much attention to the plight of the African American male. This attention has come about, in part, due to studies showing African American males are lagging behind other race/sex groups in a number of areas, including health, employment, and higher education. One particular area of concern is the disproportionate representation of African American males in the criminal justice system.

Some of the grim statistics of the overrepresentation of African American males as victims, offenders and suspects are well-known, such as:

- African American males make up 46 percent of the male prison population.
- African American males have about a 1 in 30 lifetime chance of becoming a victim of homicide.
- During the period from 1977-1990, 39 percent of the persons legally executed in the United States were African American males.

Less well-known are preventive strategies to reduce the involvement of African American males in the criminal justice system.

It is ironic that the overrepresentation of African American males is viewed by many as a "black problem," yet the lives of all Americans are impacted by this problem. Tax dollars are being used to install metal detectors in schools; merchants are passing on increased insurance costs to consumers; and families of incarcerated males are being forced on welfare rolls. In addition, the costs of administering the criminal justice system are skyrocketing at a time when local, state and federal budgets are equally strapped for funds. Clearly, there is, at the very least, a need to develop viable alternatives to the criminal justice system for African American males.

In the preparation of this article, a number of persons were asked to give their ideas on alternatives to the criminal justice system for African American males. Most of the recommendations made were in the category of alternatives to incarceration, e.g., home incarceration bracelets and community service programs. The focus of this article is much broader than alternatives to incarceration. It is the premise of the author that a review of factors outside the criminal justice system is necessary for an understanding of why African American males are overrepresented. And an understanding of the reasons for the overrepresentation is necessary before solutions can be developed.

This article is designed to present a number of recommended policies and actions that can be implemented by governmental agencies, private industry, community and national organizations, and individuals to reduce the involvement of African American males in the criminal justice system, both as victims and offenders. The first section of the article provides an overview of the nature of the problem. In the second section, some of the issues related to race and crime are reviewed. The final section is devoted to recommended policies and actions.

## NATURE OF THE PROBLEM

African American males are disproportionately arrested and incarcerated in the United States. National arrests statistics are not broken down by race and sex, but available statistics do show that African Americans make up approximately 30 percent of all arrests. This is considerably greater than the percent of African Americans in the population—12 percent.

Incarceration statistics for 1988 show that African American males made up 46 percent of the male prison population and 37 percent of the total jail population. The Sentencing Project found that on any given day, one in four African American men in the age group 20-29 is on probation, in jail or prison, or on parole (Mauer 1990). A study of Washington, D.C. residents found that 42 percent of the African American males from 18 to 35 were involved in the criminal justice system—in jail or prison, on probation or parole (Miller 1992). On the other hand, only 19.6 percent of African American men in the age group 18-24 are enrolled in college (Nelson 1991).

The FBI maintains records on murders and non-negligent manslaughters by race and sex of offender and victim, but it does not maintain race and sex data on other types of offenses. The 1990 report shows that 54 percent of the male homicide victims were African American (FBI 1991). In 1990 the homicide rate for young African American males was 84.7 per 100,000 compared to 11.0 for Caucasian males (Centers for Disease Control 1990). Homicide is now the leading cause of death for young African American males but only the fourth leading cause of death for young Caucasian males.

The involvement of African American males in the criminal justice system is costly for the African American community and for society at large. In addition to the costs associated with the loss of lives and property, there are costs such as those associated with the incarceration of heads of households. It was estimated in 1988 it cost close to $17,000 per year to keep a male incarcerated (Corrections Yearbook 1989), considerably more than the estimated $4,000 per year to educate a child. The incarceration costs are now estimated to be from $20,000 to $35,000 per inmate per year. The cost of incarceration is increased when families of incarcerated men are forced on public assistance.

African American households tend to experience greater financial losses from victimizations, including burglaries, larcenies and motor vehicle thefts (Bureau of Justice Statistics 1984). African American victims are more likely to incur injuries that require hospital care than Caucasian victims, and their victimization is more likely to result in more than one day lost from work (Bureau of Justice Statistics 1992).

The costs extend beyond monetary costs, as residents of many predominantly African American communities are forced to change their lifestyles due to fear of victimization. Businesses are more reluctant to invest in African American communities because of high insurance rates and fear of victimization. Residents are forced to seek employment in other neighborhoods due to the small number of jobs available in their communities. In addition, the extensive involvement of African American males in the criminal justice system has an impact on the African American family as many children grow up without fathers, and females cannot find husbands. One-in-four African American females will never marry (in part due to the incarceration and early death of eligible males) compared to one in ten white females (Lyons 1993).

## RACE AND CRIME

Why is a disproportionate number of African American males involved in the criminal justice system? Are African American males more criminally inclined? Can the disproportionality be accounted for solely by racial discrimination?

There is no agreement concerning what causes crime or what is the relationship between race and crime. Some of the earlier explanations used biological factors to explain the criminal behavior of African Americans (Lombroso 1911). In recent years, there has been less discussion of the biological theories, but some prominent researchers, such as James Q. Wilson (1983), have tried to discredit explanations that focus on the root causes of crime. These researchers believe discrimination and racism are no longer dominant.

Some authors argue that African American criminality is due in part to violence in the United States. Silberman (1978) explains:

> A propensity to violence was not part of the cultural baggage black Americans carried with them from Africa; the homicide rate in black Africa is about the same as in western Europe. (p. 123)

Violence is a characteristically American phenomenon that has its roots in the very foundation of this country (Brown 1979). The American connection is best captured in the phrase popularized by H. Rap Brown, "violence is as American as apple pie."

The theory that the greater involvement of African American males in the criminal justice system can be explained by race discrimination alone has not been supported by much of the research. Studies have shown that leniency is often shown to African Americans who commit crimes against other African Americans (Baldus et al. 1983). Nevertheless, some studies have shown that racial bias is a variable in explaining disproportional involvement. For example, Frazier and Hernetta (1980) conclude that:

> race bias may be passed on subtly through recommendations for sentence as well as through formal decisions such as arrest charges, bail dispositions, charges on an indictment, or the charges finally accepted in guilty pleas.

More recently, an analysis of drug arrest statistics led to accusations of disparate treatment of African Americans. The *USA TODAY* (1993) found that African Americans made up 42 percent of the arrests on drug charges—an increase from 40 percent in 1988 and 30 percent in 1984.

The subculture of violence theory popularized by Wolfgang (1967) has been criticized by many scholars as an inadequate explanation of African American criminal behavior. Harvey (1986), for example, has coined the concept, the subculture of exasperation. He theorizes that homicidal acts are caused by systemic factors such as high unemployment, low status, and substandard living conditions, and emotional factors such as frustration, anger, and powerlessness.

Other authors, such as Silberman (1978), have associated machismo and violence by African American males. He explains how the "bad nigger" myth as portrayed through "Blackploitation" movies and stories told in gatherings of African American males helped African American males to cope with oppression through fictitious violence against white people. The hero of these movies and stories was always an African American man who conquered women and used violence to prove his "manhood." Silverman argues that the "bad nigger" stories lost their appeal as other methods, such as heroin usage and muggings and robberies, were found to provide more "action."

Some African American psychologists and psychiatrists have used psychological concepts to explain the overrepresentation of African Americans in crime statistics. Terms such as self-hatred and rage have been used to explain why African Americans, especially African American males, commit crime. The term "black rage" was popularized by Grier and Cobbs (1968). They explored the emotional conflicts of African American males in America. The self-hatred concept is based on the premise that years of subhuman treatment by whites and years of living in a world in which "good" is defined in white terms and "bad" in black terms, leads to hatred of one's self and others who are similar in color. Poussaint (1983) criticizes the concept of self-hatred because it seems to blame the victim. Yet, Poussaint found it to be useful in trying to explain the murder of African Americans by African Americans.

## POLICY IMPLICATIONS AND RECOMMENDATIONS

There are no quick fix policies and programs that will address the problem of overrepresentation of African American males in the criminal justice system. Governmental responses primarily have been politically attractive actions, such as legislation increasing criminal penalties ("lock 'em up and throw away the key") and additional appropriations for prison construction. Governmental responses also have taken on racial overtones, such as use of an African American male named Willie Horton during the 1988 Presidential campaign as the symbol of what is wrong with the criminal justice system.

Outlined below are recommendations for addressing the problem of the overrepresentation of African American males in the criminal justice system. The author does not claim the list is exhaustive, rather the list is designed to provide discussion and policy development.

### Education

One of the most important tools for preventing involvement in the criminal justice system is results-oriented educational programs. Persons committing violent crime are overwhelmingly persons who are minimally educated. The Task Force on Juvenile Delinquency (1967) found that boys who failed in school were almost seven times as likely to be delinquent than those not failing.

A number of education-related factors may help to account for greater involvement of African American boys in delinquency. Kunjufu (1984) identified several education-related factors that help to destroy African American boys at an early age: a relative absence of African American male elementary school teachers; a "racist/irrelevant curriculum designed to maintain the status quo;" and the lack of quality and continuity of the teaching staff. These factors, coupled with a high dropout rate and a tracking system that places a disproportionate number of African American boys in the non-college tract and in the special education section, help make many of these boys prime candidates for the criminal justice system. After observing a school in East Brooklyn, New York, Logan (1986) found that strong administrative leadership, high expectations, strict discipline and a committed staff resulted in high achievement for African American students.

The primary education policy for the country should focus on strong educational programs that encourage students to have high expectations and to believe in themselves, while simultaneously providing them with the requisite skills to become productive citizens. Emphasis should be placed on preventing students from dropping out and on recruiting and retaining teachers who not only care about the future of their students, but also understand the needs of African American male students.

**Recommendations:**

- Every school should adopt an anti-dropout policy. Counseling should be provided to persons at-risk of dropping out, and alternative educational programs that will keep them in school or offer the opportunity for a GED should be available. Adequate funds should be given to predominantly African American schools, and those maintaining a low dropout rate should receive special recognition.

- Literacy programs should be available in every low-income African American neighborhood. National and community organizations can provide volunteer services in areas where public funds are not available.

- Alternative or supplementary educational programs should be developed by the African American community to instill cultural identity and a sense of morality. In addition to promoting culture and values, these programs should provide tutoring in academic subjects.

- African American churches, associations and organizations should embrace and promote education. Educational Olympics should be planned to give educational achievement a greater status in African American communities, such as the NAACP's ACT-SO competition.

- Educational policies that mandate expulsion of students and provide no alternative education programs should be eliminated.

- Educational institutions should establish counseling support groups that are charged with monitoring African American males. The focus should be on identifying economic problems, academic difficulties and possible disciplinary problems before they are manifested. The support groups also should develop a resource bank of role models available to regularly interact with students in the schools and in community settings.

- Civic associations and professional organizations should set up educational programs in the criminal justice process and criminal law to familiarize young African American males with their legal rights and ways to avoid confrontations with law enforcement officers.

- Parents should monitor the educational activity of their sons. They should visit their children's school at least once a semester to check on the quality of instruction, progress of the student, and related matters. They should question and challenge the rationale and procedures before allowing their children to be placed in special education classes. Parents should be required to visit schools to register their children and pick up report cards.

- Methods should be instituted to recruit and retain highly skilled, culturally sensitive, and committed teachers in predominantly African American schools.

- Students should be provided with a safe place in which to learn.

- Nonviolent conflict resolution should be a required course in every school.

- Anti-drug programs should be designed with messages that appeal to African American males living in high-risk communities. Politicians, athletes, and entertainers who have not abused drugs should be included in anti-drug programs. African American youth need to see role models who have made it without abusing drugs. The continual parade of former abusers gives the message that you can use drugs and still make it.

- Legislative support for maintaining Head Start programs should be continued and expanded.

- Every prison inmate without a high school diploma or GED should be required to pursue the requisite course of study to obtain such education prior to release.

- Uniforms have been used by some schools to remove the pressure of clothes competition from students. This concept should be adopted by more schools.

- Scholarships, loans and other forms of aid specifically for racial minorities should be maintained and restored to the pre-Reagan administration level. Businesses should also be encouraged to support educational opportunities for inner-city youth.

- African and African American history should be incorporated into public school curricula so non-African Americans can have an understanding of the contributions made by African Americans. It also would serve as positive cultural reinforcements for African American males.

**Employment**

African Americans are three times as likely as Caucasians to live below the poverty line, and over one-third of African Americans are poverty-stricken. The unemployment rate for African Americans is twice as high as it is for Caucasians. High unemployment is a particular characteristic of young African American males who live in urban areas. Even the future outlook for African American males is grim because many businesses are downsizing.

Some studies have shown a relationship between high unemployment and crime. Ehrlich (1973), using cross-sectional data on crime, income levels and unemployment, concludes that a one percent increase in unemployment results in a 5.7 percent increase in murder. Calvin (1981), focusing specifically on African American youth, concluded that there was an extremely strong association between unemployment and street crime. Myers (1983) found that higher wages for released repeat property offenders had a strong and deterrent effect on crime. Noting that African American former inmates face increasingly dismal employment opportunities, he suggested that manpower policies be expanded in African American communities.

The primary employment policy for the country should emphasize full employment and the elimination of racial discrimination in employment. There is evidence that racial discrimination still exists in the job market. For example, a study by the Urban Institute found that companies in Chicago and Washington, D.C. treated African American applicants less favorably than white applicants 20 percent of the time (*The Seattle Times* 1991). The authors of the study concluded that job discrimination experienced by African American men could prevent access to or discourage many from entering the job market.

**Recommendations:**

- State and federal governments should develop comprehensive job training programs. These programs should train in relevant job skills for current and future job requirements. The training should provide basic skills necessary for effective job searching, such as interview techniques, resume preparation and test taking.

- Local and state governments and African American businesses and organizations should develop adult and youth learning and job training centers to prepare African American males for jobs. These centers should instill the work ethic in young males. Businesses should be provided with tax incentives to encourage them to provide training.

- Jobs for ex-inmates should be a priority. Jobs will help reintegrate ex-inmates, and instill self-esteem and personal pride.

- Affirmative action should be maintained as a policy. Job discrimination still exists, and affirmative action programs have been effective avenues for opening doors of employment to African Americans.

- The present welfare system should be revised so that it fosters independence and stable families. Welfare recipients should be provided with meaningful job training and jobs after training.

- African American organizations, such as police organizations, should provide tutorial programs to help African American males prepare for specialized jobs.

- The Federal Job Corps should be expanded to include more African American inner-city males.

**Gun Control**

Increasingly, guns are being used in homicides, assaults and robberies (Uniform Crime Reports 1991). Firearms are the weapons of choice in many homicides because they are easy to use and to conceal after the crime. Some argue that the availability of handguns contributes to an increase in robberies. As guns become more readily available, and the firepower gets quicker and more devastating, there is a greater need for effective gun control.

African American males are more likely to be victims of gun-related violence than white males. More than half of the African American homicide victims are killed with a handgun compared to a little more than 40 percent of white homicide victims (Center for Disease Control 1986). The rate of suicides and homicides with guns is five per 100,000 for white suburban school age children, but it is 28 per 100,000 for inner city youth (Fingerhut et al. 1992). In addition, a U.S. Department of Justice study found that about a fourth of all violent crimes committed against African American males were committed with the use of a handgun. This compares to one-eleventh of crimes committed against white males (Rand 1990).

As the number of African Americans who are victimized by firearms-related violence has increased, verbal support for gun control from African Americans has increased. Support for gun control is evident from a recent New York Times/CBS poll which showed that the majority of Americans would favor a seven-day waiting period for the purchase of a handgun, and 41 percent would favor a ban on the sale of handguns except those issued by law enforcement officers (*New York Times* 1993). African American ministers and school children have lobbied Congress for passage of gun control legislation, such as the Brady Bill which calls for a five-day waiting period for the purchase of a handgun. The Brady Bill was recently passed. Gone are the days when Congressman John Conyers (D-MI) was almost a lone African American voice urging Congressional support for gun control. Many African Americans have finally realized that more handguns are being used in "brother" against "brother" incidents than are being used to fight the "revolution" against white America.

Law-abiding citizens maintain that they keep handguns to protect themselves from criminals. Yet, few of these persons even use their guns for self-protection. According to Lee Brown (1988, p.112), research indicates that a firearm in the home is six times more likely to be used in the fatal shooting of a family member than the shooting of a potential burglar or other intruder.

The National Commission on the Causes and Prevention of Violence (1969) noted that the "culture's casual attitude toward firearms" was partially responsible for this country's failure to adopt effective national firearms policies (p. 180). Many of the recommendations made by the Commission can be reintroduced. They probably will receive a serious review and analysis because polls are showing the public is becoming more supportive of certain forms of gun control, especially waiting periods, controls of assault weapons, and limits on juvenile possession.

**Recommendations:**

- Federal legislation should be passed that requires the registration of all handguns, periodic inspections of gun dealers, a waiting period for the purchase of a firearm, and increased penalties for illegal handgun possession and use.

- Federal legislation should be introduced that prohibits the purchase of more than one gun per month. Similar legislation has been enacted in Virginia and South Carolina.

- The number of federal gun inspectors should be increased. The Bureau of Alcohol, Tobacco and Firearms has 13 percent fewer field inspectors than it had a decade ago, yet the number of licensed gun dealers has increased by 59 percent.

- Federal legislation should be passed that bans the import, manufacture, sale and use of semi-automatic and assault weapons.

- Restrictive licensing should be required for all firearms. Citizens should be required to demonstrate an affirmative need to own the firearm and the ability to safely use and store firearms.

- African American organizations and all levels of government should launch a massive anti-handgun use public education campaign. The anti-smoking and anti-drunk driving campaigns have shown that education can be effective in changing public opinion concerning destructive behavior.

- Legislation is needed that would establish stronger guidelines for licensing gun dealers. Dealers should be prohibited from selling guns from their homes. Dealers should be required to report the loss or theft of weapons to the Bureau of Alcohol, Tobacco and Firearms. The provisions of the Gun Control Act of 1968 should be restored. Record keeping violations by dealers should be felonies, and inspectors should be allowed to inspect gun dealers more than once a year.

**Criminal Justice System**

African American males are disproportionately affected by the criminal justice system. Recommendations have been offered that may help to prevent African American males from becoming crime victims or subjects of the criminal justice system. These recommendations primarily have been aimed at institutions or agencies that are not a part of the criminal justice system. The following list is but a few of the actions that should be taken by criminal justice officials.

**Recommendations:**

- Law enforcement agencies should adopt a deadly force policy that only allows the use of deadly force in defense of life. This policy would not allow the shooting of a fleeing felon.

- Law enforcement training should include instructions in African American culture. Officers should be sensitive to the unique concerns of African American males.

- Police recruitment programs should target African American males. Test taking classes should be offered to improve the ability of African American males to score high on police entrance examinations. These entrance exams should be job relevant.

- Youth diversion programs should be expanded to allow the participation of African American males who are first offenders.

- Summer youth programs that take African American males away from high crime areas should be financed by local governments. These programs can be administered by criminal justice officials in conjunction with African American religious or professional organizations.

- Community mediation boards should be established or expanded to help resolve some neighborhood disputes and minor crimes without the intervention of the criminal justice system.

- Alternatives to incarceration should be expanded for nonviolent, first-time offenders. Increased use of such programs as job training and community service would not only help to alleviate prison and jail overcrowding but could also help provide essential city services.

- Federal drug enforcement legislation should be reviewed for its adverse impact on African Americans. The legislation has resulted in the arrest and incarceration of many low-level dealers and users for long periods of time, while many of the real drug "kingpins" who are responsible for the importation of drugs into the country are never caught and incarcerated.

## SUMMARY AND CONCLUSIONS

This article has provided an overview of the problem of the involvement of African American males in the criminal justice system along with recommendations for change. Although a number of recommendations have been presented, the discussion and list of recommendations are not exhaustive.

There is a need for more research by African American scholars on the distinctive causes of criminal behavior on the part of African American males. Not only should the research studies compare and contrast African American males and Caucasian males, it should compare and contrast African American males and African American females. There also is a need for comparative research contrasting black criminality in the United States with black criminality in countries such as Canada and Great Britain.

The study of African American criminal behavior should focus attention on the larger issue of violence in the United States. There is a need for more research on the driving forces of American violence. International studies could provide new insights and enhance our understanding of violence's prevalence in this country.

A major contribution to our knowledge base on crime can be made by research concerning the effect of racial discrimination on the disproportionate involvement of African American males in the criminal justice system. Many Caucasian researchers start from the premise that racial discrimination is not a factor, and their research is reflective of that premise. There has not been enough original research conducted by African American scholars, in part, because research grants have not been provided. There is a need for African American scholars to continue and expand their research and for them to cite research findings from other African Americans in their writings and to use publications by African Americans in their teachings.

Finally, African American scholars must join forces with other members of the African American family to aggressively attack the problem of African American male involvement in crime. The continual arrest, detention, killing and demoralizing of African American males by the criminal justice system and related systems are robbing the African American community of some of its good minds and potential leaders. An African American "think tank" could provide factual data and research documentation needed to capture the attention of policy makers in this country.

## REFERENCES

Baldus, D. C., C. Pulzaski, and G. Woodworth. 1983. "Comparative Review of Death Sentences." *Journal of Criminal Law and Criminology* 4:661-753.

Brown, R. M. 1979. "Historical Patterns of American Violence." In *Violence in America: Historical and Comparative Perspectives,* edited by H. D. Graham and T. R. Gurr. Beverly Hills: Sage Publications.

Brown, L. P. 1988. "Crime in the Black Community." In *The State of Black America,* 1988. New York: National Urban League, Inc.

Bureau of Justice Statistics. 1984. *Criminal Victimization, 1983.* Washington, DC: U.S. Department of Justice, Office of Justice Programs.

_______. 1992. *Criminal Victimization in the United States, 1991.* Washington, DC: U.S. Department of Justice, Office of Justice Programs.

Centers for Disease Control. 1990. "Homicide Among Young Black Males—United States, 1978-1987." *Morbidity and Mortality Weekly Report* 39:869-873.

_______. 1986. *Homicide Surveillance: High-Risk Racial Group—Blacks and Hispanics, 1970-83.* Atlanta: U.S. Department of Health and Human Services, Public Health Service.

*Corrections Yearbook. 1989.* Washington, DC: U.S. Government Printing Office.

Criminal Justice Subcommittee of the Governor's Advisory Committee for Black Affairs. 1987. *Crime and the Black Community: An Assessment of the Impact of Selected Criminal Justice Issues in New York State.*

Currie, E. 1985. *Confronting Crime.* New York: Pantheon Books.

Davis, R. and D. F. Hawkins. 1986. "Homicide Prevention Within the Black Community: Public Health and Criminal Justice Concerns." In *Homicide Among Black Americans,* edited by D.F. Hawkins. Lanham, MD: University Press of America.

Ehrlich, I. 1973. "Participation in Illegitimate Activities: A Theoretical and Empirical Investigation." *Journal of Political Economy* 81:521-566.

Federal Bureau of Investigation. 1991. *Uniform Crime Reports.* Washington, D.C.: U.S. Government Printing Office.

*Final Report on Crime and the Black Community: Causes, Effects and Remedial Approaches - A National Conference.* 1986. Washington, DC: National Organization of Black Law Enforcement Executives.

Fingerhut, L. A., D.D. Ingram, & J.J. Feldman. 1992. "Firearm and Nonfirearm Homicide Among Persons 15 Through 19 Years of Age." *Journal of the American Medical Association* 267:3048-3053.

Gibbs, J. T. (ed.). 1988. *Young, Black and Male in America: An Endangered Species.* Dover, MA: Auburn House Publishing Co.

Grier, W. H. and P. M. Cobb. 1968. *Black Rage.* New York: Basic Books.

Harvey, W. B. 1986. "Homicide Among Young Black Adults: Life in the Subculture of Exasperation." In *Homicide Among Black Americans,* edited by D.F. Hawkins. Lanham, MD: University Press of America.

Hirschi, T. 1969. *Causes of Delinquency.* Berkeley: University of California Press.

Jaynes, G. D. and R.M. Williams (eds.) 1989. *A Common Destiny: Blacks and American Society.* Washington, D.C.: National Academy Press.

Kunjufu, J. 1984. *Countering the Conspiracy to Destroy Black Boys.* Chicago: Afro-Am Publishing Co.

Logan, H. 1986. "Blacks Helping Blacks: Either You're Part of the Solution or You're Part of the Problem." *The Washington Post,* November.

Lombroso, C. 1911. "Crime, Its Causes and Remedies." *Criminology, Law Enforcement and Social Problems.* Ser. No. 14.

Lyons, D. C. 1993. "Why Some Younger Men Prefer Older Women." *Ebony* 48: 30-34.

Mauer, M. 1990. *Young Black Men and the Criminal Justice System: A Growing National Problem.* Washington, DC: The Sentencing Project.

Miller, J. 1992. *Hobbling a Generation: Young African American Males in Washington, DC's Criminal Justice System.* Washington, D.C.: National Center on Institutions and Alternatives.

Myers, S. 1983. "Estimating the Economic Model of Crime: Employment Versus Punishment Effects." *Quarterly Journal of Economics* 48:157-166.

Nelson, J. 1991. Racist or Realistic? *USA Weekend,* May 17-19.

*New York Times,* August 15, 1993.

Poussaint, A. F. 1983. "Black-on-Black Homicide: A Psychological-Political Perspective." *Victimology* 8:161-169.

Rand, M. R. 1990. *Handgun Crime Victims*. Washington, D.C.: U.S. Department of Justice, Bureau of Justice Statistics.

Rose, H. M. and D. R. Deskins. 1986. "Handguns and Homicide in Urban Black Communities." In *Homicide Among Black Americans,* edited by D.F. Hawkins. Lanham, MD: University Press of America.

*Seattle Times,* May 16, 1991.

Silberman, C. E. 1978. *Criminal Violence, Criminal Justice.* New York: Random House.

*Task Force Report: Juvenile Delinquency.* 1967. Washington, D.C.: U.S. Department of Justice.

*USA Today,* July 23, 1993.

Wilson, J. Q. 1983. *Thinking About Crime.* New York: Basic Books.

Zimring, F. E. 1985. "Violence and Firearms Policy." In *American Violence and Public Policy,* edited by L.A. Curtis. New Haven: Yale University Press.

# PREVENTING CRIME THROUGH ECONOMIC DEVELOPMENT OF URBAN NEIGHBORHOODS

*Anne Thomas Sulton is an attorney. Much of her law practice is in the area of small business consulting and litigation. Sulton also is a criminologist, specializing in crime prevention. She regularly writes editorial columns for newspapers. She received a law degree from the University of Wisconsin in Madison and a doctorate degree in criminology and criminal justice from the University of Maryland in College Park.*

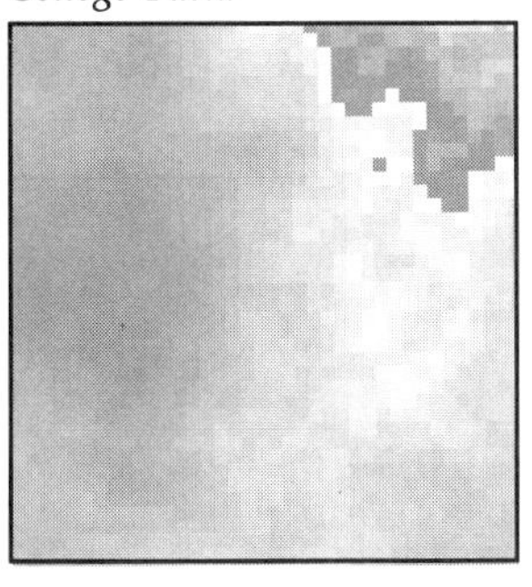

## CRIME, CAUSES AND CONTROL

According to the Uniform Crime Reports, 114,121 persons reportedly were murdered in the United States during the past five years. Since 1988, almost 72 million Americans reported to police they were victims of crime, with nearly nine million reporting victimization of violent crimes (Federal Bureau of Investigation 1989, 1990, 1991, 1992, 1993).

Although the Uniform Crime Report data are useful, they are incomplete. The data offer only a partial picture of America's crime problem because some citizens are reluctant to report some crimes to police and some police agencies choose not to particpate in the reporting project (Federal Bureau of Investigation 1993).

To construct a reasonably accurate picture of the amount of crime, other sources of crime-related data also should be reviewed. The Bureau of Justice Statistics National Crime Victimization Surveys are an important source. The Surveys indicate that far larger numbers of crimes than those reported to police actually occur. According to these Surveys, "In 1990, 24% of U.S. households were victimized by a rape, robbery, assault, theft, burglary, or motor vehicle theft" (Rand 1991).

Although we do not know how many crimes occur, we do know that most crimes are not cleared by an arrest. According to the Federal Bureau of Investigation (1993), only 21 percent of crimes were cleared by an arrest in 1992. Because we do not know how many crimes occur and most reported crimes are not cleared by an arrest, in most cases we are not cognizant of the demographic or other characteristics of those individuals committing crimes. In other words, most of the time we do not know who the criminal offenders are.

Consequently, the picture of "the criminal offender" is shaped by the faces of those being incarcerated in prisons. Most of those incarcerated are people of color, with African-Americans being in the majority in many prisons. Nearly all of those incarcerated are poor. However, one errs when concluding that crime is a non-white or a poor problem.

We also do not know what causes people to commit crime. Since the turn of this century, literally millions of pages in thousands of books and journals have been published on the causes of crime. Thousands of criminologists have advanced scores of theories.

Some of these theories claim that crime is caused by biological or psychological maladies, some type of social pathology, social disorganization, overcrowding in urban areas, unequal or differential opportunities for success, poverty, or unemployment (Lombroso 1911; Park 1921; Merton 1938; Sutherland 1947; Sheldon et al. 1949; Lemert 1951; Ohlin and Cloward 1969; Reckless 1972; Silberman 1978). More recently, blame for crime has been placed upon single-parent families or hand gun availability.

But these theories are flawed. Crime is a legally-defined phenomenon, and as such, there are many contexts in which the same or similar behavior is not considered criminal. Crimes are committed by the affluent. And most poor and unemployed people are law-abiding. Meltzer (1990) explains:

> Of course poverty does not inevitably cause criminal conduct. In most poor neighborhoods the great majority of citizens are law-abiding. Like anyone else, they want to enjoy a decent quality of life, they want peace and security. (p. 150)

Furthermore, millions of children are being raised in single-parent families and they are not engaging in criminal conduct. And while it is wise to place ownership and use restrictions on all firearms and ammunition, there is little evidence to suggest that hand guns "cause" crime.

The most obvious flaw in many crime causation theories is their failure to acknowledge that "crime" is an inappropriate dependent variable. In other words, identifying "crime" as that variable to be explained by selected independent variables is of little or no practical value.

First, even the most rigorous empirical studies are able to explain only a small portion of the variance in their elaborate equations by examining, individually or jointly, the independent variables. In other words, most of the time researchers cannot explain what caused crime. Predictably, most researchers conclude their reports by calling for additional studies.

Second, the variable "crime" has no intrinsic or inherent meaning. "Crime" simply is a term or label used to denote an entire class of socially unacceptable behaviors, specificially those behaviors found so offensive that criminal sanctions are provided through a political process involving debate, negotiation, and ultimately compromise. The conception of what "crime" is changes from time to time, with more behaviors being included with each new legislative session. Thus, employing "crime" as a dependent variable in a crime causation equation is unsound because it fails to differentiate or distinguish between or among very different types of behaviors.

Also, many of the selected independent variables are difficult to define, resist quantification, and, therefore, are not amenable to statistical analysis. For example, many crime causation theories propose that crime is caused by poverty. Before a researcher can quantify poverty, he must define it. Is poverty a function of one's personal income? If yes, how is personal income being defined? If personal income is defined as earned income, should the researcher consider income earned only through lawful means? Or is poverty a mindset or an attitude? If yes, then poverty may be an unsubstantiated belief or it may be acceptance of the reality that one is trapped in the economic underclass or is permanently relegated to a ranking high on the misery index.

Because researchers frequently disagree about how the "same" variable should be defined, definitions vary from study to study. These definitional disagreements and quantification difficulties often serve to confuse rather than to enhance our understanding of the causes of crime. This does not mean that a search for the causes of crime is an unworthy or futile endeavor. But it does encourage a sincere and honest reassessment of what is an appropriate starting point for discussions concerning crime control.

Efforts to control crime are hampered by our current inability to accurately count crime and to empirically identify the causes of crime. Thus, our ability to intelligently fashion rational and effective crime control strategies is quite limited.

Most researchers readily admit that more information is needed before firm conclusions can be reached. Their calls for additional research usually are sincere. But criminal justice practitioners, appointed government officials, and elected politicians seldom acknowledge that there is insufficient information to support currently fashionable crime control strategies. These participants loudly proclaim that more law enforcement is the best approach. But the benefits of this approach are difficult to find.

The "more law enforcement" approach has resulted in a stunning increase in the number of dollars spent to operate criminal justice agencies. For example, in 1980, this nation was spending approximately $4 billion to operate prisons. By 1988, it was spending about $10 billion. For fiscal year 1993, it was spending nearly $20 billion (American Correctional Association 1980, 1988, 1993). In 1990, the total spent to operate all criminal justice agencies exceeded $74 billion (National Institute of Justice 1992).

We also know that the "more law enforcement" approach has dramatically increased the number of persons having contact with these agencies. In 1980, about 300,000 people were incarcerated in prisons; in 1992, nearly 900,000 were incarcerated (American Correctional Association 1993).

And we know that this approach has not reduced the number of crimes committed. In 1988, 13,923,100 crimes were reported to police; in 1992, 14,438,191 crimes were reported to police (Federal Bureau of Investigation 1989, 1993).

Obviously, the "more law enforcement" approach is very expensive. And it apparently is not providing satisfactory results.

While researchers busy themselves searching for elusive answers to crime causation questions, politicians earmark billions of dollars to temporarily banish offenders from society. And the numbers of youngsters being identified by their parents in morgues across the country continue to climb.

Perhaps the right question is not what causes crime, or how many police are needed to suppress crime and apprehend offenders, or how much punishment is enough to deter crime. The most useful question may be: "What can we do to prevent crime?"

## CRIME PREVENTION

Crime prevention is not increasing police patrols of inner-city neighborhoods. Police patrol assignments are reactions to perceived currently occurring crime problems or are responses to calls for assistance, many of which are reports of criminal victimizations. Crime prevention is not expanding the penalties available for violations of criminal laws. Sentences are imposed after conviction for crimes, which already have occurred. Crime prevention is not building more prisons. Punishment by confinement in a prison cannot be crime prevention because confinement occurs after sentencing, which occurs after conviction, which occurs after the commission of a crime. In other words, crime prevention precedes the involvement of criminal justice agencies in the personal affairs of private citizens.

According to Lejins (1965), crime prevention involves "measures which are taken before a delinquent or criminal act has actually been committed and which are intended for the purpose of forestalling such acts." Lejins (1965) explains that there are three categories of prevention: mechanical prevention (which places obstacles in the way of potential offenders so that it becomes difficult or impossible for them to commit the act); punitive prevention (which forestalls crime and delinquency by the threat of punishment); and corrective prevention (which aims to eliminate the causes of criminal and delinquent behavior). Lejins (1983) maintains that discussions about crime prevention must begin with an identification of the type of prevention under consideration.

Crime prevention has a long history in this country. By the late 1970s, hundreds of millions of dollars had been spent by government agencies and private philanthropists to fund thousands of crime prevention programs (Krajack 1979). Although no firm dollar figure can be identified on the basis of currently available data, one reasonably can assume that more money has been spent since then.

Many of these programs define crime prevention as the "anticipation, recognition, and analysis of a crime risk, and the initiation of some action to remove or reduce it" (National Crime Prevention Institute 1978). Although this definition does not specify a mechanical prevention approach, many groups using this definition assume that crime can be controlled by placing obstacles in the way of potential offenders. Thus, their focus is on installing bigger locks and brighter lights, designing crime-resistant buildings and physical environments, establishing neighborhood blockwatches, increasing police surveillance, providing elderly escort services, loaning property engraving tools, improving police-community relations, and supporting police leadership or control of neighborhood-specific or community-wide crime prevention activities (National Advisory Commission on Criminal Justice Standards and Goals 1973; Law Enforcement Assistance Administration 1979; Sorrentino 1979; McPherson and Silloway 1981; Sulton 1989; Tucker and Starnes 1993).

Mechanical prevention measures, particularly blockwatch programs, have been and continue to be very popular. However, because reported crime rates consistently are high, the emphasis has shifted toward adoption of punitive measures. During the last decade, legislators, at the behest of their constituents, have increased the penalties available for commission of numerous crimes, particularly drug-related offenses. Legislators also have approved plans authorizing transfer of juveniles, age 14 and older, from the rehabilitation-oriented juvenile justice system to the punishment-oriented adult criminal justice system. And more prisons are being built to accommodate the inevitable increases in the numbers of persons sentenced under these statutes. But the threat of punishment apparently has not deterred those hundreds of new offenders being incarcerated each week.

There is little evidence to support the notion that placing obstacles in the way of potential offenders and threatening harsher penalties have controlled crime. The questionable benefits accruing under the very expensive mechanical and punitive approaches encourage some observers to suggest serious consideration of corrective prevention measures. A growing segment of the population is calling for an approach that potentially can eliminate the causes of crime. Even small children are questioning the wisdom of spending more money to build prisons than their schools.

These calls for corrective preventive programs are not new. In 1973, the National Advisory Commission on Criminal Justice Standards and Goals recommended identifying and eliminating the causes of crime. It stated: "crime prevention initially requires an attack on those conditions in society that contribute to or support crime" (p. 3). And, at the 1987 National Symposium on Community Institutions and Inner-City Crime, hundreds of citizens from across the nation called for investment in programs that eliminate the causes of crime, including those that economically develop impoverished neighborhoods (Sulton, 1989).

Interest in corrective measures has intensified. Many citizens are demanding establishment of programs that help students improve their scores on academic achievement tests, that provide safe and productive after-school environments for "latch key kids," that offer wholesome recreational opportunities for teenagers, and that provide employment training and job opportunities for teenagers and young adults. Some funds are being provided to support these ideas. But the corrective prevention approach still is not being extensively employed.

Reluctance to invest adequate funds to establish corrective prevention programs may be due to lack of supporting data. Rigorous empirical evaluations of this approach's efficacy rarely have been completed. Answers to questions concerning the potential effectiveness of the corrective prevention approach also are elusive, in part, because of theoretical limitations.

## TOWARD A NEW CRIME PREVENTION THEORY

According to Lejins (1965), corrective prevention aims to eliminate the causes of criminal and delinquent behavior. But how do we eliminate the causes when we do not know what they are? Using the best of existing theory, it initially appears that we may have reached an impasse. The dilemma with which we are faced may require the extension or expansion of Lejins's theory, or the development of a new crime prevention theory.

A hopeful sign can be found in the psychology literature. Coie et al. (1993) suggest the creation of a "prevention science" that seeks to prevent major human dysfunctions and to eliminate the causes of disorder. They contend that increasing "protective factors may be the strategy of choice," particularly where risk factors, such as dysfunctional parenting or extreme poverty, are difficult to identify or to eliminate.

This idea may have applications for crime prevention. For 25 years, the House of Umoja Boystown in Philadelphia has operated on a number of assumptions, including that when approaching the gang problem it is better to start by providing protection from harmful influences than to start by eliminating these influences (Sulton 1989, p.17). The House of Umoja Boystown is widely recognized as one of the most successful gang violence prevention programs.

Coie et al. (1993) also indicate that prevention science should search for and examine positive attributes in highly stressful environments. They argue that research projects should be designed to determine why some "people, who, in spite of exposure to major stressors, survive or thrive in their development."

For decades, Robert Woodson, of the National Center for Neighborhood Enterprise, has advocated the need to study and learn from "living models of success." He constantly reminds his audiences that more can be learned by studying the successes of inner-city residents than can be learned by focusing on their failures. Woodson (1993) supports his arguments by noting the accomplishments of community-based organizations, accomplishments that are amazing given the enormous challenges faced by these organizations.

Perhaps the most encouraging part of Coie et al.'s (1993) proposal is the suggestion that it may be possible to prevent crime without knowing what causes individuals to engage in conduct which violates criminal statutes. They argue:

> Theoretically guided prevention trials can simultaneously test the efficacy of interventions and provide answers to questions about etiology. Thus, if a specific risk factor is reduced or eliminated by an intervention but the pathogenic process is not altered, that risk factor would no longer be considered a causal factor but might be viewed simply as a marker of dysfunctional development.

Thus, it may be possible to identify a factor believed to be causally related to a specific type of criminal behavior and to develop a program providing protection from that factor or to eliminate that factor. If the targeted behavior continues after protection is provided or the factor is eliminated, then the factor would be extracted from the crime causation equation.

This approach differs from much of the criminological crime causation research. Criminologists frequently review crime-related data, such as the Uniform Crime Reports or prison population data, and then attempt to explain crime by referring to the demographic characteristics of those identified as offenders. Because poor non-white males are more frequently arrested and incarcerated than rich white females, crime causation theories often argue that poverty and crime are related, that race and crime are related, and that gender and crime are related. Completely ignored are the following: 1) the data reviewed is incomplete; 2) it is scientifically unsound to design theories around existing data, particularly when that data has been collected for other purposes; and 3) prison data does not provide an accurate picture of the entire offender population.

The Coie et al. (1993) proposal provides an exciting way of thinking about crime prevention theory and research. Their proposal is a useful starting point for the refinement of crime prevention theory because it permits consideration of a corrective prevention approach without initially requiring precision concerning the causes of crime.

However, the Coie et al. (1993) proposal may be inappropriate for crime prevention theory and research because it does not take into account the fact that crime is a legally-defined phenomenon. This proposal also may be of limited utility because it might not be capable of accurately identifying or measuring the effects of an enormous volume of dynamic and simultaneously-operating individual and institutional level variables. Whether this task can be accomplished by behavioral or social scientists remains unclear. But it is clear that until theory and research are refined the answers to many crime control questions will not be found.

Lejins's crime prevention theory, particularly the corrective prevention aspect, is a good starting point for discussions of crime control. Elimination of those factors causing crime is the best way of controlling crime. Thus, a corrective prevention approach should prove to be the least expensive and should provide the most satisfactory results.

In my view, however, before we can conclude that corrective prevention programs are effective crime control tools, the corrective prevention aspect of Lejins's crime prevention theory should be expanded to incorporate the following assumptions.

1. Programs respecting the inherent dignity and worth of every person, regardless of the value of his contributions to society or the nature of his interactions with other persons, will be more effective in providing protection from the causes of crime or eliminating the causes of crime than those programs which de-humanize or disrespect persons. An effective crime control measure must have a moral basis. Programs demonstrating respect for all persons and advocating that all persons have value will be more successful in preventing crime than programs demonstrating contempt for certain persons and advocating that some persons are disposable.

2. Programs acknowledging that crime is a legally-defined phenomenon will be more effective in providing protection from the causes of crime or eliminating the causes of crime than programs defining crime in non-legal terms. Crime is a label attached to certain behaviors by legislators. Programs recognizing this, therefore, will be more successful in preventing crime than programs defining crime in biological, psychological or other non-legal terms.

3. Programs encouraging compliance with the law will be more effective in providing protection from the causes of crime or eliminating the causes of crime than programs threatening punishment for violations of law. Encouraging people to abide by the law, by showing them the benefits and rewards of lawful behavior, is a more effective strategy than threatening severe punishment for violating the law. Offenders realize that punishment occurs after they are apprehended. They also realize that their chances of being apprehended are relatively low. Thus, programs establishing compliance with law as the goal of program activities will be more successful in preventing crime than programs advocating punishment as the goal of program activities.

4. Programs focusing on institutional or macro-level change will be more effective in providing protection from the causes of crime or eliminating the causes of crime than programs focusing on individual or micro-level change. We live in a highly complex and interdependent society wherein most individuals have little control over much of what occurs in their lives. Forces which shape our major institutions are beyond the control of any single individual. Programs focusing on the institutional or macro-level will be more successful in preventing crime than programs focusing on the individual or micro-level.

5. Programs recognizing that opportunities and access to resources are not equal and working to reduce the effects of racism will be more effective in providing protection from the causes of crime or eliminating the causes of crime than programs assuming the playing field is level. There is inequality in this country. The inequality is due, in part, to differences in abilities. But it also is attributable to racism. Racism is a

permanent part of the American experience. Thus, programs acknowledging inequality and working to reduce the effects of racism will be more successful in preventing crime than programs ignoring inequality and racism.

6. Programs designed and controlled by neighborhood residents will be more effective in providing protection from the causes of crime or eliminating the causes of crime than programs designed or controlled by non-residents. Neighborhood residents know better than non-residents which strategies and techniques will produce satisfactory results in their neighborhood. Therefore, resident participation during the planning and implementation phases is an essential ingredient of any potentially satisfactory crime prevention program. But non-residents too often assume that residents lack the ability and willingness to manage the affairs of their neighborhood. Non-residents frequently design programs in a vacuum, failing even to solicit residents' input. In some cases, forums for resident input are held and residents are encouraged to share their experiences and to offer recommendations. However, more frequently than not, when residents offer recommendations, non-residents reserve the "right" to disregard residents' recommendations. Programs designed and controlled by neighborhood residents will be more successful in preventing crime than programs designed or controlled by non-residents.

7. Programs selecting a specific neighborhood problem, such as youth gang violence or illegal drug sales, and marshalling existing community resources to address the selected problem will be more effective in providing protection from the causes of crime or eliminating the causes of crime than programs addressing "crime" in the neighborhood and relying upon temporary, short-term, external funding. Crime control efforts require a long-term, multi-year commitment of human and financial resources. Year-to-year funding encourages year-to-year planning. A short-term approach does not allow the formation of clearly stated program goals, the development of well-defined sets of procedures for achieving those goals, or time to evaluate the usefulness of the strategy. Thus, programs identifying specific problems and using existing resources to address the problems will be more effective in preventing crime than programs focusing on "crime" and relying on temporary support.

8. Programs designed to revitalize impoverished neighborhoods through economic development will be more effective in providing protection from the causes of crime or eliminating the causes of crime than programs designed to revitalize impoverished neighborhoods through non-economic development means. Economic development is the best method of increasing the number of jobs offering long-term

employment and paying wages able to sustain families. Economic development of impoverished neighborhoods will increase lawful business activities in the neighborhood and increase the number of legitimate employment opportunities available to neighborhood residents. Programs focusing on economic development of impoverished inner-city neighborhoods will be more effective in preventing crime than programs focusing on other aspects of neighborhood revitalization.

Advancements in crime prevention theory and crime control can be made. The above noted eight suggested assumptions provide a useful framework from which we can begin to refine existing crime prevention theory and to fashion potentially effective corrective crime prevention programs. If the assumptions above articulated are valid, then economic development of impoverished neighborhoods holds the greatest promise for preventing crime.

## PREVENTING CRIME THROUGH ECONOMIC DEVELOPMENT

Economic development, and the best methods of achieving it, are subjects hotly debated by economists, business persons and politicians, particularly when it concerns raising the standard of living of those who are poor, moving people out of poverty, and creating jobs. These observers generally acknowledge that wealth is not evenly distributed, that a substantial segment of the population is not participating in the economic life of the nation, and that steps should be taken to increase this segment's participation.

Since before the turn of this century, criminologists also have been concerned about poverty, as well as its causes and cures, because poverty appears to be related to crime. During the early part of this century, a quasi-Marxist analysis was popular among some. These criminologists argued that concentration of wealth in the hands of a few causes poverty among many. For example, Bonger (1916) claimed that crime was related to the poverty suffered by those unable to compete in a capitalist system. He believed crime would end when wealth was redistributed.

Although most criminologists, then and now, reject a quasi-Marxist analysis, many agree the study of crime must include an examination of those institutional or macro-level factors producing poverty. These observers remind us that the forces which shape our economy, that determine the type and location of employment opportunities, and that ultimately produce poverty are beyond the control of those who are poor. Consequently, we must look beyond individuals' experiences in the marketplace to obtain a clearer picture of the relationship between poverty and crime.

Sullivan (1989) argues that an institutional or macro-level analysis is appropriate. He contends that youth crime in inner-city neighborhoods is caused by lack of specific employment opportunities and by poor employment conditions in these neighborhoods. Sullivan (1989) maintains that these poor employment conditions "produce both the stresses of poverty and weakened social control" (p. 251).

According to Sullivan (1989) the segmented labor market theory should be applied to an analysis of the relationship between employment and crime. Sullivan (1989) reports that segmented labor market theory recognizes the existence of a primary and a secondary labor market. The primary market offers "steady employment at relatively high wages which can support families." The secondary market offers "low-wage jobs, welfare, employment and training programs, informal economic activities, and crime" (p. 11). Sullivan (1989) believes the markets are a result of the structure of the economy and society.

Other social scientists have employed this type of analysis. For example, Thomas (1993) concludes:

> At the same time, segmentation of labor markets, the movement of industries out of central cities, and the decline in the production of goods relative to the production of services have created a social and economic situation that perpetuates black poverty.

Baker (1991) identifies a similar, but larger, set of simultaneously operating factors having an adverse effect upon job seekers. Baker (1991) maintains some job seekers, particularly teenagers, face numerous obstacles. Among these are racial discrimination, a diminishing need for workers who are functionally illiterate, an evaporating supply of semi-skilled jobs, union efforts to control the number of laborers, the exodus of industry from urban neighborhoods, and the reluctance of employers to offer entry-level jobs including a training component for disadvantaged job seekers (p. 222).

Racial discrimination frequently is listed among those factors causing unemployment. Some observers point to the government's labor statistics. These data consistently show unemployment rates for African-Americans are at least twice that of whites. For example, in 1988, total unemployment reportedly was 5.4 percent (Bureau of Labor Statistics 1989, p. 7). However, 11.7 percent of African-Americans were unemployed and 32.4 percent of African-Americans aged 16 to 19 were unemployed (Bureau of Labor Statistics 1989, p. 38). And the most recent data show that while total unemployment rates are falling the unemployment rates for African-Americans continue to rise.

Thomas (1993) argues that racial discrimination even affects the amount of compensation received by those African-Americans able to locate employment. His study found that African-Americans earn less than two-thirds of the amount earned by whites. And Thomas's findings show that when African-Americans and whites have the same occupational status, the same education, and are the same age then African-Americans earn "9.3 percent or an average of $2,634 less a year in personal income than whites." According to Thomas (1993), "This represents the 'cost of being black.'"

A sluggish economy also is identified as a cause of unemployment. Kahn (1993) suggests the nation is recovering from the recession. But he maintains that job growth is particularly sluggish. Kahn (1993) contends that a "typical recovery would have produced 4.3 million jobs ... the current recovery has produced fewer than 900,000." The 1993 Economic Report of the President appears to agree. It states:

> The American economy is neither in long-term decline nor short-term contraction. It is emerging slowly from a period of sluggish growth and a short, about average, recession after the longest peacetime expansion in history. But it does face serious problems and challenges. (page 27)

The Report seems to reach a distressing conclusion. It acknowledges that "economic growth is essential to provide rising employment opportunities for new entrants in the labor force and those seeking upward economic mobility." But it also claims that economic growth alone will not "make major inroads in the poverty rate in the United States" (p. 29). This is counter-intuitive.

Unemployment is a leading cause of poverty. During the last decade, poverty has "worsened and deepened" as well-paying blue-collar jobs and training and employment programs were eliminated through plant closings and federal government budget cuts (Commission on the Cities 1988). A primary goal of economic growth or economic development is job creation. When economic development is directed toward creating jobs for those who are poor, then poverty should decrease.

For the most part, efforts have not been directed toward economic development of impoverished neighborhoods. Friedman (1988) explains:

> We have for a long time spent on the poor in this country, but we have rarely invested in them. There is a large difference there. When you spend through income maintenance or social services you maintain consumption, but you don't necessarily treat people as though they have capacity and talent and vision

> that can grow over time and return value to the community as a whole. For every dollar we spend in the name of the poor, ninety-plus cents goes for income maintenance or social services. A few pennies go for training; at most, a fraction of a penny goes for anything that can be construed as economic development or expanding the opportunity to produce. (p. 11)

Economic development of impoverished neighborhoods should reduce poverty in those neighborhoods and it might prevent crime. Although poverty is not necessarily a cause of crime, the two certainly are frequent companions. Afterall, it does not require the genius of a rocket scientist to see that economically prosperous neighborhoods experience less crime than their impoverished counterparts.

The absence of employment opportunties has long been associated with inner-city crime and other social ills (Brown 1977; Wilson 1987; Jacobs 1989). Therefore, we need, as Congressman Ron Wyden (1991) suggests, "new models for tackling the interrelated problems of employment, deteriorating neighborhoods, crime and inadequate housing" (p. 2). One of these "new models" should feature economic development of impoverished neighborhoods, with a goal of creating employment opportunities offering long-term employment and paying wages able to sustain families.

Few will argue against this goal, in part, because there is broad support for the idea that every person seeking employment should be able to find a job. But there is not a consensus on how employment-related goals should be reached.

Many observers recommend that government should take the lead by implementing some type of public jobs and training program (Pepinsky and Jesilow 1984, p. 149; Commission on the Cities 1988; LeVert 1991, p. 130). But these multi-billion dollar programs have had limited success in reducing the number of people living in poverty. In fact, it appears that the number of people living in poverty is increasing.

The value of these jobs and training programs also are questioned because there is little evidence supporting the notion that they decrease crime. Studies evaluating the success of jobs-related demonstration projects, at best, have given mixed signals (Nettler 1984, p. 127). Many of these projects' employees soon quit after being hired or continued engaging in illegal conduct. A few projects were successful. But their success usually was due: 1) to their selection processes, wherein those employees likely to succeed in the absence of the projects were selected for participation by project staff; or 2) the projects were designed so jobs offered were not low-prestige dead-end jobs, but rather jobs providing some hope of advancement and pride.

It appears that short-term, government-sponsored jobs and training programs are unable to create long-term employment opportunities paying wages able to sustain families. They are laudable attempts to fill the gaps. But they simply cannot be designed to do the things that private sector economic growth or development can do - create and maintain long-term employment opportunities.

According to the 1993 Economic Report of the President, "The private sector of the economy is where most of the jobs are created and income earned" (p. 30). And it is the small business portion of the private sector that is "the backbone of the American economy" (Swain 1988). Small business accounts for 99.8 percent of the total number of businesses in our economy and 56 percent of workers employed in nongovernmental, nonfarm employment. Most of these businesses employ fewer than 20 employees and have gross revenues of less than $100,000 per year (Swain 1988, p. 9; Fleury 1992, p. 6).

Future job growth most likely will occur in the small business sector (Timmons 1990). According to Swain (1988):

> We find that the job growth that we all like to brag about comes not from the business that has 50 employees moving to 100 employees, but from businesses that are new start-ups, adding their first 5 to 10 to 15 employees. That's really where the dynamism of the economy is. (p. 9)

Small business also is the "lifeblood" of neighborhoods. They provide needed services to neighborhood residents. They provide employment opportunities. And they are an anchor for neighborhood stability (Wyden 1991, p. 45).

Small businesses are uniquely positioned to play a potentially monumental role in this nation's crime control effort because they are the primary vehicle for job growth. But how do we enable small businesses to participate in crime control efforts?

Providing a small tax incentive to encourage small businesses to set up shop in impoverished neighborhoods and to train and hire neighborhood residents, as suggested in the 1993 Economic Report of the President, is a good beginning. But a small tax incentive is not enough to enable the average small company to take such a big business risk.

Being in business is risky. Over half of all businesses fail in their first five years of operation (Goldstick 1988, p. 2). Reasons for failure frequently include inadequate capitalization to commence business operations, inability to secure lines of credit from financial institutions and suppliers, and absence of technical assistance or professional advice. The physical location of a business also may doom it to failure (Fleury

1992, p. 12). Features of successful businesses usually include adequate capital to commence operations and lines of credit to continue operations, detailed planning, technical assistance provided by professionals such as lawyers and bankers, a talented workforce, and a great location.

Few business advisors would recommend to a successful or potentially successful business that it set up shop in an impoverished high crime neighborhood. Most of the reasons are obvious. Insurance premiums would be higher. Building security costs would be higher. Because of fear of crime, it would be more difficult to recruit non-resident employees. Because of fear of crime, customers or clients might be reluctant to travel to the neighborhood to transact business. And office/retail space, even if comfortable and attractive, probably would be surrounded by mostly older and unattractive buildings.

Also, few business advisors would recommend that a company spend a substantial portion of its tight budget to train and employ un-skilled or semi-skilled residents of an impoverished high crime neighborhood. There also would be concerns about whether these workers would pilfer from the company, be loyal to the company, and be committed to the success of the company.

Businesses take risks every day of their existence. Most try to identify and minimize their risks. Few are willing to increase their risks unless the potential for success increases by an amount equal to or greater than the risks assumed.

Setting up shop in an impoverished high crime neighborhood is a risky proposition, one most small businesses simply are unable to take. Thus, offering a small tax incentive is unlikely to result in a substantial increase in the number of jobs available in impoverished high crime neighborhoods.

However, the number of jobs available to residents of impoverished neighborhoods can be increased if federal and state governments are willing to enable small businesses to bear the risks of doing business in impoverished high crime neighborhoods. The government could assist small businesses by establishing more "new business incubators."

According to Smilor and Gill (1986), incubators "seek to leverage entrepreneurial talent, respond to a hypercompetitive environment, and implement new institutional relationships for innovative economic development" (preface). By increasing the likelihood that these emerging businesses will succeed, these incubators can assist in job creation (Smilor and Gill 1986, p. 131). Smilor and Gill (1986) maintain these incubators are essential "because of the dynamics of entrepreneurship and the thrust of hypercompetition, the nature of economic development has fundamentally changed" (preface).

In addition to increasing the number of "new business incubators," the government could provide direct grants or loans to businesses willing to work from impoverished high crime neighborhoods. This would not be a novel undertaking for the government. It already is doing this in other areas of the economy. Many businesses receive some sort of subsidy enabling them to carry the risks associated with certain types of business activities. Furthermore, the government has a long history of helping small businesses through the Small Business Administration. This federal government agency guarantees loans made to those small businesses unable to obtain private financing. In 1992, the Small Business Administration spent almost $107 million on business development (United States Office of Management and Budget 1993).

Most small businesses are familiar with the Small Business Administration. Although it has critics, the efforts of the Small Business Administration generally are appreciated by members of the business community. Of all the government agencies concerned with helping small businesses, the Small Business Administration probably is best suited to helping small businesses bear the risks of doing business in impoverished high crime neighborhoods. But its current budget is too small to accomplish this task.

For 1994, the Small Business Administration will receive only $100.3 million for business development. But over $13 billion will be spent on federal drug control efforts (United States Office of Management and Budget 1993). Because economic development of impoverished high crime areas (a corrective prevention measure) holds greater promise for reducing crime than federal drug control efforts (primarily mechanical and punitive prevention measures), funds could be shifted from the federal drug control efforts budget to the Small Business Administration business development budget.

Assuming only a 50 percent shift, the Small Business Administration would have a total of $6.62 billion for business development. With these funds, the Small Business Administration could establish an innovative "loan to grant" program. Such a program would offer loans to small businesses located in or willing to re-locate to impoverished high-crime neighborhoods. Under this program, each business would be eligible to receive a $100,000 loan if it agrees to hire and train at least three neighborhood residents. The loan would be forgiven or converted to a grant if the business maintains operations in the neighborhood for five years and continuously employs at least three neighborhood residents during this five year period. This program would target the 50 largest cities in this country, equally dividing the $6.62 billion among these cities.

In the event such a shift occurred and such a program were established, we could expect to see at least 66,208 new businesses established or existing businesses expanded in impoverished high crime neighborhoods. We also would expect to see at least 198,625 neighborhood residents obtain jobs offering long-term employment.

In other words, under this proposed program, each of the largest 50 cities in this nation would have an additional 3,972 jobs available to residents of impoverished neighborhoods. Obviously, cities like New York or Los Angeles might not notice the effects of such a small number of jobs. But smaller cities would.

Some may argue this idea does not make sense because it is too costly. But these critics should keep in mind that under this proposal no new funds are being sought. This proposal recommends shifting funds from one budget category to another and using an existing government agency to administer the funds.

Also, the actual cost of the proposed business development program is less than $6.62 billion because workers would be paying taxes and the businesses, if successful, also would be paying taxes. A substantial portion of the money invested by the government would be returned to the government in the form of taxes paid.

Unemployment in impoverished high crime neighborhoods would decrease. This would provide some savings in other areas of the government's budget. According to Dunbar (1988), "A respected estimate is that a 1 percent rise or fall in unemployment costs or saves the government about $36 billion in aid payments." Thus, we could expect to see some savings in the amounts spent to fund welfare and unemployment compensation programs. And, if crime and unemployment are related, we also could expect to see some savings in the amounts needed to operate criminal justice agencies.

The potential benefits of economic development are enormous. The proposed program has the potential of saving taxpayers billions of dollars. It would enable small businesses to help impoverished high crime neighborhoods by providing jobs to neighborhood residents. It would reduce unemployment in those neighborhoods. It would reduce poverty in those neighborhoods. It might reduce crime in those neighborhoods. It might have a positive effect on school children to see their parents or their schoolmates going to work in the neighborhood. It might have a positive effect on other aspects of the neighborhood in that small businesses routinely support the civic activities occurring in the neighborhood. And, over the five year period, we might just see some neighborhood residents buying their first homes because they can show steady employment.

Does this proposal, which essentially recommends investing in the poor, have the potential to break the cycles of poverty and welfare dependency and to reduce crime? Perhaps. Does our current "more law enforcement" approach? Absolutely not. As Pepinsky and Jesilow (1984) note: "the key to government success in managing the crime problem is to invest in businesses and programs best suited to providing social peace and welfare in American communities" (p. 155).

## CONCLUSION

Crime is one of the most pressing problems facing this nation. In the coming months and years, legislators will consider a wide variety of crime control proposals. The introduction of these proposals presents unique opportunities for making progress in controlling crime. A healthy and rigorous debate about crime and its control is a step in the right direction. Not because it promises to provide answers to those questions already known, but rather because it encourages a search for those questions which have not yet been asked. For it is in these unasked questions that we will find the key to and locate that door through which we must pass if all neighborhoods are to become safe havens for their residents.

Many of the recommended crime control measures will be based on emotional responses to specific criminal incidents, personal opinions, or political expediency. "More law enforcement" likely will be the demand most frequently made. But those advocating mechanical or punitive measures can offer little concrete evidence of the viability of such approaches to control crime. And there is clear evidence that the mechanical and punitive-oriented approaches are increasing the number of African-Americans perceived as offenders, treated as suspects, arrested and incarcerated.

Crime control efforts must be guided by reason. To make all neighborhoods safe, we need a carefully crafted, long-term plan that builds on this nation's strengths. Small business is one of our strengths. This segment of society is responsible for nearly all the new jobs created. Small business should be enabled to create jobs in impoverished high crime neighborhoods because job creation holds the greatest promise for preventing crime.

## REFERENCES

American Correctional Association. 1980. *Directory*. Laurel, MD: Author.

_______. 1988. *Directory*. Laurel, MD: Author.

_______. 1993. *Directory*. Laurel, MD: Author.

Baker, F. 1991. *Saving Our Kids from Delinquency, Drugs, and Despair: Solutions Through Prevention*. New York: Cornelia and Michael Bessie Books.

Bonger, W. 1916. *Criminality and Economic Conditions*. Boston: Little Brown.

Brown, L. 1977. "Causes of Crime." In *Black Crime: A Police View*, edited by H. Bryce. Washington, D.C.: Joint Center for Political Studies.

Coie, J. et al. 1993. "The Science of Prevention: A Conceptual Framework and Some Directions for a National Research Program." *American Psychologist* 48:1013-1022.

Commission on the Cities. 1988. "Race and Poverty in the United States - and What Should Be Done." In *Quiet Riots: Race and Poverty in the United States*, edited by F. Harris and R. Wilkins. New York: Pantheon Books.

Dunbar, L. 1988. *The Common Interest: How Our Social Welfare Policies Don't Work, and What We Can Do About Them.* New York: Pantheon Books.

Federal Bureau of Investigation. 1989. *Uniform Crime Reports.* Washington, D.C.: U.S. Government Printing Office.

_______. 1990. *Uniform Crime Reports.* Washington, D.C.: U.S. Government Printing Office.

_______. 1991. *Uniform Crime Reports.* Washington, D.C.: U.S. Government Printing Office.

_______. 1992. *Uniform Crime Reports.* Washington, D.C.: U.S. Government Printing Office.

_______. 1993. *Uniform Crime Reports.* Washington, D.C.: U.S. Government Printing Office.

Fleury, R. 1992. *The Small Business Survival Guide.* Naperville, IL: Sourcebooks Trade.

Friedman, R. 1988. Testimony at "Self-Employment for the Poor: The Potential of Micro-Enterprise Credit Programs," a Hearing before the Select Committee on Hunger, U.S. House of Representatives, April 20, 1988. Washington, D.C.: U.S. Government Printing Office.

Goldstick, G. 1988. *Business: How to Get in the Black and Stay There.* New York: John Wiley & Sons.

Jacobs, J. 1989. "Black America, 1988: An Overview." In *State of Black America*, National Urban League. New York: Author.

Kahn, G. 1993. "Sluggish Job Growth: Is Rising Productivity or an Anemic Recovery To Blame?" *Economic Review* Third Quarter.

Krajack, K. 1979. "Preventing Crime." *Police Magazine* November.

Law Enforcement Assistance Administration. 1979. *LEAA Tenth Annual Report: Fiscal Year 1978.* Washington, D.C.: U.S. Government Printing Office.

Lejins, P. 1965. *Recent Changes in the Concept of Prevention.* Reprint from the Proceedings of the 95th Annual Congress of Correction of the American Correctional Association.

______. 1983. Personal Interview. October.

Lemert, E. 1951. *Social Pathology.* New York: McGraw-Hill.

Levert, M. 1991. *Crime.* New York: Facts on File, Inc.

Lombroso, C. 1911. *Criminal Man.* Montclair, NJ: Patterson Smith (Republished 1972).

Meltzer, M. 1990. *Crime in America.* New York: Morrow Junior Books.

Merton, R. 1938. "Social Structure and Anomie." *American Sociological Review* 3:672-682.

McPherson, M. and G. Silloway. 1981. "Planning to Prevent Crime." In *Reactions to Crime,* edited by D. Lewis. Beverly Hills, CA: Sage.

National Advisory Commission on Criminal Justice Standards and Goals. 1973. *Community Crime Prevention.* Washington, D.C.: U.S. Government Printing Office.

National Crime Prevention Institute. 1978. "The Practice of Crime Prevention." *Understanding Crime Prevention* 1.

National Institute of Justice. 1992. *Sourcebook of Criminal Justice Statistics.* Washington, D.C.: U.S. Government Printing Office.

Nettler, G. 1984. *Explaining Crime* (3rd ed.). New York: McGraw-Hill.

Ohlin, L. and R. Cloward. 1969. "The Differentiation of Delinquent Subcultures." In *Delinquency, Crime, and Social Process,* edited by D. Cressey and D.A. Ward. New York: Harper & Row.

Park, R. and E. Burgess. 1921. *Introduction to the Science of Sociology.* Chicago: University of Chicago Press.

Pepinsky, H. and P. Jesilow. 1984. *Myths That Cause Crime.* Cabin John, MD: Locks Press.

Rand, M. 1991. *Crime and the Nation's Households, 1990.* U.S. Department of Justice Bureau of Justice Statistics Bulletin. August 1991, pp.1-7.

Reckless, W. 1972. *The Crime Problem* (5th ed.) New York: Appleton-Century-Crofts.

Sheldon, W., et al. 1949. *Varieties of Delinquent Youth.* New York: Harper & Brothers.

Silberman, C. 1978. *Criminal Violence, Criminal Justice.* New York: Vintage Books.

Smilor, R. and M. Gill. 1986. *The New Business Incubator.* Lexington, MA: Lexington Book.

Sorrentino, A. 1979. *How to Organize the Neighborhood for Delinquency Prevention.* Chicago: DePaul University.

Sullivan, M. 1989. *"Getting Paid." Youth Crime and Work in the Inner-City.* Ithaca, NY: Cornell University Press.

Sulton, A. 1989. *Inner-City Crime Control.* Washington, D.C.: Police Foundation.

Sutherland, E. 1947. *Principles of Criminology* (4th ed.) Philadelphia: J.B. Lippincott Company.

Swain, F. 1988. Testimony at "Self-Employment for the Poor: The Potential of Micro-Enterprise Credit Programs," a Hearing before the Select Committee on Hunger, U.S. House of Representatives, April 20, 1988. Washington, D.C.: U.S. Government Printing Office.

Timmons, J. 1990. *New Business Opportunities: Getting to the Right Place at the Right Time.* Acton, MA: Brick House Publishing Company.

Thomas, M. 1993. "Race, Class, and Personal Income: An Empirical Test of the Declining Significance of Race Thesis, 1968-1988." *Social Problems* 40:328-341.

Tucker, M. and B. Starnes. 1993. "Crime Prevention Through Environmental Design: The Tallahassee Model." *The Police Chief.* October.

United States Department of Labor Bureau of Labor Statistics. 1989. *Handbook of Labor Statistics.* Washington, D.C.: U.S. Government Printing Office.

United States Office of Management and Budget. 1993. *Budget of the United States Government: Fiscal Year 1994.* Washington, D.C.: United States Government Printing Office.

United States President. 1993. *Economic Report of the President.* Washington, D.C.: U.S. Government Printing Office.

Wilson, W. 1987. *The Truly Disadvantaged: The Inner City, the Underclass, and Public Policy.* Chicago: University of Chicago Press.

Woodson, R. 1993. "Our Agenda." *Agenda: The Alternative Magazine of Critical Issues* 3:1.

Wyden, R. 1991. Statement at "Assisting Neighborhood Businesses In the Minority Community: Strategies for Community Reinvestment, 'Project Alberta,'" a Hearing before the Subcommittee on Regulation, Business Opportunities, and Energy of the Committee on Small Business, U.S. House of Representatives, October 26, 1991. Washington, D.C.: U.S. Government Printing Office.